Yasmine BOUABDALLAH

Cognitive-semantic representation of actions

Yasmine BOUABDALLAH

Cognitive-semantic representation of actions

Lexico-semantic study of action verbs in aphasia

ScienciaScripts

Imprint

Any brand names and product names mentioned in this book are subject to trademark, brand or patent protection and are trademarks or registered trademarks of their respective holders. The use of brand names, product names, common names, trade names, product descriptions etc. even without a particular marking in this work is in no way to be construed to mean that such names may be regarded as unrestricted in respect of trademark and brand protection legislation and could thus be used by anyone.

Cover image: www.ingimage.com

This book is a translation from the original published under ISBN 978-620-6-70191-0.

Publisher:
Sciencia Scripts
is a trademark of
Dodo Books Indian Ocean Ltd. and OmniScriptum S.R.L publishing group

120 High Road, East Finchley, London, N2 9ED, United Kingdom
Str. Armeneasca 28/1, office 1, Chisinau MD-2012, Republic of Moldova, Europe
Printed at: see last page
ISBN: 978-620-7-62967-1

Contents

Acknowledgements

My thanks go to my masters who have been with me since I started out as an apprentice researcher;

I would like to thank Professor ZELLAL Nacira for her scientific rigour, her extensive experience in all fields and her constant encouragement, which has been invaluable to me. Her sound advice, her attentive and demanding reading and her guidance have been of great use to me in my training and in my life, including the two CMEP-TASSILI, URNOP/Université Paris 8- Labo Chart internships.

I would like to thank Mme BENHAMLA Zoubeida for the trust she placed in me by agreeing to supervise this doctoral work, for her many pieces of advice and for all the hours she devoted to re-reading this research work. Her availability, her human qualities, her attentiveness and her understanding have been a great support to me.

Thank you to Professor AMOKRANE Saliha for her unfailing support, her scientific guidance, her demanding readings, her comments, her advice, her availability and her directives. She accompanied me relentlessly throughout the years of my doctorate.

I would like to say a very special thank you to Mr KACEMI Salah, PhD, lecturer in speech therapy at the University of Annaba, with whom I spent my two CMEP-TASSILI scientific placements. Thank you for introducing me to his patients using the "Give me back my words" software. It was a real pleasure to work with him.

Thanks to Professor Catherine Tessier, who welcomed us into her office at the Salpetriere Hospital during the CMEP-TASSILI course, for her scientific guidance and for sharing her practical and theoretical research with us.

I would like to express my sincere gratitude to all the members of the jury for giving up their valuable time to judge my work.

Thank you to my parents, who have worked so hard to ensure my success. Thank you for all the sacrifices you have made and your invaluable advice.

Thank you to my husband, who has encouraged me for so many years and whose enthusiasm and support have kept me going.

Thank you to my brothers, whose support has kept my spirits up in difficult times.

Resume

The semantic representation of action refers both to the organisation in memory of knowledge about actions and their processing. The semantics of action relates to representations of a sensory-motor nature linked to execution, and is expressed by verb and gesture. Any representation of the lexicon expressing actions (verbs, verbal expressions, nominalisation) forms explicit knowledge about functional objects. This view is in line with the perspectives of linguists who demonstrate the presence of cognitive primitives (Jackendoif, 1983, Descles, 1985). The meaning of the sign in a discourse is a *representation* in which the *semantic* value in language is combined, and this representation is constructed by the cognitive relationships of the brain with reference to the objects around us.

Asking someone to close an open door is expressed as "close the door", and more often in colloquial language as "la porte! We also note that if a travel scenario can be expressed as "pack your bags, book a plane ticket, book a hotel, take the plane, rest in the hotel room", the list of nouns "baggage, plane ticket, hotel and hotel room" alone is enough to understand the scenario, whereas "do, book, take, rest" is not enough to grasp the scenario. With this in mind, we will focus on action verbs in aphasics in order to understand: Which of the verb or object most affects the mental construction of the verbal lexicon in language acquisition?

To answer this question we used the computer programme "Rendez Moi Mes Mot" by Dr. KACEMI Salah, a computerised version of the "MTA 2002" test by Pr. ZELLAL Nacira applied to five cases of aphasia whose major language disorder is represented by semantic paraphasias. The aim was to show the cognitive elasticity of oral language in aphasics based on semantic approximations.

Key words: semantic paraphasia - lack of words - aphasia - semantic representation - action verbs - objects - context.

*"Language reproduces the world, but by subjecting it to
its own organisation.*
own "Emile Benveniste

Introduction

The language faculty represents a predisposition for socialisation specific to the human species, characterised by functional traits or a linguistic transcoding protocol. Thus, a good exchange strategy is at the heart of any communication process, through the choice of words that convey the information decoded by a semantic representation of language. Aphasia implies a difficulty in oral production (lexical, syntactic or articulatory), hence the dysfunction of linguistic transcoding.

The lack of words represents one of the major language disorders in aphasia and manifests itself in various forms: anomia, lexicalisation disorder (Nespoulous § Virbel, 2003; Basso, 1993).

In our previous research - a lexico-semantic study of oral language in aphasics (Broca-Wernicke)- (magistere 2009), we identified a significant presence of word substitutions reflecting semantic paraphasias in oral production in aphasics. In the present study, we wanted to go further in our investigations, and we propose to work on verbal paraphasias based on action verbs in oral naming, a subject of study that remains little exploited. We have chosen to analyse aphasia in which the oral language disorder is represented by semantic paraphasia. In particular, we are interested in verbal paraphasia in aphasia based on action verbs in oral nouns. The aim is to interpret the psycholinguistic and neurolinguistic aspects of the oral action verb lexicon.

The lack of words in aphasia is generally compensated for by compensatory strategies that reflect lexico-semantic approximations. These lexical production problems are linked to semantic deficits and can be verbalised by modalising statements (Tran, 2007).

In our study, we are interested in the faculties preserved in aphasics which allow the creation of semantic flexibilities at the level of the verbal lexicon.

Aphasics produce semantic approximations that consist of using one verb in place of another (both being semantically close). These communicative strategies highlight the semantic flexibility of verbs and make flexibility a fundamental cognitive principle (Duvignau, 2003; Duvignau et al. 2004).

According to K. Duvignau, there is cognitive flexibility in children during language acquisition, which manifests itself in semantic approximations, productions that favour a relationship of "semantic proximity" between verbs (Duvignau., & al, 2004). In our research, we refer to the results of studies by Duvignau et al (2008), Nespoulous and Virbel (2003) and Charles Albert Tijus and Elisabetta Zibetti.

The presence of these semantic paraphasias would be synonymous with a construction of the verbal lexicon under an aspect of semantic proximities and would generate a phenomenon of semantic approximation, which plays a crucial role in the hierarchisation of the mental lexicon. The lack of words in the aphasic allows us to orient our study towards two dimensions. The first relates to the study of semantic paraphrases of verbs (or verbal semantic approximations), for example:

"elle a casse le journal" for "dechirer le journal". The second relates to the lexico-semantic hierarchisation that emerges from these utterances, through generic verbs such as "diviser des steaks" for "trancher des steaks" or specific verbs such as "couper des steaks".

Generally, verbs are polysemic if they are not produced in a given context. We start from the following assumption: the use of objects facilitates the production of action verbs (Van Elk, Van Schie., & Bekkering, 2009). The hierarchical organisation of object categories applies to all verbs in hierarchical networks. The functional properties are explained by the structural properties of the objects, which play a role in the construction of semantic categories and which can be lexicalised.

Asking someone to close an open door is expressed as "close the door", and more often than not, in colloquial language, as "the door", but rarely as "close".

We also note that if a travel scenario can be expressed as "pack your luggage, book a plane ticket, book a hotel, take the plane, rest in the hotel room", the list of nouns "luggage, plane ticket, hotel and hotel room" alone is enough to make us understand the scenario, whereas "do, book, take, rest" do not make it possible to grasp the scenario. This observation prompts us to ask whether it is the verb or the object that most affects the mental construction of semantic representations.

Research on the semantic-cognitive dimension of verbs is scarce and most has focused on its syntactic aspect and on agrammatism in aphasics. In the present study, we propose to use the nominal lexicon to analyse lexical disorders, in particular semantic paraphasias, which are characteristic of the language of aphasics who adapt language strategies to compensate for the loss of their ability to express themselves.

Our problem is underpinned by the following questions:

-Is the mental construction of semantic representations of actions most affected by the verb or the object?

-What are the processes that can lead to a lack of words in aphasics?

-On what basis are lexical substitutions made by aphasics?

In an attempt to answer these questions, we put forward the following hypotheses.

-Cognitive elasticity in aphasia is the fundamental strategy used to structure the mental lexicon. This is based on semantic approximations in the oral naming of action verbs.

-We hypothesise that the lack of words in aphasics is caused by impairments in lexical production in the oral naming of actions.

These problems are compensated for by approximations in the aphasic's responses. This leads us to suppose that this is a palliative strategy for aphasics, in order to structure and adapt their statements.

-We assume that the aphasic will produce and recover the verbal class more easily, in relation to their semantic representation (object vs. action).

-   Our first objective is to account for the presence of semantic-cognitive elasticity based on oral lexico-semantic disorders in aphasics by analysing semantic paraphasias.

-Our second aim is to find out whether the functional properties of objects are justified by their structural properties and whether they are involved in the construction of semantic categories, which may or may not be lexicalised from an oral action naming task (action with object manipulation). This will explain the entanglement between the action verb and the object derived from the named verb.

-   Our third objective is to observe whether the context of the object has an influence on the production of action verbs in aphasics.

To carry out our work we will analyse the oral productions of five cases of aphasia represented by three different types of aphasia: Broca's, transcortical and subcortical, whose medical report showed a cerebrovascular accident (ischemic stroke), using the aphasiogram "Rendez-moi mes mots "1 designed by S. Kacemi (computerised test software (MTA) adapted and calibrated by Professor Zellal Nacira). In an attempt to achieve the objectives we have set ourselves, we will draw on two approaches: psycholinguistics and neurolinguistics.

The psycholinguistic approach focuses on the production of verbs through an oral description task in aphasics.

The aim of the neurolinguistic approach is to highlight the brain areas involved in the oral description of an aphasic subject, based on the different approaches to classifying aphasia. We start from the premise that there is no single cerebral region that acts, but rather a neural network (Zellal, 2011).

We have structured our research in two parts.

The first part, comprising five chapters, presents the theoretical elements to which we will refer in our study.

In the first chapter, entitled *L'organisation du langage oral chez l'aphasique (The organisation of oral language in aphasia),* we will first define aphasia and its different approaches, then report on the structural and neuroanatomical organisation of language in aphasia, then delimit aphasia in relation to the liguistic sign, and finally discuss the neurolinguistic characteristics of the different clinical forms of aphasia.

In the second chapter, entitled *Oral production and its disorders in aphasics,* we will describe the different lexical deficits, then explain language in relation to the brain, and finish with the different approaches to therapy.

In the third chapter, entitled *La hieharchistion lexico-semantique des verbes (The lexico-semantic hierarchy of verbs),* we define the hierarchisation of the mental lexicon, explain the notion of semantic proximity in relation to the word, and finally determine the forms of categorisation in the production of verbs in aphasics.

The fourth chapter, entitled *Cognitive Flexibility in Aphasia: Semantic Approximations,* outlines the characteristics of semantic approximations, then explains the concept of semantic approximation as a proof of cognitive flexibility, and finally delimits semantic approximation in relation to pragmatics.

The fifth chapter is entitled *Oral Action Naming.* In this chapter we will define oral action naming in relation to neurpsychological models, then we will outline the different variables that influence oral naming, and finally we will report on the modular organisation of language.

The second part is devoted to the study and analysis of oral denomination cases, and also comprises five chapters.

In the first chapter, entitled *Oral action naming in aphasic subjects,* we present the experimental protocol, the analysis criteria, and the representative sample. We then present the study of five cases of aphasia in oral action naming, and finally we discuss the results.

The second chapter, entitled *Cognitive interpretation of the results,* will be devoted to a cognitive representation of comprehension disorders, central production disorders and access deficits to phonological disorders, followed by a presentation of syntactic disorders from a cognitive point of view. We will explain the semantic system, analyse the modelling of oral production and naming, delimit categorisation in relation to over-extensions, and finally show the influence of action on the processing of manipulable object concepts.

In the third chapter, entitled *Lexico-semantic interpretation of the results,* we explain how the lexicon is recovered, give an account of the word mark, show the role of preserved knowledge in lexicon recovery, explain over-extension as a compensatory strategy, and end with the valid responses in lexico-semantic processing.

In the fourth chapter, entitled *Pragmatic interpretation of the results,* we will relate the two cognitive and lexico-semantic interpretations. We will report on the semantic approximation from a pragmatic point of view, we will define the action verbs in relation to pragmatics and finally we will explain the semantic approximation from a cognitive-pragmatic point of view.

Finally, the fifth chapter, entitled *Nature of semantic dissociations and conceptualisation,* will be devoted to proposed explanations, followed by an attempt to identify the influence of association forces on matching choices in aphasia, and ending with cognitive factors and category structure in the recovery of language in aphasia.

Theoretical part

Chapter 1 The organisation of oral language in aphasics

1. Aphasia

Any linguistic disturbance in communication during comprehension (encoding) or production of oral or written language (decoding) is synonymous with aphasia (A. Roch-Lecours & F. Lhermitte, 1979). This lexico-semantic disorganisation is the result of a lesion in the dominant hemisphere of language, generally the left hemisphere.

Depending on the location and extent of the lesion, cerebral damage impairs or even eliminates several aspects of oral and written language, as well as oral and written comprehension. In aphasiology, we identify several deficits affecting lexical, semantic, phonological, morphosyntactic and pragmatic language. These deficits vary according to the brain areas damaged and the type of aphasia.

In the disorganisation of language, oral production can be seriously impaired compared to comprehension, which remains intact. Aphasia is characterised by a major symptom: the lack of a word. This is an inability to produce the word that corresponds to the psycholinguistic context of the moment (conversation, story, directed exercise, etc.).

We will go into more detail about disorders of oral production in Chapter 2. There are various causes of aphasia: cerebrovascular accident, trauma or tumour. We have confined ourselves to the oral aspect in aphasics whose etiology is vascular in adults. This was done in order to determine the objective of our study.

The evolution of aphasia varies according to the extent of the lesion, the causes, the lesion location and personal criteria (age, socio-cultural level, stress, etc.).

The diagnosis of aphasia is determined by the neurological context. To target the areas specialised in language functions and better understand their role, progress in cerebral imaging is attempting to establish neuroanatomical correlations.

In the human brain, there are various cerebral areas that are characterised by different functions. As a result, aphasia is rarely isolated and
often coexists with neuropsychological and neurological disorders.

This oral and/or written language disorder depends on its etiology, and a regression of the disorders will be observed thanks to spontaneous recovery and rehabilitation if the causes have stabilised.

Regardless of the type of aphasia, the nature of the brain lesion and the age of the aphasic, he or she presents a plural linguistic disorder and a single cognitive disorder (N. Zellal, 2011). Control over language is deregulated by a brain lesion, which has been established on the basis of performance on neuropsychological tests, hence the dissociation of the dual cognitive operations of analysis and synthesis.

2. Classification of aphasia according to different approaches

The presence of several types of aphasic disorder has led to a large number of classifications of clinical forms, using a variety of criteria.

The study of language impairment in aphasia involves several fields of investigation: neurology, speech therapy, psychology and linguistics. This interdisciplinarity explains the diverse classification of the different types of aphasia and the interpretation of the different language processes.

2.1 The empirical approach

This approach is based on a simple dichotomy to classify the different forms of aphasia and determines two categories: fluent vs non-fluent aphasia[2] (J-M. Mazaux, 2007). This approach is descriptive and starts from a clinically observable point of view.

2.2 The linguistic approach

Given that aphasia is a pathology of language, our approach is based on linguistic foundations (Jakobson & Halle, 1956), (Kremin & Nespoulous, 1994).

The aim was to address language disorders. The linguistic approach was based on clinical hypotheses, i.e. on studies of the processes and structures of non-pathological language, and to use this clinic to better understand language. In this approach, we are unable to understand how the brain works, since anatomical and clinical principles are not taken into account.

2.3 The neuroanatomical approach

In this approach, the classification of aphasia refers to the neuroanatomical aspect of the brain and each cerebral area represents a distinct cerebral area with specific functions. It is a connectionist localisation theory which reveals that distinct cerebral centres have specific functions. This concept is based on a neuroanatomical classification of aphasia (Bonin, 2003), and confirms the linguistic approach. Neuroanaotomic classifications do not take linguistic assumptions into account.

Furthermore, the localisationist conception shows that language disorders are categorised on the basis of neurological lesions. Localisationist classifications include aphasia related to the motor functions of the oral-phonatory apparatus, hence motor aphasia, and the second type of aphasia related to lesions of the acoustic areas, including sensory aphasia. Advances in imaging are attempting to establish neural networks based on cerebral localisation for each aphasia. Studies by Chomel, Leloup, & Bernard (2010) reveal that the semantic and syntactic disorganisation of language cannot be explained by localisationist classifications. In addition, medical imaging research is attempting to find the link between neural networks and the cerebral lesion in aphasia.

However, the current perspective assumes that various cerebral areas involve several cerebral areas in the language process. The current view is much more dynamic and admits many cerebral areas for any language process (Shallice, 1988).

---

[2] - Fluent aphasias are characterised by logorrhea (a rapid flow of verbal output), while non-fluent aphasias are characterised by a reduction in verbal output, leading to mutism.

2.4 The neurolinguistic approach

Research in functional anatomy (Germin, Ricordel, 2017) shows that in the neurolinguistic approach, cerebral knowledge is closely related to linguistic models (Sabouaud, 1995). This classification model considers that extra-linguistic disturbances are at the origin of the disorganisation of language performance. This approach is defined by the level of performance and skills; the generative linguistic conception (Chomsky, 1957). As a result, the aphasia clinic is taken into account in the neurolinguistic approach. The link between cerebral degeneration and language theory has been developed on the basis of the processes that construct phonemes and semes, morphology and syntax (Chomesy & Piaget 1982).

2.5 The neuropsycholinguistic approach

In this approach, we refer to language disorders as well as to the cognitive linguistic system, hence its multidisciplinary nature. Neural networks represent a strategic system in relation to language, as has been confirmed by research into medical imaging (J-N. Nespoulous, 2016).

In the neuropsycholinguistic approach, we rely on the anatomoclinical approach. For example, agrammatism is characterised by a deficit in functional words, whereas lexical words are preserved in the linguistic system of the aphasic Basso & al. (1985). This reflects the hypothesis that these two types of class are treated differently by the cerebral system. The neuropsycholnguistic approach is based on the cerebral, structural and functional architecture of language. The aim is to determine the various types of cognitive dissociation in aphasia. Today, studies in neuropsycholinguistics have enabled us to gain a deeper understanding of the linguistic cognitive system and brain activity during language processing in the brain.

3. The structural and neuroanatomical organisation of language in aphasia

In the present study we will explain aphasia on the basis of two models representing the structural organisation of language. A model comprising three levels of articulation and four types of linguistic unit (Gil, 2006) and the model based on linguistic and psycho-cognitive concepts (Zellal, 2011).

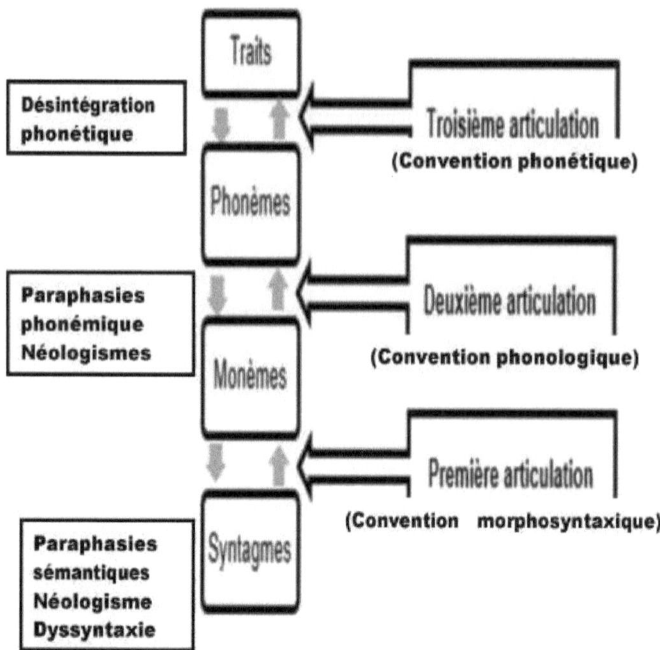

Figure 1: Representation of the three levels of articulation (Gil, 1989)

The units of the first articulation represent the monemes, i.e. the minimal units of meaning, the smallest meaning-bearing units. This significant unit is divided into two types of unit: lexemes (with lexical value, referring to an empirical concept such as nouns and verbs), and morphemes (referring to the grammatical class representing number, tense, gender, mode and logical connectors).

The signifier (the sonic aspect) and the signified (the semantic aspect) are the two components of the moneme

For example, in the word courais, we distinguish two distinct units of meaning: the action of running and the indication of temporality: cour and ais. These two units carry meaning. The combination and choice of these monemes, with reference to syntactic rules, form syntagms and sentences.

The units of the second articulation are the phonemes, the distinctive units that enable words to be distinguished from each other. The phoneme represents an abstract entity that corresponds to several sounds. In each language, there is a limited number of phoneme combinations that make up the monemes. In aphasiology, language disorders can be detected in the first and second articulations.

-Cognitive-behavioural model (N. Zellal, 2011)

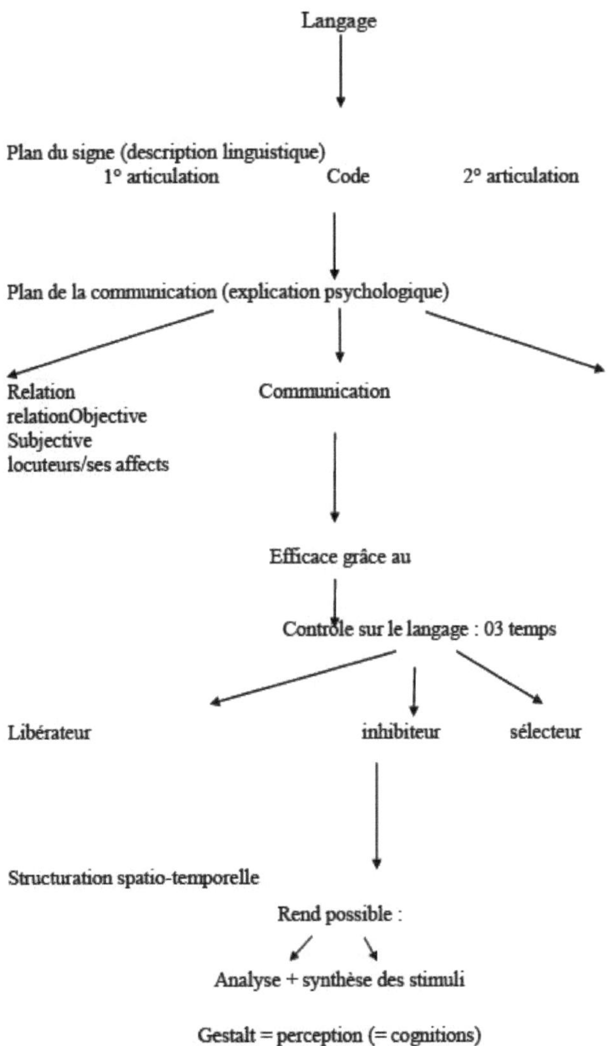

Figure 2 - Elaboration of a definition of language taken from Zellal (2011) This model takes into account concepts from developmental psychology and the theory of perception, which explain aphasic language disorders as a unique phenomenon. Aphasics have the ability to analyse language but have difficulty synthesising it (its gestalt) [2].

Gestalt represents language, which is made up of precise words whose meaning varies according to context. The creation of meaning is a conscious process in aphasics.

In their communication and creation of meaning, aphasics present a temporal disorder, experiencing difficulty in the use of their code, manifested by an exaggerated release time (or diffluence) or despotic inhibitory control (reduction), which leads to a disturbance in word reading time (paraphasia and jargon) or inhibition (severe psycholinguistic reductions).

4. Aphasia and the linguistic sign

The language disorder in aphasia reflects a disorganisation between the signifier and the signified in linguistics. As a result, we can explain aphasia on two levels, representing the two sides of the linguistic sign (Alajouanine, 1968): the signifier or the acoustic form of the linguistic sign, which represents the second articulation (selection and arrangement of the phonemes that make up the monemes), and the conceptual aspect or the signifier, which refers to the first articulation (construction of syntagms and sentences from sectioned monemes).

The linguistic unities of each side of the linguistic sign are determined by these two aspects: the axis of choice (paradigmatic) and the axis of construction (syntagmatic).

So the production of a word or a sentence is determined by these two ways of organising linguistic units: on the paradigmatic axis, it is characterised by the choice of phonemes (second articulation) and words (first articulation), and on the syntagmatic axis, it is characterised by the choice of phonemes (second articulation) and words (first articulation).

[1] - https://urnop-alger2.com/images/labo/redefinition.aphasie

and words (Jakobson, 1963). Moreover, in our study, articulatory disorders are not taken into account, nor is movement of the phonatory apparatus (mouth, organ of phonation)-third articulation- (Bouquet, 2012). In addition, we are interested in the linguistic contribution in relation to the clinic of the aphasic.

- **The neuroanatomical hierarchy of language in aphasia**

The neuroanatomical structure of language is located in the dominant hemisphere of the brain (left). We will note two axes: an expressive axis representing oral and written production, and a receptive axis encompassing input modalities (hearing, vision) as well as comprehension of oral and written language.

- **The expressive axis of language**

The area of the expressive axis (Broca's) represents the seat of articulate language, and damage to this area causes what is known as "Broca's" aphasia. Broca's area is responsible for phonological and semantic processing and corresponds to the opercular and triangular parts (Brodmann's areas 44 and 45) which are part of the inferior frontal gyrus (Seron and Latter. 1986). They are linked to the insula and basal ganglia and are involved in phonetic programming.

The prefrontal cortex is composed of promoter areas. The mediodorsal nucleus of the thalamus has connections with the prefrontal cortex (LeMinor & Dillenseger. 2019). Thus, the entire communicative mechanism in relation to the context of language is directed by the prefrontal cortex, which handles several cognitive and language activities (Kail, Fayol. 2000).

- **The receptive axis of language**

The inability to understand spoken language reflects Wernicke's aphasia, which is characterised by a lesion in Wernicke's area. Karl Wernicke (1874) showed that language sounds are recognised in the posterior part of the first temporal convolution. This is done in order to attribute meaning to them (Campolini § al. 2003).

Medical imaging shows that phonological and articulatory word processing is performed by the **supramarginal gyrus**. In addition, semantic processing is handled by the angular gyrus, which is active in language in relation to the right hemisphere.

The identification and categorisation of objects is determined by the phonological and semantic aspects of language, and is managed by the neurons of the angular and supramarginal gyrus (a multimodal associative region receiving auditory, visual and somato-sensory inputs).

The auditory system's processes of hearing words spoken or visual perception of words read are not processed by the language areas. Language comprehension is performed by the auditory cortex, which enables sound recognition, an essential prerequisite. At the same time, object recognition and the identification of names during reading are performed by the visual cortex, which is responsible for the conscious vision of the language context.

- **A central associative region**

All the associative fibres of the arcuate bundle anatomically form Broca's and Wernicke's areas. The central associative areas group together various cerebral areas; the insular cortex, the opercular portion of the motor areas (areas 4 and 6) and somesthetic areas (areas 1, 2, 3) as well as the parietal opercular area, which consists of the somesthetic area, (Falten, 2011). Impairment of the cerebral components that anatomically form this area will result in aphasia.

The areas of each language centre have their own specificity and act in parallel Broca's area and Wernicke's area are connected by the nerve fibres of the arcuate bundle. The emotional connotation of words is processed by the right hemisphere. These two areas, which are essential for language production and comprehension, have a multimodal function that is at the same time distinct (Rondal & Seron, 2003).

Dahene (2015) has shown in his research that a complementary motor area outside the perisylvian area located on the inside of the frontal lobe[3] plays a relevant role in the language process. This reflection reflects the observation that a lesion in this area, which is characteristic of the word pronunciation process, causes a language disorder that may develop into mutism (Posner and Raichle, 1994). Therefore, language is not simply an interaction between two essential areas of language production and comprehension (Broca & Wernicke). The production of language represents a whole complex cerebral organisation involving various areas interacting with the language process. This explains why other forms of aphasia

3 appendix 4, p 290.

cannot be grouped under expression and reception (Lechevalier, 1989; Joanette & Roch Lecours, 2000).

5. Neurolinguistic characteristics of the different clinical types of aphasia

In order to present the main forms of aphasia, we have drawn on the interdisciplinary theories of Sabouraud (1995), Roch-Lecours & Lhermitte (1979) and Gil (2006), Rondal & Seron (2003).

The following criteria: non-fluent/fluent, motor/sensory as well as expression/reception, anterior/posterior[4] represent relevant data in the structure of the different forms of aphasia as well as in their classification:

Fluency and non-fluency are the two traditional classification criteria used to distinguish the two main categories of aphasia (Lecours & Lhermitte, 1979).

It's about making a comparison through the abundance of oral language production: quantity is measured by the rate of fluency.

The categories of Wernicke's aphasia are defined by fluency versus non-fluency, while Broca's aphasia is characterised by non-fluency.

Logopenic aphasia is characterised by a near-normal verbal flow. This type of aphasia is therefore not taken into account by this form of distinction (fluency and non-fluency). [3]

Conductive and anomic aphasias present a speech rate slowed down by interruptions and hesitations caused by a lack of words, but the aphasic is able to produce sentences of normal length.

5.1 Aphasias defined by classic cerebral language areas

In order to define these cerebral areas, we will refer to lexico-semantic disorders in oral names of action[4][5] .

- Broca's aphasia

Broca's aphasia is characterised by a deficit in the combination of phonemes and syntagms, which implies a reduction in speech revealed by brief, sparse production with long pauses, agrammatism, perseverations, elisions and arthric disorders. In this type of aphasia, language is affected at the level of the relationship between signifier and signified.

We can also find central and subcortical lesions due to damage to the territory of the sylvian artery (Alexander & Hillis, 2008) (middle cerebral anterior and posterior branches).

- Wernicke's aphasia

In Wernicke's aphasia, all the components of language are affected: comprehension and production. This is due to damage to the middle cerebral artery in the territory of the posterior and inferior branches of the first left temporal convolution, and to associative fibres (Mazaux et al. 1987). This damage results in a disorder of the language of meaning and signifier, revealed by a disturbance in the selection of

---

[4] -See appendix 3, p 285.
[5] -See appendix 4, p 286.

phonemes and monemes, at the level of taxonomic capacity.

Aphasic language is characterised by lexical disturbance: neologisms, phonemic paraphasias in spontaneous speech and in oral naming tasks.

- **Conductive aphasia**

The disconnection between the inferior frontal gyrus and the temporo-parietal cortex caused by a lesion at this level results in conduction aphasia. During oral naming, conduction aphasia produces phonemic paraphasias and palliative strategies, which will be the focus of our research in this study.

The main characteristics of language in this type of aphasia are fluidity of speech punctuated by palliative strategies (logopenic). The conduction aphasic makes various attempts to name the object, while being aware of his or her errors, and his or her oral naming productions are close to the target word. This means that conduction aphasics refer to a model in which they cannot break down all the components (D. Forest, 2005 p. 125).

5.2 Aphasias outside the language areas

• **Transcortical aphasias**

Transcortical aphasias are distinguished from other types of aphasia by the repetition of words. These types of aphasia are due to lesions outside the language areas that are connected to language-related pathways. This results in several symptoms (Alexander & Hillis, 2008).

In this group of aphasias we have three forms:

• **Transcortical motor aphasia**

The lesion in this form of aphasia is located in the supplementary motor area, more precisely in the prefrontal cortex of the left hemisphere, and consequently this cerebral area is found in the pre-motor region in front of Broca's area. From a linguistic point of view, language in transcortical motor aphasia is marked by pauses, resulting in short sentences with little syntax.

The major symptoms of language deficit in this aphasia are reduced language and lack of prompting.

It is characterised by a significant reduction in spontaneous language (which may develop into mutism), although the ability to repeat words is preserved (when it is massive, it is an echolalia) (Freedman, 1984).

• **Sensory aphasia**

Language is much more fluent in this form, which is made up of semantic paraphasias. While comprehension is affected, this is due to the area of impairment being located behind Wernicke's area (Rondal & Seron, 2003).

• **Mixed (global) transcortical aphasia**

This form of aphasia is represented by the two main classic types of Broca's aphasia, which involves a lesion in the left sylvian artery, with general inhibition of communication. The second form, Wernicke's aphasia, is defined by lesions in the left posterior cortical and subcortical areas, with an excessively fluent, jargon-filled speech rate and a comprehension disorder.

From a linguistic point of view, speech in this type of aphasia is virtually impossible. This is due to the cerebral lesions responsible for speech.

-Anomic aphasia

The lack of the word is important in this form of aphasia, and the speech of the aphasic is characterised by a fluency of speech that is even normally grammatically correct; adorned by periphrases and long pauses due to the lack of the word. Word repetition and comprehension seem to be preserved. From a cerebral point of view, the lesions causing this type of aphasia are located in the c level of the inferior temporal gyrus, which is most often the origin (Goodglass & Kaplan, 1972).

- Subcortical aphasia

Various cerebral areas are affected in subcortical aphasia, specifically the dominant hemisphere of language (thalamus, putamen, pallidum, caudate nucleus), the internal capsule, the external capsule and the anterior and posterior white matter (Pitre, 1989).

The variability of the regions affected in this type of aphasia gives rise to various linguistic disorders (Roch-Lecours, 1979). In terms of oral production, there is a high rate of verbal paraphrases, verbal incoherence, and spontaneous fluent logopenic speech, while comprehension is relatively preserved.

Chapter 2 Oral production and its disorders in aphasics

1. Lexical disorders in oral production

Oral production disorders in aphasics are manifested by articulatory disturbances; arthric disorders ..., syntactic disturbances; agrammatism, dyssyntaxia ..., lexical disturbances; missing words, paraphasia...

We will be looking at the process of word loss in the aphasic subject, and our analysis will focus on word selection (lexical level). The aim is to distinguish lexico-semantic disorders.

The aphasic presents various compensatory strategies representing linguistic phenomena that manifest themselves in the form of paraphasias in order to compensate for his or her language dysfunctions. Aphasic language is defined by several forms of phonemic, morphological and semantic paraphasia, manifested by lexical derivations. In our study, we will focus on semantic paraphasia, where the word produced retains a semantic proximity to the target word, for example "casserole for marmite" (Tran, 2000, p.176).

We will analyse this lexico-semantic language disorder through the oral production of semantic paraphrases of action verbs in relation to the functional properties of objects to be named in aphasics. The aim was to analyse the relationship between action verbs and the functional properties of objects to be named in aphasics.

All forms of aphasia are characterised by deficits in spontaneous language, reflected in an inability to produce a lexicon appropriate to the context of speech.

In this chapter, we will briefly present the various linguistic studies on lexical access difficulties in non-pathological adults (Tran, 2000, p.35-40), in order to highlight the characteristics of lexical production disorders.

1.1 How non-pathological adults find their words

Speech represents a system of relationships in which two types of relationship are manifested on two axes: the syntagmatic axis constitutes an ordered chain of lexical units, which a speaker must respect in order to be understood. On this axis, linguistic signs are linked in succession to their surroundings (Saussure, 1995). The second axis is the paradigmatic or associative axis, where lexical units are represented outside the discourse chain, i.e. at the level of language.

In order to produce the target word, several operations are carried out by the speaker. The speaker draws on a "lexical store" or "paradigm" comprising different exchangeable lexical units.

Aphasics are not the only ones to suffer from this linguistic malaise. Memory lapses in oral production can be observed in normal speakers:

According to Blanche-Benveniste, quoted by Tran (2000, p.36), various forms of word failure can occur in a non-aphasic speaker, for example lapses (substitution), reflecting the fact of having a word on the tip of the tongue (Bonin, 1995, p.23), hesitations, hyper-corrections and approximations which do not affect speech. On the other hand, the over-abundance of these transformations in aphasics makes their speech pathological.

1.2 Encoding and decoding
a. The speech process

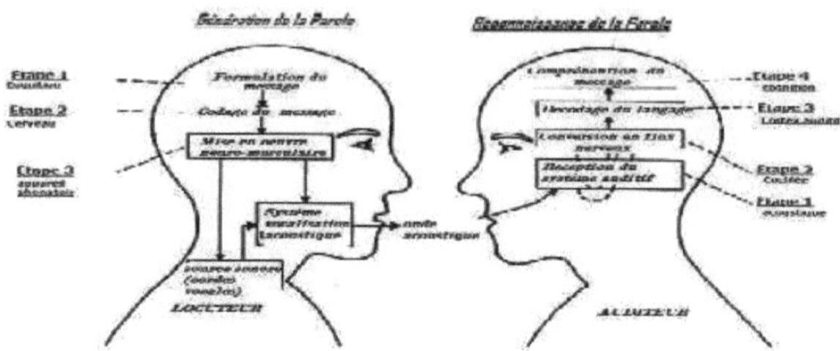

Any act of utterance intended to inform, question or explain to an interlocutor represents the speech process. The naming of a situation involves setting up the elements of a socialised linguistic code on a sound substrate with a view to a dialogical action. This is achieved by weaving semantic and pragmatic reasoning between the self and the world.

(A. Bertrand, & P. Henri Garnier, 2005). In other words, speaking is: naming objects, naming others, describing and predicating, i.e. carrying out transformations, reasoning, convincing and arguing. So speech is not just a simple exchange of information; it is a cognitive process that takes account of the state of the world (context).

1.3 The lack of words in aphasia

All the disorders of lexical production (semantic paraphasia, jargon, neologism or no response) represent the lack of words in aphasia, which can go as far as mutism (Nespoulous, 1980).

The inability to name words or situations in spontaneous language is a major synonym of the word deficit found in all forms of aphasia (Pillon, 2002). This lexical deficit manifests itself in various forms: empty words, periphrases and circumlocution "It's the object where we put our things to go to school" for satchel designer, pauses in the production of words, sometimes going as far as mutism.

The lack of words can affect either spontaneous or induced language. During induced language, the speech therapist gives the aphasic oral naming tests in order to assess the different cognitive processes (Moreaud & al. 2010).

During an oral image naming task, we detect various linguistic behaviours that reflect a lack of words. Abbreviated sentences, long pauses, indecision and the use of general lexical forms (machin, chose, etc   ) all reflect a lack of words.

This lack-of-word disorder is defined by the production of empty words, manifested by an inability or even an inability to produce the target word.

(C. Bogliotti, p.99).

This symptom of aphasia is manifested by periphrases and circumlocutions, or approach behaviours.

In his article "Les troubles de la denomination orale" C. Bogliotti (2012, p.99) summarises the different linguistic manifestations of word failure in the following table:

Manifestations of the lack of words in speech	Definitions and examples
Empty words	Meaningless lexical units " machin, chose, truc, bidule " (thing, thing, thing, thing)
Crosstalk	Oral language disorder resulting from neurological damage, in which the subject replaces one linguistic unit (phoneme, word) with another.
Phonemic paraphasias	Modification of the order of phonemes within a word Addition (/debabyla/ for deambulant) Omission (/San'p~ c / for champignon, /kapab/ for capable)
Verbal paraphasia	Use of one word for another without there being any relationship of meaning between the two, this word often coinciding with an existing word in the language "echelle" for office "Il faut recoudre mon mouton".
Semantic paraphasia	Use of one word for another, but which are related in meaning "cup" for glass "pear" for apple.
Circumlocution	"It has a point" for knife.
Approach drive	Successive attempts to produce the target word, generating phonemic or semantic paraphrases, spontaneously corrected "per... pare... parapi... parapli" for umbrella (phonemic approach in a phonemic paraphrase).
Commentaries metalinguistics	"It starts with an 'o' for orange.
Filled breaks	"hum", "euh
Delayed evocation	
No production	

Synonymous approximations" are part of the way we approach things

(Gil, 2003), for example, for the target word "ciseau", the aphasic responds as follows: "euh...c'est; pour le papier on coupe".

The lack of words can be compensated for by periphrases, e.g. for the word "refrigerator": "It's the object in which I put all the food to preserve it" (Pillon & De Partz, 1999), and sometimes by explanations or gestures interpreting the action.

1.4 Characteristics of anomie

The inability to produce a word corresponding to a psycholinguistic context is an anomaly which represents the main symptom in aphasia. Goodglass. H and Wingfield. A (1997, p.3) reveal in this sense that among the language disorders in aphasia, anomia is the most prominent aphasic symptom.

Absence of response, long pauses, various paraphrases and palliative strategies are synonymous with anomie, which takes different linguistic forms. In her research, Nespoulous & al (2008) cite five forms:

- **Sorting anomia**: In this type of anomia, the aphasic possesses semantic features concerning the object to be named but is unable to produce the target word. In this case, the aphasic presents a lack of the separated word (cut), and productions are accentuated by periphrases and mimes.

- **Construction anomia:** is characterised by phonemic decouplings that are not produced correctly (phonemic paraphasias, neologisms); if there is no motor impairment, the deficit may be articulatory.

In the motor area, we will see frontal lesions which give rise to so-called motor aphasias. Furthermore, if there are phonological disturbances, this implies conduction aphasia. As a result, the production anomaly is not affected by semantic disturbances.

- **Conceptual (semantic) anomia:** in this context, the aphasic has comprehension problems.

-**Conceptual anomia**: concerns lexical encoding disorders in lexico-semantic categories (Damasio et al. 1979). We will go into more detail on this concept in Chapter 4, of categorial disorders in relation to the nature of the word: grammatical/semantic category verb versus noun (Tranel et al. 2008).

- **Sensory anomia**: this results from a specific sensory cause and causes difficulty in naming the word.

2.lexicalisation deficits in neuropsychology

Research in neuropsychology and cognitive psychology has shown that acoustic analysis and lexical activation in the cognitive system and language represent precision in the processing of information. This processing takes place in both the phonological and semantic systems.

Thus, from the observation of cognitive disorders following brain injury, it is possible to make inferences about cognitive processes in relation to normal cognitive activities. From these concepts, models of information processing can be constructed.

In order to interpret how language functions, these processing models will specify the different components of language functions in oral production, with the aim of interpreting the disorders observed in aphasics.

2.1 Oral production

Several processes make up oral production (Tran, 2007):

-The definition of concepts in oral discourse reflects **the stage of conceptualisation of** the discourse.

- The transformation of the conceptual structure into a linguistic or lexical structure **represents the stage of linguistic enunciation** (Nespoulous & Vribel, 2003).

Another highly relevant process in oral production is based on two axes:

The choice of lexicon corresponding to the context of utterance is made on the paradigmatic axis, in order to associate and arrange words in syntagmatic discourse (Chapter 1).

Two types of retrieval are involved in the lexical selection process: retrieval at the lemma level, which encodes the semantic information of words. The second type of retrieval concerns morphology, and retrieves information about the word form which represents the lexeme level while encoding phonological properties. The process of activating representations stored in memory constitutes the mode of word retrieval.

-The selected lexical units are combined in the mental lexicon, arranged according to the syntactic rules of the language.

-The last phase of production in this stage consists of the structuring of the linguistic message, which is represented by a sound form and a sequence of articulated words. Various models have been proposed to account for lexical production, and these conceptions of lexical production access diverge. Each type of processing is specific to the model of lexical production (Caramazza & Hillis, 1990), (Levelt et al. 1999).

2.2 Lexicalisation and its disorders

We distinguish two types of lexicalisation disorder on the basis of neuropsychological models of lexical processing: lexico-semantic and lexico-phonological.

-The lexical system

The classic model devised by Caramazza & Hillis (1990) represents the lexical system, which is defined as a modelisation of the components and stages involved in word production (Tran, 2007). Several lexical categories make up the lexical system where input (auditory/visual) and output (oral/written) modalities are interconnected. Any disorganisation of these processing methods results in difficulties in producing the target word in relation to its context.

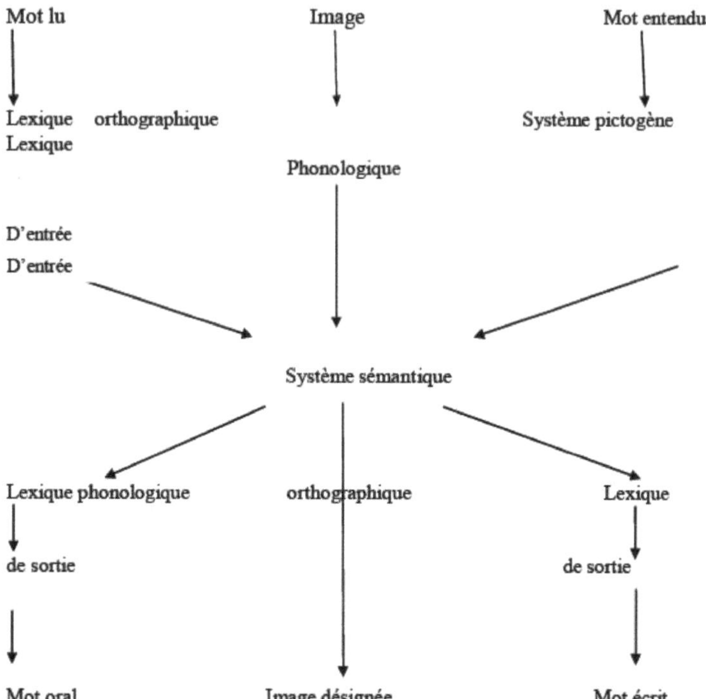

Figure 4: Lexical processing of language (Tran, 2007, p.16)

We will describe the constituents involved in oral production, focusing on the semantic system and the phonological output lexicon in relation to the disruptive effects which lead to semantic paraphasia.

- **The semantic system**

The various modes of input (oral, written, visual ....) and output (oral, written, gestural...) are involved in the production of words in the language system.

In order to access semantic representations of words, we use the semantic system. Semantic representations store words via this system. During processing, the semantic characteristics are activated in relation to the word (heard, read), in order to access the meaning.

The semantic system input provides access to lexical representations of words. It stores the semantic representations corresponding to the words (in various modalities).

Difficulties in activating the correct semantic representation are observed when one of these components is impaired. These difficulties are manifested either by impossible production or by semantic paraphrases due to partial activation of semantic associates sharing semantic features with the target concept.

We distinguish two types of lexicalisation disorders in oral production when the semantic system is impaired: lexico-phonological disorders in which the semantic system is unaffected, and lexico-semantic disorders in which the semantic system is affected.

Two points of view relate to this concept, and researchers have not used a reference model of semantic processing: a single semantic system common to all input and output modalities (Caramazza & Hillis, 1990), (Morton & Patterson, 1980), multiple semantic systems specific to each input modality (Shallice, 1988). We refer to the model presented above.

- The phonological lexicon in the output lexical system

When an oral response is available, the phonological output lexicon is activated. It stores phonological representations of terms and receives knowledge from the linguistic system.

Several inputs are possible, with the exception of the linguistic system. During processing, the phonological representation corresponding to the evoked linguistic representation is activated.

When the phonological output lexicon is determined in isolation, a number of errors appear: problems activating the phonological output representation that corresponds to the linguistic representation being addressed (the words are phonologically close), oral language would be almost impossible, we notice neologisms, semantic paraphasias, circumlocutions.

These disorders show that the aphasic possesses semantic information about the object to be named, and are related to the phonological output disorder.

Partial activation of the semantic system gives rise to semantic paraphrases sharing semantic features with the target concept, which in turn activate the phonological representations corresponding to these semantic associates. In this case, we will have a response semantically related to the target word. Comprehension is preserved in aphasics with a disturbance of the phonological lexicon. We use Tran's (2007) presentation of the lexical system to describe lexicalisation disorders.

3. Brain and language

3.1 The organisation of language in the brain

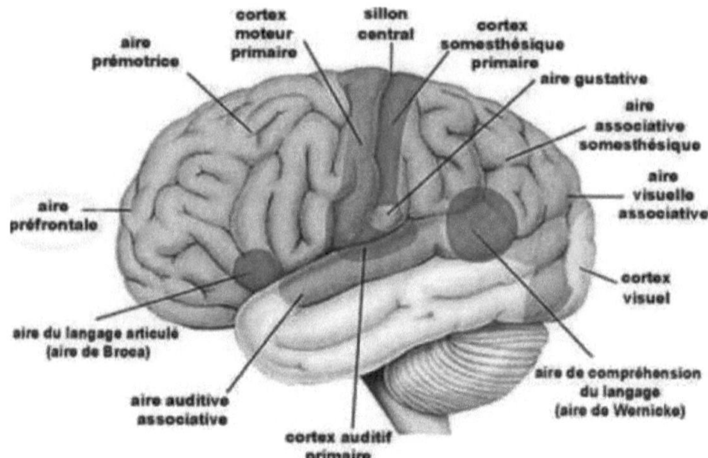

Figure 5: Representation of cerebral areas [5]

By perceiving the messages emitted by others and in the controlled articulation of the sounds emitted in order to attribute meaning to them. The brain is the conductor of human communication.

Language is regular if, on the one hand, the phonatory organs (mouth, tongue, pharynx and nose) are not impaired and, on the other hand, the nerve structures, mainly the brain, are functioning correctly.

Any order transmitted by the brain to the phonatory organs results in what we call language. However, the end result is speech, which involves the brain making a number of decisions at different levels.

What's more, the way language is organised in the brain is as follows: the brain is made up of two hemispheres, the left and the right.

In the majority of individuals, the language areas are located in the left hemisphere. Two of these areas are particularly important: Broca's area and Wernicke's area. Broca's area is located in the anterior part of the brain and is mainly responsible for articulate language (expression).

Wernicke's area is located in the posterior part of the brain; it is mainly responsible for the receptive aspect of language (comprehension) (Nouveau Larousse Medical, cerveau, p.200).

Language, like other cognitive activities, depends on specialised regions of the brain:

1.1 -www.questmachine.org/article/Notre_cerveau

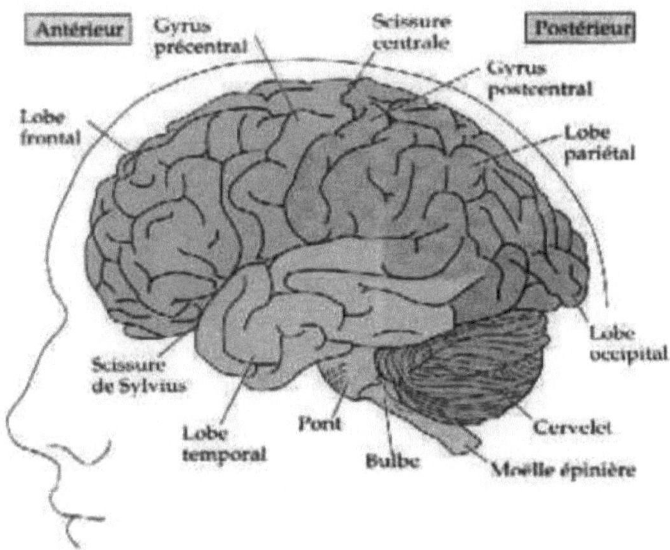

Figure 6: Mapping of areas related to oral communication (speech and hearing) in the brain [6]

1.2 The brain, a complex organ

The oval-shaped brain is the largest organ in the human body, weighing around 1,300 kilograms, equivalent to 2 to 3% of the body weight. It contains 74% water and is made up of two main hemispheres separated by a deep median groove, each specialising in a particular set of tasks:

The left hemisphere governs the verbal, the abstract, the temporal, the rational, the analytical, the symbolic, the numerical, the logical and the linear.

- The right hemisphere, for its part, directs the consciousness of things, synthesis, concreteness, analogy, the irrational, the spatial, the intuitive, the global and the timeless.

The brain is a general area of the central nervous system, controlling our ideas and thoughts. There are over a hundred billion interconnected nerve cells that transmit and receive messages from different parts of the body.

These cells are the seat of intellectual, sensory and motor functions. The hemispheres are divided into four parts or, more commonly, lobes - The frontal lobe, which is located in the anterior part of the cerebral hemispheres, contains the centres responsible for muscular control, such as chewing, licking and swallowing, as well as the centres for thought, memory, reasoning and associations;

- The parietal lobe, which is located in the upper part of the brain, behind the frontal lobe, receives information related to touch and orientation in space;

- The occipital lobe, located at the back of the hemispheres, contains the centres responsible for vision;

- The temporal lobe, which is located on the side next to the temporal bone in the lower part of the brain, contains the hearing, taste and memory centres. The functions of each lobe are coordinated by commissural fibres that link the two hemispheres. The right hemisphere is therefore opposed to the left.

1.3 The distinction between the right and left hemispheres

Left Hemisphere	Right Hemisphere
Verbal name, describe, define	**Non-verbal** Awareness of things, but limited connection with words.
Analytical Discovering things step by step, element by element.	**Synthetique** Placantles choses together to form a whole.
Symbolic To use a symbol to replace something.	**Concret** Connect with things as they are at the moment.
Abstract Extracting information and using it to represent the whole.	**Analogical** relates the links between things, including metaphors.
Temporal Keeping track of time, organising things sequentially and executing them in order.	**Atemporal** does not refer to time
Rational Drawing conclusions based on facts and reasoning.	**Non-rational** Does not need facts and reasoning; inclined not to judge.
Digital or digital Using numbers and their instructions.	**Spatial** Seeing where things are in relation to others and how the parts form a whole.
Logic Drawing conclusions based on logical organisation.	**Intuitive** Proceeding in leaps and bounds, from impressions, feelings, visual images and pieces of information.
Linear Thinking in terms of linked ideas, convergent thinking.	**Global** Perceiving wholes, associating parts, diverging conclusions.

Table 1: The distinction between the left and right hemispheres (Claude-Pierre Vincent, p. 162).

1.4 Areas of the brain

The brain comprises several areas corresponding to different functions.

If we look at the left hemisphere of the brain from the forehead upwards, we can see that the **prefrontal cortex** contains **the thinking area**, which plays an important role in decision-making, problem-solving and self-awareness, and is also involved in **immediate memory**, accounting for 30% of the cortex.

We then move on to **the pre-motor area**, which has a single role, that of designing gestures. The secondary area is closely linked to the pre-motor area. **The primary sensory area** perceives the pressure of objects on the skin, the position of muscles in space, pain and temperature.

The secondary sensitive area translates the sensations perceived by the preceding area. The **secondary visual area** combines information about colours, shapes, etc. , and gives meaning to the image.

In **the primary visual area,** we perceive shapes and colours without trying to relate them, unlike **the secondary sensory area.**

The role of the **cerebellum** is to collect the messages that **the motor area sends** to the muscles and to correct them in order to carry out a harmonious movement.

Next to it is **the secondary auditory area**, which identifies sounds, and then **the primary auditory area**, which perceives sound waves.

Finally, the last area of the cortex is **Broca's area (language expression area),** which is essential for pronouncing words (Nouveau Larousse medical, 2000).

The motor area of language or **Broca's area** is located in front of the premotor area (frontal lobe).

Wernicke's **area of integration of written and** spoken **language** is located in the posterior part of the temporal lobe of one hemisphere (usually the left in right-handed people).

1.5 Para-verbal aspects of language

Language is not just verbal; a great deal of information is expressed through non-verbal channels. According to Aryle (1985) non-verbal language comprises five aspects (Argyle, 1985, p.173) whose function is to punctuate, modulate, accentuate language and/or provide feedback to the speaker;

1-vocal accompaniment of language 2- facial expressions of language 3- gaze 4-kinetic signals, postures and gestures 5- occupation of space.

-Vocal language aids

We distinguish two kinds of vocal signs ".... Accompanying oral utterances according to whether or not they are related to the semantic content of verbal remission" (Argyle, 1985, p.173).

Firstly, the idiosyncratic aspects not directly related to the semantic content of the verbal message, which deal with the **vocal** properties of **the speaking subjects;** they include the timbre of the voice used to communicate attitudes and emotions, voice types and national, regional and individual accents.

-Speech signals acting as modulators of semantic language content: These signals make it possible to complete the meaning and provide synchronisation of verbal productions. However, these signals are independent of the phonetic characteristics of the language. Argyle presents **intonation,** as the constituent of vocal patterns, for example the ascending and descending contours marking either interrogation or declaration, the sound accentuation of certain elements of the utterance (to be distinguished from the tonic accent whose place is fixed in French and therefore non-contrastive) and the tempo, or variations in the rhythm of verbal utterances. Expressive sentence stylistics, characterised by pauses at the end of sentences and the separation of phrases and clauses in complex sentences.

-Prosody is made up of: intonation, accentuation and tempo and are used simultaneously or separately in verbal utterances.

Argyle shows that the status of prosodic signals remains a controversial issue in psycholinguistics. There is no general rule for defining the criteria for the production of prosodic contexts in a language, because the use of prosodic contexts remains dependent on the individual characteristics of the partners in the interactive episode, such as motivation, social status, affective components of the personality, etc.

However, there are relationships between prosody and utterance structures, while intonation and stress modulate certain types of utterance.

(Declarative, interrogative, etc.).

On the other hand, verbal utterances are modulated by prosodic signals which have meaning only insofar as they adorn these verbal messages. Unlike gestures and postures, which can be emitted independently of any verbal language, but as a set of more or less precise characteristics serving to modulate the meaning of the verbal message and sometimes to alter it in certain conditions of the[7] interactive 'episode'.

-Facial expressions

The human face is one of the most important parts of the non-verbal signal.

Facial expressions represent both certain individual characteristics and various aspects of emotional life, that is to say; that in oral discourse, they have a modulating function on the verbal between two people, in other words during a dialogue the facial movements between the speaker and the listener serve to complete the meaning of the verbal messages, for example if the listener does not understand what the speaker is saying, or doubts the veracity of the message, he will adopt a questioning mimic or will puff out his cheeks to express his incomprehension and/or his sceptical air with regard to the message.

-The look

Argyle considers that a person looks at another person primarily to obtain information rather than to provide it (Rondal, 1985, p.176), because people are a means of receiving signals. In a communicative action between two individuals (speaker and listener) the gaze has the function of modulating interactions because the gaze and the act of speaking are always in association from the moment the gaze provides feedback. It should also be noted that Aryle has shown in his research that a person looks twice as much at their partner when they are listening than when they are speaking.

-Postures and gestures

When speaking, each person adopts postures and makes hand gestures in order to modulate the language. The postural and gestural modifications accompanying the verbal act can be generically referred to as kinetic signals, which translate the occupation of space in non-verbal communication.

1.6 Memory

Human memory represents a complex cerebral activity that our brain possesses to record, store and retrieve information in order to use this acquired knowledge. The sequence of events since our birth forms the elaboration of our identity (Domart § Bourneuf ,1986). Memory enables us to retain the information we have stored and consciously retrieve it at a later date.

- Encoding, storage and retrieval

Memory is responsible for storing information and retrieving it. It should also be pointed out that information can be lost, recounted or imagined. Factors relating to affectivity (motivation, attention or emotion) are important in the formation of a memory.

The memory is based on a storage system or several storage modes, each with its own capacity and duration.

The following are the different stages in memorisation: **a. Encoding**

In order to give meaning to information, the process of processing is implemented by encoding it and turning it into a real memory. This is done by interpreting the information in neuron language. Encoding represents sensory stimulation in the form of an electrical current (Bertrand § Garnier, 2005, p. 122), (For example, our mouths detect a taste through the taste buds, which involves stimulation of the nerves in contact, which then send an electrical current to the brain and then to the memory in order to attribute a meaning to the taste).

b. Storage

Once the information has been assigned a meaning, it must be stored in the appropriate area of the brain by the cerebral activity we call "storage".

7-The word "episode" refers to the speech sequence in a communication

Certain factors have an effect on the retention of information: the greater the affective charge, the longer it will be stored, and the longer the storage time (Bertrand § Garnier, 2005, p.122). If information is not constantly reused, its storage time will remain unlimited.

c.Consolidation

The transition from short-term to long-term memory represents the consolidation of information so that it can be forgotten (Bertrand § Garnier, 2005, p.122). This process is slow and continuous, lasting up to more than 10 years.

d. Recovery

The process of "recuperation" (Bertrand § Garnier, 2005, p.124) is the bringing together of several constituent elements in order to reuse information that has already been stored. For example (remembering the journey to the bakery comes back to us when we go to buy bread). If one of the stages in the memorisation process is poorly carried out, either encoding or storage, there will be a retrieval problem, what we call a 'memory gap'.

3.7 Different types of memory

According to the different interconnected neural networks, there are five types of memory: **working memory** (short-term memory at the centre of the neural network), **semantic** and **episodic memory** (two systems of long-term conscious representation), **procedural memory** (which refers to unconscious automatisms) and **perceptual memory** (which relates to the senses).

a.Short-term memory

Short-term memory is used to recall information from 1 second to 10 minutes after the encoding process, and is a memory of the present. This type of memory is constantly active, for example to retain a telephone number long enough to dial it. On average, the human being is capable of remembering seven different elements simultaneously in the short term.

Short-term memory represents a pre-memorisation of long-term memory. There are in fact interactions between these two memory systems. For example, when we learn a song, we trigger a voluntary learning process by repeating it several times in order to store and consolidate it in long-term memory in interaction with short-term memory. When certain areas of the prefrontal, occipital and parietal cortex are altered, short-term memory is affected by 'antegrade amnesia'.

b.Working (or immediate) memory

The manipulation of information stored in our short-term memory is controlled by **working memory,** sometimes called immediate memory.

It is activated when we want to do two things at the same time, such as driving a car while talking on the phone.

It performs processing operations on information stored in memory on a one-off basis, for example, **sorting names in alphabetical order.**

c.   Long-term memory

Long-term memory is characterised by long-term storage within certain areas of the brain (Bertrand § Garnier, 2005, p.118), storing information for the **whole of** a **person's life.** Long-term memory has a considerable capacity, and depending on the nature of the information to be remembered, it can be broken down into different memory systems.

We distinguish between explicit and implicit memory:

•   **Explicit memory, or declarative memory**, encompasses semantic memory and episodic memory. It stores information expressed in language (a personal memory, for example).

•   **Implicit memory, also known as non-declarative memory** or **procedural** memory, is involved in the acquisition and use of motor skills (e.g. driving a car or playing a sport).

Long-term memory and short-term memory play an essential role in learning.

d.   Semantic memory

This memory is responsible for storing general knowledge about oneself (personal experience) and information about the world (geography, nature, names of objects, their functions, uses or characteristics. It is a memory of facts and theoretical concepts.

The information is organised in the form of a semantic network; the search for information depends on **the distance between the "subject of the question" node and the node where the information is located.**

Semantic memory is the memory of "definitive knowledge", representing a second declarative memory (Bertrand § Garnier, 2005, p.118). It is considered to refer to language, evolving over the course of research towards the knowledge we possess of the world around us.

In this conception, semantic memory is a system necessary for language and general knowledge. This memory stores the cognitive referents of input signals.

e. Episodic memory

Long-term memory activates **episodic memory**. This memory enables us to travel mentally through time and **project ourselves into the future**. It has the capacity to store information about **events experienced** and their context (place, date or emotional state).

In amnesia, this memory is altered. If we ask a person to recall a memory or to think about the next holiday, this memory is called upon.

f. Procedural (or motor) memory

Procedural memory is implicit memory *and* represents the second part of long-term memory. It is a memory of automatisms, skills and know-how. The execution of habitual gestures is automatic, which activates procedural memory, which is said to be unconscious: for example, when we walk, we do not consciously mobilise our muscles to walk and keep our balance.

g. Perceptive (or sensory) memory

It corresponds to the **memory of sensations experienced through our five senses**. It is activated when we store images (faces and places) or sounds (voices) without realising it. For example, a person goes home by habit, using visual cues.

Perceptual memory is activated by visual, auditory, tactile, gustatory and auditory perceptions, enabling us to recall events in a brief manner.

Based on our five senses, we distinguish between various sub-categories of perceptual memory: **visual memory** (which accounts for 80% of the information transmitted to the brain), **auditory memory** (which is crucial to musical creation), **tactile memory** (also known as kinesthetic memory), **gustatory memory** and **olfactory memory.**

4. Lexico-semantic deficits

Lexico-semantic disorders are manifested by lexical paraphasias "cahier" for motorbike (Tran, 2007, p.6), semantic lexical paraphasias "chaise" for table; (Tran, 2007, p.6) periphrases that do not necessarily have a semantic link with the target, e.g. "c'est pour le voyage" for a "valise". The difficulty in accessing the semantic system is marked by the variability of responses for various tasks.

4.1 Lexico-phonological deficits

In this type of disorder, aphasics refer to gestural compensation strategies that are informative, periphrases. This type of disorder is indicative of a post-semantic disorder in phonological retrieval.

Phonemic paraphasias present in all oral production situations characterise disorders of access to the phonological lexicon. Conduction aphasias due to impaired access to the phonological lexicon are characterised by this type of paraphasia.

We found that amnesic aphasia, where only lexical production is affected, is characterised by impaired access to the phonological output lexicon.

A semantic relationship with the target word is present in the errors produced.

4.2 Mixed lexical deficits

A number of symptoms reflect different levels of disturbance in the processing of comprehension and writing. Impairments in semantic and phonological recovery represent mixed disorders which are very frequent in aphasia. We thus observe the presence of these mixed disorders in so-called severe aphasias: Wernicke's aphasia, transcortical sensory aphasia, and even global aphasias where the disorders are relevant.

5. Compensatory approaches to lexical deficits

The various types of paraphasia are part of the compensatory strategies that aphasics use to overcome their linguistic handicap. Thus, the presence of paraphasia in lexical production is a symptom of a lexical disorder. The aphasic's difficulty in producing the target word in its appropriate context represents a language disturbance manifested by paraphasias of various types.

Paraphasias are classified according to their distinctive features, phonemes and monemes. These linguistic criteria will limit the categorisation of paraphasias. Hence the diversity of the different terminologies used to classify paraphrases. This is based on the structural analysis of language[8] (chapter 1, p. 30):

5.1 The different types of paraphasia

At the level of the third articulation of language, there are disturbances due to articulation deficits, reflecting features that make up phonemes unsuited to the target word. In this case, we speak of phonemic paraphasia. This is a form of phonemic disorganisation resulting in omission of phonemes and addition or reversal of phonemes. At this level, the disorder is located in the second articulation of language.

For example: /potaj/ for armchair; /malen/ for madeleine (Tran, 2000, p.161). If the word structure is no longer recognisable, we speak of a neologism.

All productions in which the phonological structure (phonetic and/or phonemic) is affected are called "segmental paraphasias" (Tran, 2000).

•   **Verbal or lexical paraphasia: the** replacement of one word by another, verbal paraphasia represents a lexical selection disorder. To explain this disorder, we drew on the work of Tran (2000), who used the term lexical paraphasia instead of verbal paraphasia, which could be confused with the verb.

It is at the level of the first articulation of language that this type of lexical disorganisation manifests itself.

We distinguish between two types of lexical paraphasia:

• **Formal lexical paraphasia** or (morphological verbal paraphasia): the word produced is formally related from a sound point of view to the expected word. For example: 'tulipe' for 'tuile'. They represent a disorder of the second articulation.

• **Semantic lexical paraphasia** or (semantic verbal paraphasia): the disorder corresponds to the choice of words, the product has a semantic relationship with the target word. For example: apple for tomato. This is a disorder of the first articulation, in our study we will focus on semantic lexical paraphasia affecting verbs.

• **Constructional paraphasia is the** poor production of words by the speaker that have not been built on the rules of word construction that determine the use of bases, suffixes and/or morphological procedures Tran (2000, p.172- 173) For example: "attache- gosier" for museliere; "debouchade" for tire-bouchon; "arrosier" for arrosoir.

This table summarises the different types of paraphasia according to Tran (2000).

Target word	Answer	Analysis level	Type of disorder	Denomination
Lezard	Frog	Meaning of the word	Lexical selection disorder	**Lexical semantic paraphasia**
Wild boar Fork	Ashtray	**Word form**	Disorder of selection, arrangement and/or	**Formal lexical paraphasia** / **Segmental paraphasia**
Mushroom	/puriit/		phoneme articulation	**Logatome**
Kettle	Boiler	**Word structure**	Word construction disorder	**Constructional paraphasia**

Table 2 The different types of Tran paraphasia (2000 p. 177).

Tran (2000) represents complex paraphasias which are manifested by various transformations between several paraphasias; this is a "dynamic" approach: in the table Tran presents :

Complex paraphasias: in this type of paraphasia, we use several levels of analysis. For example, an aphasic tries to name the word "fourche": "une peche", "une beche". Peche is a segmental disorder of beche and beche is a disorder of lexical selection of the target word, so we speak of formal semantic paraphasia. The last aspect of lexical deficits that we will discuss is neologisms and logatoms (Tran, 2000).

Neologism: Neology is "the process of forming new lexical units" (J. Dubois et al. Dictionnaire de linguistique et des sciences du français).

Language). In addition, the neologism expresses the consequence of this process which concerns a new word and its meaning, new word or new meaning of a word. Superordinate units of words are considered to be neologisms (J.-F. Sablayrolles,

2000, p.225), for example: neological productions by allusion. In aphasiology, if the word produced has no structural or semantic similarity, we speak of a neologism. However, in language sciences, J. Dubois defines a neologism as a new signifier and a new link between signifier and signified, i.e. a new lexical unit in unconventional communication in linguistic usage (Dubois § al. 2002 p.322).

Logatome : A logatome can be defined by a syllable (sounds) or sequence of sounds that are related to phonological rules and have no meaning (they do not form a word); e.g. probita, idarbula.... J. Dubois et al (2002 p.290).

A logatome can represent a formal lexical paraphasia, in that it is composed of a series of phoneme that have no meaning in the language Tran (2000 p. 162).

Lexical deficits define the oral language of aphasics. The aphasic has knowledge of the word to be produced. In order to compensate for the disorder, the aphasic will call on his lexical information, which is not altered, leading to various palliative approaches to the lack of the word (Nespoulous, 1980).

5.2 Compensatory approaches for aphasics

Compensatory approaches (or strategies) such as synonyms and periphrases represent a situation of naming difficulty due to the lack of words in the aphasic. This condition encourages them to use these compensatory approaches.

Lexicalisation could be compared to a dynamic contextual process (Nespoulous & Virbel, 2003). These paraphrases, which represent lexicalisation strategies, are constructed from a dynamic phenomenon of analogy.

In the productions of people with aphasia, we therefore distinguish verbal behaviours that are integrated with communication strategies. This is done in order to compensate for their disorder. Nespoulous (1990) classified these manifestations by linguistic categories, as cited by Tran (2000, p.74):

- Aphasic in origin: in the form of manifestations of language disorder.
- In the form of preserves language components;
- In the form of communicative interactions, in order to build palliative strategies, despite the language deficit".

Linguistic faculties that are not impaired will be the subject of palliative strategies for the lack of words in aphasics (Nespoulous, 2008 & Tran, 2000).

- Using Tran's (2000) classification[10] we have identified various types of strategy:

- The information preserved is evoked in the form of: paraphrases, empty words (truc, machin, chose), periphrases (bijou for bracelet).
- Circumlocutions are classified as **adaptive strategies,**
- To make themselves better understood, people with aphasia use a variety of **facilitative strategies:**
- Linguistic approaches :
- Formal :
- Phonological: the aphasic produces a word that is phonologically similar to the target word.
- Graphics: If the aphasic has severe difficulty speaking, he will try to spell or

write the target word.

- Homophonic: It will define the concept of the word, for example (I know that ?a is drunk for "a glass of juice").
- Structural: present data on the structure of the target word.
- Contextual: Presenting the context in which the objects are used (for example, for the action of driving a car) "he will mime a person driving a car".)
- reference strategies ;
- Definitions: Define and explain the use of the   target word (put food to preserve it for the fridge)
- Experiential: T h i s f o r m o f   a   pp r o c h t h e a p p h a s i c s
- e r e f e r e n c e o n t h e r e p o r t b e t w e e   n t h e s   u j e c t a n d t h e object
are based on the relationship between   the toy and   the object (I bought some Tuesday "for plates")
- **Gestural strategies:** The aphasic shows or mimes the action or use of the object.
- **Compensatory strategies**: In the case of naming difficulties, the aphasic will involuntarily produce neologisms, gestures of use and naming. Their productions are sometimes adorned with explanations (Tran, 2000, p.232), hence :
- **Modalising behaviour** to compare its name with the target word.
- **Metalinguistic behaviours** where they use data on the target word in their production

5.3 Semantic paraphasias and over-extensions

a. Definition of semantic paraphasia

All substitutions of one word by another in semantic proximity reflect semantic lexical paraphasia or semantic paraphasia.

A deficit in accessing the output phonological lexicon, the semantic system or a disorganisation of the semantic system itself results in semantic paraphasias in (Morin, 1993).

Kremin (1990) classifies verbal paraphasia by referring to the links between the utterances and the target word.

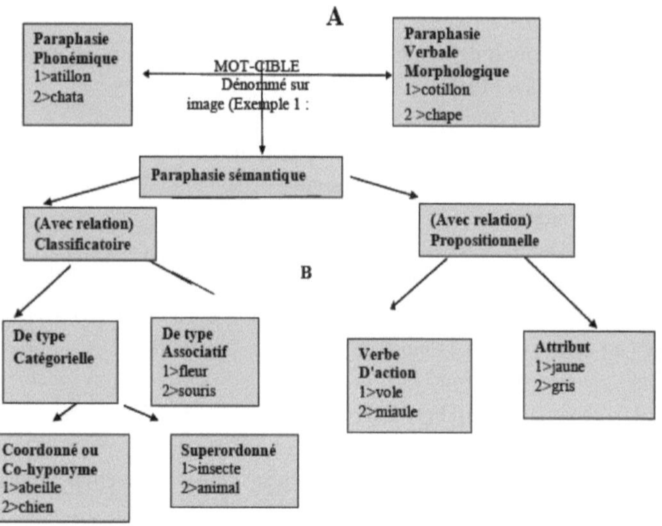

Figure 7: Model by H. Kremin (1990) Hierarchy of semantic verbal paraphasias (lexical substitutions) (cited in M. Manchon, 2011)

The diagram below shows two main forms of semantic paraphasia:

- When they are classified in relation to the noun to be named and an adjective of the target word (substantive / attribute), we speak of a propositional link.

- Two forms are described in a relationship; the first is a linking relationship between two concepts of the same semantic category (animals) 'cat' for 'dog'. The link between two concepts represents a relationship of co-hyponymy which applies to both, as hyponyms of the same semantic nucleus "animals".

which represents the hyperonym. The second relationship expresses a categorisation link

concepts ;

- Co-hyponym: "abeille" for butterfly
- Superordinate: 'animal' for dog. This link is explained by a hyperonymic relationship.

This concept of hyperonymy/hyponymy and co-hyponymy will be used in our study to describe the lexico-semantic classification of action verbs.

b. Over-extensions

The process of word substitution referring to semantic relationship is the result of categorial or analogical over-extension. This is the result of semantic paraphasias. On the other hand, we have noted that the lexico-semantic links established in semantic paraphasia constructions are not clear.

c. Category over-extensions

In her studies, Nespoulous (2005) found that most aphasics produce words that belong to the same semantic category as the original word.

For example, Nespoulous (2005, p.7):

Plate for cup, animal for tiger (Nespoulous, 1992).

"Tree" for plant, house for pavilion (Tran, 2000).

These examples are proof of the de-contextualisation established between words by links of the same semantic category.

d. Analogue Extensions

The aphasic is able to identify with the linguistic means at his disposal by referring to the similarity between two phenomena. This update highlights the essential role of proximity in communication and the mental lexicon.

The ability to paraphrase the use of a word is found in the use of analogical over-extensions, which consist in producing words that are semantically similar but do not belong to the same semantic concept. The referents used do not belong to the same notional domain, for example: "devetir pour eplucher", "detruire pour couper" (Jakobson, 1963), (Duvignau et al., 2005, p.8).

5.4 Over-extensions in aphasia (metaphors or analogies)

We found similar results between aphasics with lexical selection disorders and children during language acquisition whose lexicon is still developing and who do not always have the right word for the speech context.

Analogical over-extensions of words in semantic proximity, which do not have the same semantic concept, have a metaphorical aspect.

Metaphor involves a semantic proximity between two utterances. In aphasiology, we draw on the research of Duvignau (2002), who analysed metaphorical utterances with a verbal pivot in children and adults learning a new foreign language. She classified the different points of view on this subject: we will speak of the ability to create semantic proximities between two elements of different semantic categories, if the word is known. These statements can therefore be considered as metaphors. If the word is not known, then we will say that they are analogical over-extensions, characterised by an unconventional semantic load in the discourse, which aphasiologies describe as errors in relation to the lack of the word.

Elie's research (2009) corroborates the notion of "semantic approximation" by confirming that it is impossible to attribute errors to the utterances of children in the process of lexical construction:

"The child would be able to relate representations of events or actions in the world to each other, and therefore to use one verb for another because of their semantic proximity. In spite of this, the child, who is still in the process of constructing a lexicon, has not developed a sufficiently elaborate verbal repertoire. These different arguments tend to show that unconventional utterances with verbs, produced by the child, can carry neither the status of error, nor the status of metaphor and must rather be considered as semantic approximations". (Elie, 2009)

Modelling plays an important role in communication, in that it either weakens or confirms the incredibility of the statement in question. Furthermore, the ability to categorise represents a relevant process in the hierarchisation of the mental lexicon in the non-pathological adult, which will enable him to create metaphors. In this way, a metaphor is assigned by an intentionally produced semantic tension constituted by modalisers.

In this case, the aphasic is deliberately producing a metaphorical stylistic effect. The aphasic expresses himself according to the linguistic means still available to him. This makes modalisation a metalinguistic activity, and it is represented in various ways with terms such as "a way of   ", "Pour faire du....", "Se servir pour...". (Tamba, 1994, p.27).

Here are a few examples taken from our corpus: - /I didn't put the right word/, /I find these things/ /?a coince, ?a sortir pas/.

- /No I'm not going to say she's undressing, that's not the word, no she's opening, that's not the word/ to say peeling a banana.

Nespoulous (1981) and Tran (2000) define two types of modaliser, those in which the speaker positions himself on the content of his discourse in order to provide clarification, and those in which the speaker indicates whether or not he is satisfied with his discourse. Hence the propositional relationship (called referential).

The disorders associated with aphasia represent a relevant field of research for defining unconventional verbal statements such as metaphors. This type of modalisation is not the result of a desire to mark a figure of speech. The possibility that metaphorical statements with a verbal pivot exist is not considered.

Nespoulous specifies that sometimes speech including modalisations is less disturbed than referential speech. Nespoulous (1981) suggests that non-verbal behaviours such as gestures and mimicry should be taken into account as modalisers in aphasic speech.

The modalisations show us that the word is present in the aphasic's lexicon and that he possesses the meaning of the word that he cannot express.

To compensate for their lexical difficulties, aphasics deliberately construct denominative strategies with the aim of reaching the target verb, resulting in unconventional utterances.

5.5 Semantic and verbal paraphasia

The semantic break between the verb produced by the aphasic and the original verb highlights semantic paraphasia in aphasiology. Duvignau (2002) noted a syntactic focus in the spontaneous utterances of children aged 2-4 years, revealing the existence of a verbal configuration: For example (Duvignau, Gaume, & Nespoulous, 2005, p. 9):

- Destroy book/ point to torn page.
- Je broie la glace de la fenetre/ breaking the ice on the window.

The verb that the child produces generates a relationship of meaning with the target verb, even though it does not belong to the same semantic concept. Duvignau (2002) describes these verbal-based metaphorical utterances as "semantic approximations".

Other similar types of utterances are produced by aphasics:

- She **destroys** the book, the book in two/ for: she tears the book apart
- Er, she's peeled the skin off the tangerine/ for: she's peeling a tangerine.

Jakobson (1963) attributes to this linguistic form in discourse the status of "Parasynonymy of deficit words", and their use in communication gives them the role of "semantic approximation", through the notion of comparison (quoted by Duvignau et al., 2005 p.11).

10 -These strategies are proof of Tran's (2000) deviant responses. On the other hand, research by Nespelous and Valdois attributes to them the status of palliative strategies.

Problems with lexical production are a central feature of aphasia, known as word failure or anomia, and affect all types of aphasia. It involves difficulty in producing the appropriate word corresponding to the target lexicon.

Referring to neuropsychological models of lexical processing, we distinguish two types of lexicalisation disorder: lexico-semantic and lexico-phonological. Research in neuropsychology and cognitive psychology reveals the presence of a semantic relationship with the target word.

From a neuropsychological point of view, semantic paraphasias are due to impaired access to the phonological output lexicon, impaired access to the semantic system or disruption of the semantic system itself.

This manifestation of semantic paraphasia reflects the fact that the aphasic is capable of establishing relationships between terms of the same category, a fundamental skill that translates into analogy.

We will focus on the organisation of the verb lexicon in aphasics. This phenomenon highlights the essential role of semantic proximity between words. Semantic paraphrases have different relationships with the target word. They are the result of substitutions created from categorial or analogical over-extensions.

Chapter 3: Lexico-semantic hierarchisation of verbs

1. Hierarchising the mental lexicon

1.1 Classification in the form of a hyperonymy-hyponymy network: semantic representation

We will focus our study on the type of verbal hierarchy in aphasia, based on oral productions of non-conventional action verbs, for example, "undress the banana" for the action "peel the banana" (Duvignau et al., 2004). We will analyse the different forms of semantic links between action verbs in the linguistic organisation of language based on the hyperonymy-hyponymy relationship. We will focus on the lexico-semantic organisation of action verbs in aphasics in order to understand the types of semantic relations established between action verbs (general verbs vs. specific verbs) in the process of speech degeneration of general and specific verbs such as (to go) and (to walk) (Pinker &al., 1989).

We are focusing our research on the organisation of semantic representations in non-aphatic subjects, in order to understand how the mental lexical hierarchy works. The aim is to prove that aphasics possess cognitive-mental flexibility, which allows the lexical organisation of verbs by proximity.

The hierarchy of words in our brain represents the mental lexicon (Le Ny, 2005). The semantic representation network is made up of our concepts, which are classified by a process of categorisation. In this network, the lexicon, the representations conveyed by the words are not next to each other, but are connected by more or less strong links of meaning and organised in the form of a network. We are capable of establishing relationships between the words in our mental lexicon. Our brain is capable of analysing and semantically classifying words on the basis of a lexico-semantic hierarchical performance.

This concept will be supported by the work of Collins & Loftus (1975) who show the presence of an activation of the semantic node, whose elements are semantically linked to other nodes and which will be active, in other words these categorisation nodes form what we call a "semantic network".

These nodes represent semantic representations (categories) of the arc, which differ according to the semantic proximity between the nodes.

Transmission takes place according to the distance between the nodes, and this relationship can be staggered. According to Collins and Loftus (1975), concepts are represented by nodes. A network is made up of a set of basic units, the concepts, which are the media that enable meaning to be conveyed by language. The nodes are linked by arcs, represented by semantic links between the concepts. Linguistic representations function as infrastructures in the mental lexicon (Collins & Quillian, 1970; Collins & Loftus, 1975).

Hyperonyms and homonyms form a semantic organisation, which was demonstrated by Collin § Quillian (1969) by highlighting the semantic influence which goes from the particular to the general by linking the different semantic categories in the linguistic infrastructure.

A hyperonym encompasses one or more synonyms and is superordinate in the lexical hierarchy. The hyperonym is made up of a hyponym, which represents a distinctive synonym whose meaning is part of another more general meaning (the hyperonym), it is subordinate. Hence, in the category of dogs, "Poodle" is the hyponym of "dog"; the word "poodle" is more specific than the word "dog", which is general.

The vertical inclusion of concepts represents a lexical categorisation, based on a subordinate and superordinate hierarchisation of the lexicon. In particular, 'Animal' is the hyperonym of 'poodle'.

Roche (1978) defines the ability to classify as a taxonomy. The semantic network is interpreted on the basis of the hyperonymy-hyponymy link, which is represented in the form of a taxonomic tree.

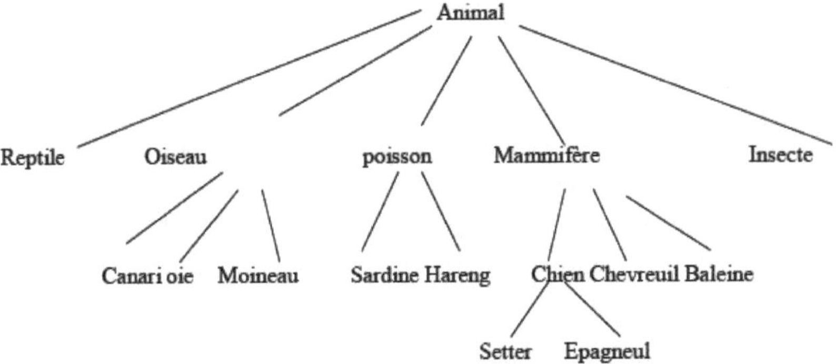

Figure 8 - Illustration of a concept hierarchy (Le Ny, 2005, p. 203)

This schema represents a lexico-semantic hierarchy, from the most specific to the most general at a higher level, which we call a categorisation in lexical organisation. So the word "animal" is a general synonym, in other words a hyperonym, so the lower levels are hyponyms of the higher categories and "reptiles, birds, fish, insects, mammals" are hyponyms of the concept "animals".

"Canary, goose, sparrow" are co-hyponyms of the same category of animal hyperonym. In aphasics, categorisation allows them to create cognitive flexibility in order to obtain a semantic approximation to the original word.

Flexibility allows for the semantic enrichment of lexical categories through cognitive adaptation of the semantic context (Mc Closkey & Glucksberg, 1978, Roth & Shoben, 1983).

1.2 Representations

The implicit and explicit knowledge stored in long-term memory (LTM) forms what we call "cognitive representations" in the brain. One of the characteristics of the human brain is that it creates representations from symbols, leaving iconographic or pictorial traces.

There is another form of psycho-cognitive representation in which our knowledge is constructed at the level of long-term memory. Any information retained by the individual in interaction with the world represents a cognitive representation, and constitutes "a general function of active mental integration of our external and internal relations with reality" (Linard & Prax, 1984, p.204). We distinguish various representations:

Occurrence representations are constructed for a specific purpose and from different contexts; they are circumstantial and transitory and activate working memory, the frontal region and decision-making areas.

Conceptual representations are responsible for object recognition and are stored in declarative memory. They are conscious and explicit representations. There are three types of conceptual representations: -Structural representations (image representations).

-Lexical and/or phonological representations (names of objects).

-Semantic representations (meaning, categorisation).

1.3 Categorisation

Categorisation represents a basic cognitive process in which the perception and comprehension of concepts and images are active. It is a mental activity that classifies concepts (objects) into different categories (classes, types, taxa) on the basis of their semantic proximity or common criteria. Among the most relevant models, this is the one developed by Eleanor Roche (1975), because it introduces typicality concepts in a hierarchical form.

There are three hierarchical levels in each category:

Superordinate level: animal.

Basic level: dog.

Subordinate level: poodle.

The typical concepts of a class are categorised at the base level, the less typical at the sub-ordinate level.

The basic level corresponds to :

Perceptually: similar shape, single mental image, shorter recognition time

Lexically: the shortest and most frequent nouns (first learned) **Semantically:** the models have most of the characteristics (attributes) of the class.

The semantic network

Figure 7: Representation of semantic memory based on hypothetical semantic memory, Collins and Quillian (1969).

We see class inclusion ratios. The characteristics presented are representations that we have about animals. Collins and Quillian's principle is to form conceptual representations as a network.

2. Semantic proximity to words

The concept of semantic proximity was revealed by Collins and Quillian (1969), which appears in the mental lexicon in the form of an arc and nodes, creating a general semantic network prototype.

The arc representing the semantic distance between prototypes reflects semantic proximity.

The word "plate", for example, is semantically closer to "dish" than to "glass", and still further from the concept "car", for the simple reason that the first two belong to the same sub-category of "kitchen utensils", while the third belongs to the sub-category of "means of transport".This example explains the semantic gap between two representations at the same level ("plate" and "dish"), hence the semantic belonging to the superordinate class Le Ny (2005).

2.1 The notion of decomposition in relation to semantic criteria

The semantic features show approximate links with the minimal units of meaning (semes) and are classified into categories. This internal aspect of the prototypes stems from semantic proximity.

The similarity and difference of the prototype in question in relation to various prototypes has been studied by Le Ny (2005, p.83). This was done in order to identify semantic features.

The meaning of words can be broken down into smaller cognitive units (semantic features). They can be likened to homonyms, and Baylon and Favre (1978) confer semantic features on the "atom of meaning". Pottier (1964) defines semantic characteristics: "The meaning of a word is not an indivisible unit, but a compound word. The same semantic element is found throughout the dictionary".

The concept of semantic function completes the concept of semantic network. By analysing the semantic features of the word 'car', we will find that it shares semantic characteristics with the concept 'skateboard', as well as the meaning of the word represented in the brain.

The creation of semantic features is based on variations in meaning, polysemy, new concepts and semantic flexibility, all of which are key factors. In this way, the mental lexicon is organised through cognitive functioning.

To show that semantic features can be semantic, Le Ny (2005) gives the example of a child who points to a "rock" and describes it as a "seat" or "chair". The child thinks of the word "chair" in relation to the use of the concept "rock", which is the action of "sitting down", hence the use of the object "chair".

The relationship between semantic knowledge of the world and the knowledge of language that we create in our brains represents the theory of semantic proximity, which can be implicit or intuitive. For Miller (1976), the concept of semantic features represents primitive elements that can be verbalised, and are therefore explicit, hence the notion of semantic decomposition. Thus, we will have fewer semantic features characterising the concept in question if we are at the general level in the semantic hierarchy and vice versa, the more we move towards the specific class, the more semantic features we will have. Consequently, on the same level, co-hyponyms share common semantic features.

Semantic features constitute logical relationships of superordination and infraordination, of inclusion, of co-hyponymy, of general to specific. Semantic networks translate the semantic links that reveal a prototype relationship.

The organisation of the verbal lexicon is based on the notion of semantic proximity, which is represented by nouns linked by hyperonymy-hyponymy relationships. In the following chapter we will present various studies that describe the organisation of the verbal lexicon through semantic proximity. In most of the research we have cited, we find that the principle of semantic proximity is built on the noun. This type of relationship has been studied by Duvignau (2004), who confirms the absence of explicit information between hyperonymy-hyponymy and semantic paraphasia.

2.2 Semantic proximity in the organisation of the verb lexicon

Nouns represent the links between words in the description of concepts. Thus, the semantically decomposable lexical unit would be the result of the analysis of the verb. After presenting the theories on the hierarchy of the mental lexicon, we found that the non is preeminent in the semantic approximation between general verbs and specific verbs in categorisation.

A distinction between semantically simple (generic) verbs like "se dinger" and complex verbs like "marcher" (specific).

The verb "to walk" includes the verb "to move" and the characteristics of the nature of the movement. Miller illustrates this semantic hierarchy with the example "to walk" and "to move": (to walk) is semantically more complex than (to move). He defines the semantic constitution of the verb as decomposable into smaller semantic units.

Other studies present a taxonomic organisation of verbs (Jackendoff, 1983; Miller & al., Pinker & al. 1976, Miller & Fellbaum, 1991; Pinker, 1989). This is based on the decomposition of the semantic representation of verbs.

2.3 Notion of semantic features and hyperonymy-hyponymy relationship a. Organisation as a semantic network (word net)

Verbs are often represented in the form of a tree linked by semantic features, forming a hyperonimy/hyponymy relationship. This concept was developed by (Miller 1990, Miller & Fellbaum 1991, Fellbaum 1998), by building an electronic lexical database containing English nouns, verbs, adjectives, and adverbs whose word semantics are not represented in the same way as in an ordinary dictionary. This notion reveals that verbs can have a more general definition, linked by a hierarchical relationship known as a 'troponym'.

For example, a tree structure for the verb 'Give', which represents a hyperonym. In this diagram, we use the concept hierarchy and the definition associated with each of these concepts.

"Give

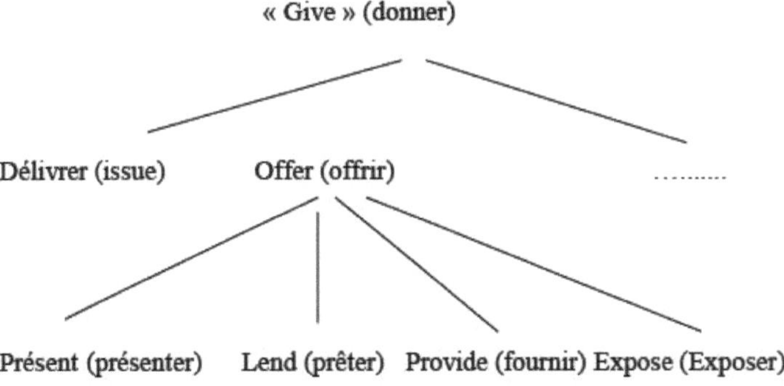

Present (presenter) Lend (preter) Provide (fournir) Expose (Exposer)

Figure 10- Representation of the semantic hierarchy of the verb "Give" by tree structure (WordNet) (Fallbaum, 1998).

By analysing the semantic features of verbs, Chibout & Vilnat (1999) illustrate the theory of semantic flexibility, asserting that verbs with very different meanings correspond semantically. This is based on a relationship of hyponymy and hyperonymy between verbs. They represent this approach using the verb 'to feed', which they assign as a hyperonym of other verbs (to eat, to chew and to drink). In the example they propose, the aim is to detect a common semantic feature between various verbs, which will make it possible to distinguish a core of common meaning and features specific to each verb, so that they can then be classified. For example, for "eat": "/feed/ + /process of tasting food/ + using mouth, tongue, teeth/...". For "drink" we replace "/teeth/" with "/throat/".

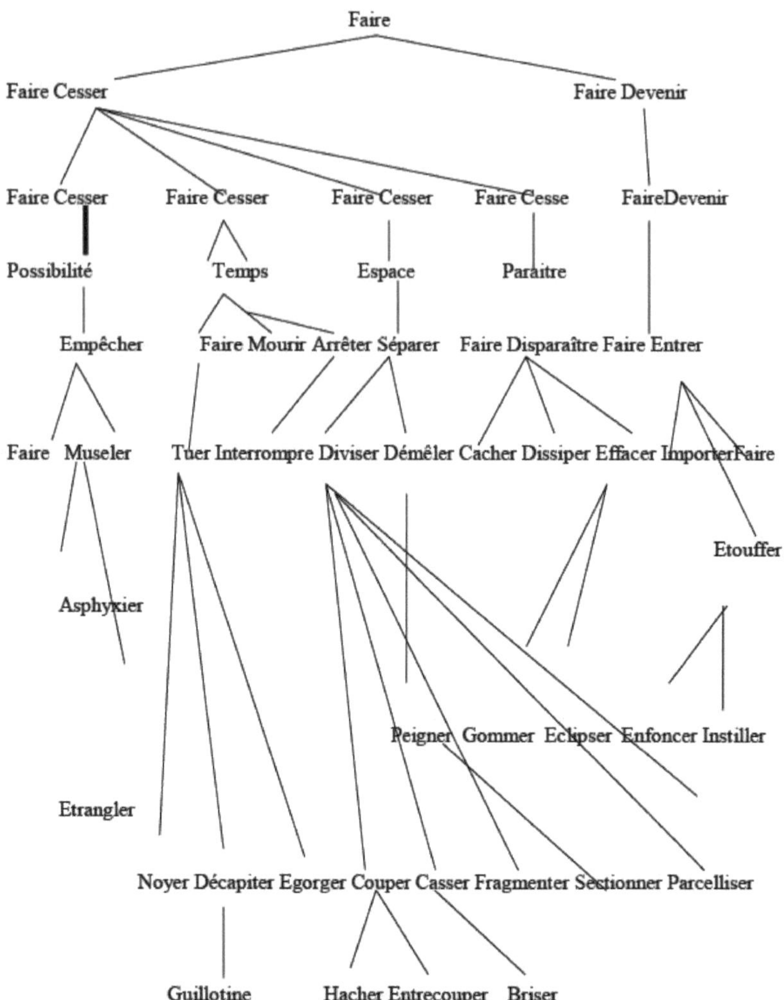

Figure 11: Lexico-semantic tree structure of verbs according to Chibout and Vilnat (1999).

This diagram shows the semantic features that each verb shares with the general class of the first verb. Chibout and Vilnat (1999) draw on the same concept developed by Miller & Fellbaum (1991).

The super-ordinate class represents the highest verb in the hierarchy, 'faire', while the intermediate level groups together the verbs in the middle. Finally, the subordinate class illustrates the lowest level verbs such as "cut" and "break" in relation to the verb "separate".

Another taxonomic form that Kim & Thompson (2004) represent semantically for the verb "to clean" is a classification between general and specific levels, such as "to polish" and "to brush".

Semantic features can be explained by the constitution of a network based on semantic proximity. In Le Ny's classification (2005), for example, the verbs "deplacer", "catapulter" and "envoyer" contain semantic features of the verb "deplacer", in other words the semantic network of the verb "deplacer".

Even if the verbs do not belong to the same semantic concept, they reveal a semantic approximation relationship. This has been confirmed by studies on the hierarchisation of the verb lexicon, highlighting the presence of a semantic proximity created from the categorisation of verbs.

b. Hyperonymy-hyponymy in the organisation of the lexicon: the links of co-hyponymy

The lexico-semantic relationship between verb and concept was the subject of a study by Duvignau et al (2004). The study was based on verbs produced by children at the language acquisition stage. The study involved analysing 216 utterances in which the verb produced presented an unconventional relationship with the target verb:

"Deshabilles la banane?" / His mother peels a banana (in a 2-year-old child), the difference in apparent semantic potential between "deshabiller" and "banane" results from the fact that "deshabiller" and "banane" correspond to two different semantic fields: /human/ and /vegetal/". (Duvignau & al., 2004 p.4).

We note that the relationship between concept-verbs is based on hyponymy and hyperonymy. The common core of meaning for the two extra-concept co-hyponyms "deshabiller" and "eplucher" is the hyperonym "enlever", referring to different semantic concepts /human/ for "deshabiller" and /vegetal/ for "eplucher".

This type of link shows semantic proximity between verbs that do not belong to the same semantic concept.

Co-hyponyms are at the same hierarchical level and are partially synonymous since they share semantic features. For example: "aller" and "conduire" (Duvignaud, 2005) are intra-concept co-hyponyms. Hyperonymy-hyponymy links are built from synonymy, hence the core of common meaning of co-hyponyms, which represents the hyperonym. Two types of cohyponymy have been identified on the basis of an analysis of the organisation of the verb lexicon using semantic approximation Duvignau (2005).

The different types of verb concepts are derived from the fields of action that represent the core of common sense (table 3).

If the verb produced : "break, briser", is part of the same semantic concept and translates the same hyperonym (deterioration), we speak of an intra-concept co-hyponym.

For the verbs "fissurer, deprimer", we see that they belong to different semantic concepts but refer to the same hyperonym (deterioration). They therefore illustrate extra-conceptual co-hyponyms.

Action Concepts

Domain objects	Deterioration	Repair
Glass, plate,	Break, Ebrecher, Feler	Putting things back together,
Book, paper,	Tearing, Decoupage, Crumpling, Ripping	Treat ,
Clothing, dress, /sewing/	Tear, Hole, Deteriorate,	Repairing, Mending, Sewing, Darning
Body, psyche,... /medicine/	Break, Pierce, Hurt, Lie, Depress, Demoralise, Guillotinate, Upset, Gener,	To care, to dress, to treat, to medicate,
Car,... /mechanical/	Accessing, Denting, Crashing, Damaging	Repair, Rebuild, Reassemble
House /Batiment/	Fissurer, lezard, Detruire, se delabre	Restore, Repair, Renovate, Rewrite

Table 3 - Classification of the verb lexicon by semantic approximation (extra and intra-concept co-hyponymy links) (Duvignau et al. 2005, p. 5) (quoted by M. Manchon, 2011).

We note that all the verbs represent co-hyponyms with links that are either intra-domain ("decoudre"/"detacher"), or extra-conceptual ("detacher").

"dechirer"/"casser". These co-hyponymy links were developed by Elie (2005), illustrating the verb 'alterer' by tree structure. In the verbal lexicon, 'alterer' represents a hyperonym and is made up of different concepts:

"clothing", "body", "paper". Hence the hyponymous verbs "decoudre" and "denouer", which are derived from this hierarchy.

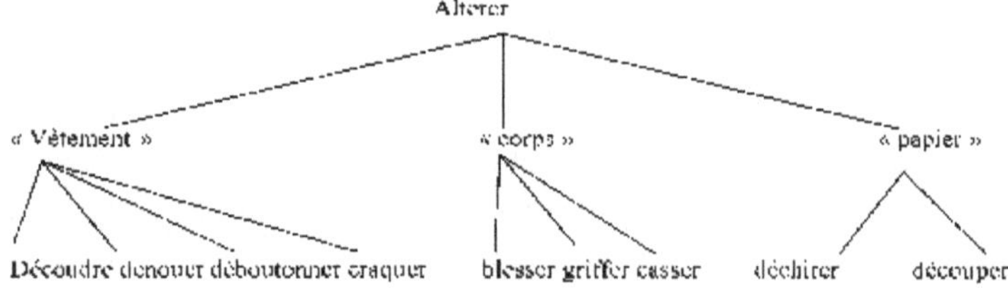

Figure 12: Semantic hierarchy of the verbal lexicon of the verb "Alterer" (Elie, 2005, p.29).

The presence of cognitive-semantic flexibility reflects the ability to produce and detect a difference in semantic potential between verbs of different concepts. The difference in semantic potential is bounded by various domains, forming a lexical structuring of verbs that are linked by an 'action concept'. Duvignau et al (2005) show that this hierarchisation is based on an extra-concept co- hyponymy relationship, which represent semantic approximations.

3. Syntax in the organisation of the lexicon in aphasiology

The syntactic aspect of the verb during oral production is of primary importance in aphasiology studies (Berndt et al, 1997). Consequently, agrammatism in aphasia represents a fruitful field for studying disorders of verb production. Furthermore, syntactic disorganisation at the level of verbs is a sign of difficulty in verbal production in aphasia.

Indeed, the study of the relationships that the verb maintains with the agent confirms the presence of a syntactic dimension specific to the verb, including semantics in verb aphasics (Kim & Thompson, 2000; Thompson, 2003).

We can compare the verb to a nucleus, around which the components of the sentence orbit. If, through the presence of an agent, the verb assigns as a process an act, a property, to a subject, we will speak of semantic valence. Verbs respond to a syntactic construction that cannot be ignored even when we decide to focus on semantics. There are two types of process: action verbs and state verbs. Tesniere (1959) associates the notion of process with the verb. Syntactic information is linked to semantic information, and vice versa.

Valency is quantitative, assigning a finite number of arguments to a predicate (Grimshaw, 1990). The most actancially rich action verbs can have one, two or even three actants (monovalent, bivalent, trivalent).

By the notion of semantic valence we are referring to the valential concept of structural linguistics, otherwise known as argument structure. For example, a bivalent verb has two actants: F. Papillaud (2008, p.18) gives the following example: "Le garcon dechire sa feuille". Bivalent verbs are verbs involving two actants that transfer the process from an agent to a patient undergoing the process.

Agrammatics show deficits in the production of verbs vs. nouns in oral naming; for them, this means that the lexicon is organised by word class (Miceli & al. 1984; Zingeser & Berndt, 1990). There would therefore be disturbances in the lexico-syntactic representations of the verb. Thompson et al (1997) show that these difficulties increase when the number of arguments linked to the verb increases. This particularity of the verb explains why, in aphasiology, studies have focused on agrammatics on the one hand, and on syntax in this population on the other.

The relationship between verb retrieval and the properties of the argument structure of verbs in agrammatics, in comprehension and oral production

They used a lexical access model by Bock et al (1995), adapted from Bock and Levelt (1994). In order to separate lexical access into two sub-processes :

1. This choice of lexical item is called a "lemma". The phonological form is not specified, but the grammatical information is available. A lexical item that corresponds to what the speaker wants to say is selected.

2. The lemma is a lexeme formed from the phonological form which is activated by the lexical representation.

Based on the results of Thompson et al (1997), they assume that there is a hierarchy of difficulty in naming verbs. The more arguments verbs are associated with, the more difficult they are to name, which would allow verbs to be classified according to the lexical-syntactic criterion. They classify verbs on the basis of the number of arguments attached to the verb, so they assume that they are hierarchised in a lexical-syntactic dimension.

The long and exaggerated focus of linguistics and psycholinguistics on problems of syntax has helped to mask this necessity. "The heart of language is what is said [...] what the speaker is thinking about, what he wants to say, and what his interlocutor understands and retains in his mind, the person who has heard or read him" Le Ny (2005).

Studies attempt to correlate semantic and syntactic features. We agree with Le Ny (2005), who puts forward the idea that semantic interpretation is more cognitively fundamental than syntactic description. However, syntax and semantics can correspond to two distinct levels of analysis, with the verb possessing its properties at each level (Tesniere, 1959). Chomsky (1965), defending generative grammar, considers the verb to be a syntactic element.

4. Forms of categorisation in the production of verbs in aphasics

4.1 Lexico-semantic disorders in the production of verbs in aphasia

The results of research by Berndt et al (1997), Miceli et al (1984), Williams and Canter (1987) reveal the presence of lexico-semantic disorders at the level of the verbal class in Wernicke's aphasia. In addition, these disturbances could be syntactic in nature.

Brading et al (1998) hypothesised that in the verb retrieval phase of aphasics whose lesion remains in the frontal and/or parietal lobe. These results were established across a diverse population, not only limited to grammatical deviations, but also observed different types of semantic variation.

In the story completion task, aphasics retrieve verbs that group together various semantic forms more easily. This confirms that aphasics are better at retrieving specific verbs than general verbs.

Research by Breedin et al (1998) focused on all types of aphasia, whereas the focus of research by Kim & Thompson (2004) was agrammatism. The results obtained in the two studies are similar. This is despite the differences in tasks and stimuli.

The semantic complexity effect is linked to the language deficit during language recovery in aphasics. These observations were confirmed by two studies, Kim & Thompson (2004) and Breedin et al. (1998), which focused on agrammatism.

Furthermore, Kim & Thompson (2004) consider that these results are reasonable, given that non-pathological individuals score lower on narrative and sentence completion tasks than aphasics. For them, from a connectionist point of view, it makes sense to have more convenience when restoring semantically complex verbs.

4.2 The co-hyponymy relationship: unconventional utterances in aphasics

Analysis of oral utterances has revealed a new type of connection in the organisation of the mental lexicon, in the classification between hyperonymy and hyponymy: co-hyponymy relationships.

Research by Duvignau (2005) has revealed the existence of unconventional verbal utterances with a verbal pivot during language acquisition in children, which are the embodiment of the basic lexico-semantic relationship that constitutes the structure of our lexicon. In the research cited above, the theoretical regimes governing the organisation of speech and vocabulary in aphasic patients are not taken into account.

The concept of semantic proximity in the lexicon emerged from a general organisation of concepts into a semantic network. Words are linked in this semantic network by a categorical relationship such as hyperonymy, hyponymy and co-hyponymy. Semantic representations function as networks in the mental lexicon. In this classification process, general terms and specific terms between units can be classified, which does not allow us to consider the organisation of the verb vocabulary. This concept inserts concepts that drive changes in polysemy and semantic flexibility of the mental lexicon into the cognitive function.

Verbs are semantically linked by semantic relations of hyponymy and hyponymy. Noting this, Duvignau (2002) studied this type of link and showed that the verb can also be analysed as a semantically decomposable lexical unit. The organisation of the mental lexicon is mainly described by its name. The meaning of words can be decomposed into smaller cognitive units: semantic features.

Duvignau (2005) examined the organisation of verb vocabulary as a function of semantic approximation and identified different types of co-hyponymy (synonyms). In lexical semantics, research focuses on verbs, but more on syntax. According to the research, aphasics recover specific verbs more easily. Other studies have also provided data on the structure of verbs in aphasia. However, these data do not take into account the types of co-hyponymy caused by lexical disturbances. We will focus our research on the phenomenon arising from co-hyponymy: semantic approximations.

Duvignau (2005) considers the organisation of the verb lexicon by semantic proximity, and distinguishes different types of co-hyponymy. In aphasiology, research focuses on verbs, but more from a syntactic perspective. Aphasics recover specific verbs more easily. Other studies have provided data on verb production by aphasics. However, these data do not account for the types of co-hyponymy that arise from lexical disorders. We will focus our study on a phenomenon arising from co-hyponymy: semantic approximation.

Chapter 4 Cognitive flexibility in aphasia: semantic approximations.

1. Characteristics of semantic approximations

1.1 Intra- and inter-concept semantic approximation

The co-hyponymy links that cause semantic tensions between verbs that do not belong to the same semantic domains have led us to assign these context-decoupled productions a place in the hierarchy of the verb lexicon, and the status of semantic approximations.

A semantic paraphasia in aphasics, we will study the production of verbs in aphasics, in order to consider differently the organisation of the verb lexicon in this population.

In the previous chapter we saw that the verb lexicon is structured by semantic proximity with hyperonymy-hyponymy relationships. It seems that semantic approximations are not random and haphazard productions, but that they correspond to a hierarchical organisation, which is probably disturbed, but which remains to be explored in order to understand how it works. We have seen that lexical deficits force aphasics to implement strategies to produce a semantically close verb when they are unable to produce the target item.

Research by Duvignau (2002) has shown the presence of "semantic approximations with a verbal pivot" in children during the construction of their lexicon. Semantic approximations consist of substituting one verb for another, both of which are semantically close. We will describe the characteristics of these approximations and define the different types of semantic relations that co-hyponymous verbs can have.

Research into semantic approximation has highlighted the semantic flexibility of verbs and human cognitive flexibility. The use of semantic approximations demonstrates the ability to make lexical categorisations.

This notion applies to verbal statements, such as "je deshabille l'orange" ("I undress the orange"). The lexical relationship between the verbs is either a hyperonymy-hyponymy relationship, e.g. the hyponym "deshabiller" has the hyperonym "enlever"; or it is a co-hyponymy relationship, e.g. "deshabiller" and "eplucher" are co-hyponyms, with the common meaning of the hyperonym "enlever".

We distinguish two forms of semantic approximation:

They may be of the intra-concept co-hyponym type, in which case the verb emitted belongs to the same semantic concept as the noun with which it is combined and in relation to the extra-linguistic situation described, but does not correspond to the reality of the action. For example: "the lady cuts the orange" instead of "peels the orange".

- The extra-concept semantic approximant /deshabiller/ belongs to the semantic concept "textile-habit", while the target verb corresponds to the domain "fruit-orange". The verb used belongs to a different semantic field, for example "la dame, elle deshabille l'orange" to say "peel the orange". Or a synonym in an extra-conceptual co-hyponymic relationship with a conventional verb. The statement produced looks like a metaphor with a verbal pivot.

/deshabiller/ and /eplucher/ are co-hyponyms. Both converge on the same hyperonym /separer/.

We represent semantic approximations using this schema

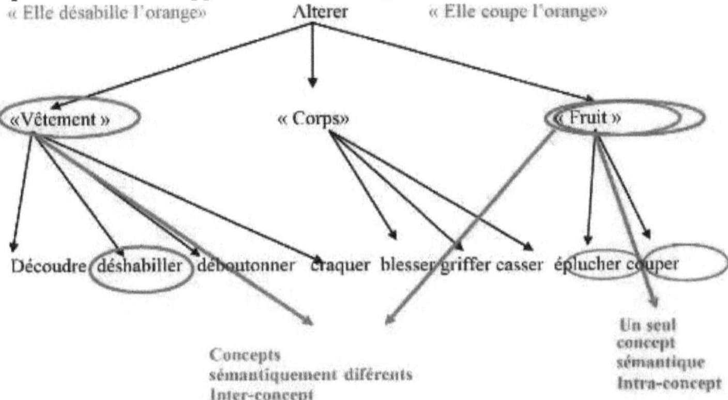

Figure 13 - Schematic representation of the notions of intra- and inter-concepts (Elie, 2008).

Studies by Duvignau et al (2008) reveal this semantic flexibility of the verbal system in children during normal development and in aphasics with lexicalisation disorders (54 children aged between 2 and 4, and 17 adult aphasics). The results of this study show that the production of verbs with intra- and extra-concept co-hyponymy in children and aphasics is greater than in controlled adults, with even more intra-concept co-hyponyms.

Studies of semantic paraphasia in verbs provide little information about the lexicon of action verbs in aphasia. The literature on the notion of semantic approximation in aphasia is sparse.

This study is part of the first research into semantic approximation. In this sense, we collected a corpus of verbs. This was done during a naming task and oral reformulation of actions.

Here are just a few examples:

Intra-concept co-hyponym:

"The lady knits a brioche" for the "emietter_Brioche" action

"She deforms the leaf" for the action "crumple_leaf" Co-hyponym extraconcept :

"She undresses the banana" for the action "eplucher_banane" "She destroys the magazine" for the action "dechirer_revue".

These observations led us to attribute to these verbal utterances the criterion of semantic approximations by action verb analogy, according to Duvignau's taxonomy (2004). The comparison of the linguistic aspect of children and aphasics leads us to determine the presence of a lexical performance in aphasics which translates into a lexico-semantic flexibility based on an extra-conceptual conception of synonymy.

1.2 The semantic approximation analogy between aphasics and children a- Errors and semantic approximations in children

During language acquisition, from the age of two and a half, children use words with different referents. They over-extend their words, hence the notion of metaphorical status (Duvignau, 2002). For example :
-   In a categorical form, "cuillere" for "fourchette".
-   Referring to the analogy "moto" for "velo". (Clark, 1993 &Bassano, 2000). The verbal utterances produced by children represent an erroneous discourse due to their poor vocabulary (Cordier, F. & Labrell, F., 2000). Moreover, this form of the first lexical stage in children (analogical over-extension) may take on a metaphorical aspect.

b- Error status

The notion of semantic approximation arose from research by Duvignau § al, (2004) on 100 children. It was found that the children's spontaneous productions were close to the appropriate utterance in relation to the context. This is explained by the presence of statements with a metaphorical aspect, for example "je deshabille la banane" (I undress the banana) for the action "peel the banana" (I peel the banana), which are considered to be errors on the basis of noun analysis.

In her studies, Duvignau (2002) asserts that children's analogical competence is present at the level of nouns and extends to verbs. Duvignau does not accept that this is an error, because she found that adults use this analogical competence from a semantic proximity when they want to make themselves understood with their 2-3 year old children:

"Children do not make mistakes: they produce a verb that conveys the same core meaning as a verb the adult would have used" (Duvignau, 2000, p.232).

Duvignau (2003) admits that semantic approximations with a verbal pivot in children are synonymous with the development of language acquisition in children who are in the process of lexical construction, where semantic categories are formed. Given the paucity of the lexicon at this stage of acquisition, the child does not know the target verb, so to compensate for his lexicon, he will use a common hyperonym between the verb produced and the target verb. This is based on a general categorisation, while not distinguishing between verbs that are semantically close; the verbal categories in his lexicon are not well formed:

As a result, verbal utterances that are not adapted to the context do not take on the aspect of metaphors or over-extensions; they represent semantic approximations with a verbal pivot (Duvignau, 2003).

This is explained by a general categorisation of verbs, such as "casser", "dechirer", "decoudre", etc., which are included in the same concept of "deterioration" (Duvignau, 2003, p. 236).

c. Semantic paraphasias in relation to error status in aphasics

The status of semantic paraphasia is pathological. This phenomenon results from a lexical deficit, and the semantic tensions formulated by the aphasic with the aim of reaching the meaning closest to the target verb may be similar to what the child produces. The modalising statements are evidence of an awareness of the lexical deficit that aphasics possess, unlike the productions of children. This is the case during their language development (Kemmerer & Tranel, 2000; Bormann & al., 2008).

These semantic paraphrases are considered to be erroneous over-extensions without lexico-semantic structuring. The analysis of responses after the oral naming test assigns error status to semantic paraphrases.

The semantic difference between the pathological response and normal speech is one reason why they are considered errors. Most research in aphasiology considers semantic paraphasias as errors (Deloche & al., 1996).

d.Semantic paraphrases with verbal pivot approximation in error form

A large number of studies question the attribution of error status to over-extensions (Duvignau, Gaume & Nespoulous, 2005). Aphasics use over-extensions to compensate for a lack of words. Nespoulous affirms that ;

"the cerebral lesion that causes aphasia also causes aphasia.
a deficit and creates a communicative handicap in everyday life...But yes, too...raphasic|ue - in the presence of his handicap - will try, and in many cases succeed, in deploying a panoply of strategies to adapt to his deficit and try to get around it in order to satisfy his everyday communicative needs" (Nespoulous, 1996, p. 423).

In this sense, the "palliative strategy" is used to communicate because the aphasic cannot naturally access his or her lexicon; it represents a form of linguistic competence (Duvignau, Gaume & Nespoulous, 2005).

As a result, the concept of over-extension has taken on the status of a palliative error strategy. We refer to the work of (Duvignau & al., 2000, p.177-191) in order to analyse verbal utterances whose linguistic structure is provided with semantic over-extension of the type.

We refer to the work of Tran (2000, p.177-191), which enables us to address from a lexico-semantic point of view the question of the linguistic structuring of verbal utterances such as "la dame divise la carotte" ("the lady divides the carrot") and "elle deshabille la banane" ("she undresses the banana").

2. Duvignau (2002) has shown that the same verb can be used differently and take on a new meaning from the action, depending on the context, while preserving the semantic core of the target verb. Duvignau defines the semantic flexibility of verbs as follows: "It is a matter [...] of emphasising the potential of a verb used in an unusual way to adapt to a new linguistic environment while retaining the essence of its meaning, or as Gentner (1981) puts it, while preserving its meaning as far as possible". (Duvignau, 2002, p241): As an example, the verb **'demolir'** is used with 27 different meanings by 17 children. In his corpus, Duvignau classified all the utterances in which the verb **'demolir'** was used, with the aim of confirming the theory of semantic-cognitive flexibility:

- The skin of the tomato is peeled off/ about a tomato that is **split**.
- Oh.the trousers are demolished / showing a hole on his trousers (**dechirer**).
- Ton manteau, il est demolie/ about an open coat, **"deboutonner"**.
- Careful you don't break your fingers, eh?/ an adult cutting cardboard with a box cutter **"hurts"**.

We find that most of the verbs produced share the same semantic core with the target verb. This preservation of meaning is due to the semantic features that the co-hyponym shares.

The results of this research confirm the presence of semantic-cognitive flexibility in the oral production of aphasics, based on the similarity of the types of utterances they presented with children during language acquisition. The aphasic possesses analogical capacities despite the language deficit.

Meligne et al (2011) noted a high production of generic verbs of the type "remove" for "peel" in non-pathological subjects from the same task of oral naming of actions in all the studies included in the "approx" part of the plan (Divignau, 2002).

This research proves that all subjects with semantic disorders compensate for this lexical lack by semantic approximations. These statements therefore reflect a deterioration in the semantic processes of the verb in aphasia.

- **Cognitive flexibility**

Duvignau (2002) defines the semantic-cognitive elasticity of verbs as : "This omnipresence of semantic approximations makes them crucial productions in that they manifest a fundamental aptitude: analogical competence, the grasp of resemblance in difference". This description was determined by the performance of aphasics in constructing semantic approximations with a verbal pivot by analogy of action.

Children possess an analogical aptitude that provides them with the ability to construct verbs that are not adapted to the context, and whose meaning is approximate. These semantic approximations represent an analogical skill that creates semantic-cognitive elasticity in children in the language acquisition phase and in aphasics.

3. From pragmatics to semantic approximation

Innovative uses often contain conversational cues sought by the speaker and/or deciphered by listeners who guess at the communicative strategies employed by the speakers (Detges & Waltereit, 2002).

Semantisation is triggered by an innovative use of an expression, which can be adopted by an increasing number of speakers and thus become routine. Such innovative uses are called 'invited inference'.

Semantics and pragmatics therefore differ in the degree of conventionality of certain functions and concepts - and it is conventionality that represents the diachronic link between meaning and signification, a process we might call 'semantisation'.

Conventionality arises when we can detect specific contexts that allow only the new reading, the "switch contexts" according to Heine (2002) or "isolating contexts" in the terminology of Diewald (2002).Approximation, both for modulations at the discourse level and for the use of specialised approximation markers, clearly shows that the distinction between semantics, i.e. the meaning of an expression, and pragmatics, i.e. the meaning arising from the interaction between meaning, context and communicative rules, is not based on the distinction between what affects the conditions of truth and what does not (Recanati, 2004, p.134) and that, on the contrary, meaning does not always contribute to truth conditions - connectors are another typical example (Traugott & Dasher 2002).

The frequent use of these inferences can then lead to the weakening of the original meaning and the increasing preponderance of inference (Heine, 2002, p.84). As soon as the cue is conventionalised, the new meaning can appear in new and much more varied contexts.

We distinguish three types of semantisation, depending on the linguistic category: lexicalisation, grammaticalisation and pragmaticalisation.

At the syntactic level, a good number of pragmatic markers have variable scope, are often syntactically unintegrated and remain free morphemes, whereas grammatical morphemes act at the level of the proposition, become obligatory and have a fixed and reduced scope, some even becoming affixes (Brinton, 1996, p, 34 ; Mosegaard, H., 1998, p, 73-74 & Waltereit, 2002). This term is rather misleading, because it is more precisely a process of conventionalisation or semantisation of pragmatic functions, i.e. procedures which organise linguistic interaction. Grammaticalisation and pragmaticalisation are generally triggered by innovative uses that a speaker creates in order to achieve certain communicative goals.

Grammaticalisation is the type of semantisation that has been most extensively studied in recent years, describing the process by which lexemes become grammatical morphemes or by which grammatical morphemes become even more grammatical.

Grammaticalisation and pragmaticalisation can be explained by the emergence of pragmatic markers, which is often considered as a specific type of grammaticalisation (Auer & Gunthner, 2003 , Brinton, 1996 & Traugott, 1997). Grammatical morphemes represent pragmatic markers and belong to the non-lexical word classes (Mosegaard,H., 1998, p238). In a diachronic perspective, this term describes the process by which complex units are integrated into the lexicon by losing their morphological transparency, but also the processes by which borrowings are made from the lexicon.

integrated into the lexicon of a language or by which lexical units become more central lexical units (Mihatsch, 2006, p16-23).

Lexicalisation produces stored lexemes as relatively fixed concept-designing units, whereas grammars, as well as pragmatic markers, are procedural elements, i.e. they do not design concepts, but trigger often unconscious and automated procedures that serve to manipulate and guide the interpretation of conceptual linguistic units and their semantic representation (Blakemore, 1987, Mosegaard, H., 1998, p.244).

We express concepts by lexemes, a process that denotes the phenomenon of lexicalisation, which is what distinguishes pragmaticalisation from grammaticalisation.

3.1 Communicative strategies and approximations

There are approximations in French which do not represent pragmatic effects. In most cases, these approximations represent markers of communicative strategy. Approximative strategies are very useful for diachronic studies of language, as well as for understanding the cognitive and communicative mechanisms involved in lexical approximation. During the approximation process, there are other means that represent certain communicative strategies, such as praverbal strategies.

3.2 Paradigmatic projection on the syntagmatic axis

An important cognitive source for several subtypes of approximators lies in the particular difficulties that may arise during lexical access. With respect to successful and non-approximative lexical access, experiments have shown that during an instant the speaking subject activates several lexical candidates: Lexical access is not automated, in situations of word shortage when we have difficulty finding an adequate expression for a given concept or referent. This is true for most communicative situations, except when there is insecurity in the naming process. This invisibility was already described by Saussure when he defined syntagmatic relations as associative or paradigmatic relations in absentia (Saussure, 1972, pp. 170-175). The speaking subject usually proceeds very quickly to select the most appropriate expression. In this case, the selection process does not materialise, only effects generated in the laboratory, such as priming, bear witness to this prior selection. These productions may be the consequence of a palliative strategy, which counteracts the error status attributed to them in the literature.

Duvignau (2002) brought out the notion of semantic approximation through the structuring of the verb lexicon in children in the process of language acquisition. Verbal semantic approximations are of two types, intra- and extra-conceptual. Semantic paraphasias affecting the verb in aphasics represent verbal semantic approximations. The presence of these semantic approximations in aphasics demonstrates the preservation of their analogical capacities, as well as the semantic flexibility of verbs and, more generally, the cognitive flexibility of subjects.

Chapter 5 The oral denomination of shares

1. Oral naming of actions and neuropsychological models

1.1 Definition of the oral name

In order to observe and analyse the different types of aphasic language deficits, oral naming represents a primordial task in the lexico-semantic analysis of pathological oral language (aphasia) (Bock & Levelt, 1994). Its objective is to name objects, by means of instructions to the affected subjects (S. Henrard, 2014).

In this chapter we discuss the different phases of information processing during oral naming, with reference to psycholinguistic and neuropsychological models of oral production.

Cerebral areas are located by oral naming in relation to the different models of information processing;

In Chapter 2, we described the lexical system on the basis of different models of language processing and the cognitive approach to naming disorders, depending on the degree of impairment;

If the aphasic has difficulty retrieving semantic and syntactic information (lemma level), then the impairment is in semantic encoding, and if the difficulty is in phonological information (lexeme level), then the impairment is in phonological encoding.

Research in psycholinguistics has developed three levels of representation during oral naming (Bock & Levelt, 1994; Dell, 1986; Ferrand, 2001). We refer to the work of Hammelrath, C. (2001) in order to summarise object naming processes and his main theoretical models:

-Identifying the different concepts related to the image.

- The mental concretisation of the word corresponding to the concept is retrieved from the mental lexicon and comprises: semantic-syntactic and morpho-phonological encoding.

-Articulation is based on phonological representation.

We will describe the different stages in the oral naming process on the basis of neuropsychological research. Neuropsychological models of naming imply an additional stage, upstream of the lexicalisation stage, namely the perceptual stage of image analysis.

This includes several levels of representation:

1.2 The different phases of information processing

a.Structural visual representations

All structural representations are stored in long-term memory, and activation of this type of representation is based on the object that corresponds to the representation stored in long-term memory (Riddoch & Humphreys, 1987). The selection of visual characteristics plays a role in the construction of the percept. This is the first level of recognition; the structural identification of objects by the selection of visual features corresponding to the object.

The mental processes involved in lexical production represent the phases of the search for the word to be named (see Chapter 2). This takes place at two levels: semantic and phonological.

b.Semantic representations

The semantic taxonomy groups together syntactic information in order to decipher semantic information.

c.Phonological representations

At the level of this representation, we interpret the different phonological forms of utterances. Sequential models assume independent processing, whereas connectionist models assume interactivity between stages. This is the stage of interpreting information about the phonological form of the word. Not all models agree on the temporal sequence of these processing stages.

Once these representations have been put in place, the final phase consists of lexical production.

d.Conceptual semantic representations

A cerebral lesion may affect a particular category. A word can be represented by various pieces of information that constitute a concept (Bierwisch & Schreuder, 1992). As we saw earlier, the notion of categorisation determines the semantic system (Rosch, 1975): for example, objects, living/non-living, in each category are classified by subcategories (animals, objects,   ).

semantic knowledge (Bonin, 2003). Concept analysis takes place at several levels, the first of which is visual. The second phase relates to the conceptual semantic representation in relation to the word to be expressed (Levelt, 1989 & Nickels, 2000). Boyer (2006) presents different models for the stages of word production in oral naming.

• The "sensory/functional" (Silveri & Gainotti, 1988) and "visual/functional" (Warrington & McCarthy, 1987) theories.

These theories have been called into question because they were not established on the basis of clinical observations, giving way to the classical theories:

• A neural sub-system in which concepts are classified in the form of categories; hence the design of the "Animals" hierarchy.

"Vegetation" "objects" (Shelton & Caramazza, 1999).

• When the semantic features of the concept are active, the lexical representation will be activated, for example (cat is a living being, mammal, feline) (Caramazza, 1997; Dell, 1986; Morton, 1969). These distinct primitive features are the components of "compential" semantic representations.

The semantic and phonological representations reflect two processes whose role is relevant to lexicalisation (Bonin, 2003). The lexical representation is composed of the lexical semantic representation, which is different from the conceptual semantic representation. The semantic and visual identification of the object is dealt with at the level of the structural and conceptual representations.

Conceptual.

1.3 Lack of words and naming disorders: neuropsychological models

Oral disturbances and comprehension disorders are the consequence of alterations in the semantic system due to brain damage in aphasics. Neurospychological models have classified two types of disturbance (comprehension and production), which are responsible for naming disorders in brain damage. Hence, lexical parphasia. Deficits in semantic representations or access to them are at the origin of these lexical or semantic paraphasias. In addition, a disorder in access to phonological information indicates an alteration in the phonological system, meaning that semantic information is preserved.

The lack of the word (anomie) has various definitions (chapter 2). Thus, if we refer to the different neuropsychological models of oral production during oral naming, we will be confronted with several presentations of the lack of the word Tran (2005, p.49). In our research, we will focus on semantic paraphasias, as well as their orign of the semantic or phonological system.

2. Variables influencing oral naming

The variable plays a crucial role in determining the lack of the word, in our research, we are interested in the variables that determine the oral denomination and that could affect the oral production of verbs, or in the interaction in the organization of the lexicon of verbs. We will explain only those variables that are relevant to our study. We draw on research by Ferrand (1997) in oral naming, in order to analyse the lack of the word.

2.1 Linguistic variables of the stimuli

Boyer (2006) has developed psycholinguistic norms to explain the variables affecting oral naming. In oral action naming, we are interested in the metalinguistic components that affect language retrieval: frequency, age of acquisition, familiarity, the

latency and imageability.

And linguistic variations of the morphosyntactic type: length, grammatical class, transitivity/intransitivity, morphology (suffix, prefix); semantics: the link to the name of the image, concreteness.

a. Frequency of use

Garett 2002 defines frequency as a linguistic multitude of manifestations in relation to a given concept. It is not related to the processes of visual or articulatory identification (object recognition). Frequency of use, on the other hand, relates to naming. Done, any study of the lexicon relies on this variable.

Words have different frequencies, from low to high. In French, there are several tools that present frequency tables: Tresor de la langue fran^aise (1971); lexique (New & Pallier, 2001), manulex (Lete et al.,2004), lexique 3 (New & Pallier, 2006). Several studies have demonstrated the frequency effect in oral naming of objects: Ferrand & al. (1997), Humphreys & al. (1988). During oral naming, high-frequency nouns are named significantly faster than low-frequency object names.

b. Frequency in aphasiology

Impaired lexical production can lead to long response times between stimulus presentation and production. Image latencies decrease in relation to word frequency if the latter is high (Jescheniack & Levelt, 1994; Goodglass § al. 1984). The frequency effect has been observed in different types of aphasics (Rochford & Williams, 1965). The decrease in latency in an aphasic may also be an indicator of recovery (Croskey & al., 1970).

We can assess oral object naming from word frequency in aphasics, with high-frequency object names being produced more easily (Kay & Ellis, 1987; Zingeser & Berndt, 1988). In the clinic, frequency will be studied in terms of latency (based on the characteristics of the images, we observe differences in the speed of naming) and the rate of correct responses. In this case, frequency will have an impact on language recovery.

- **The origin of the frequency effect**

Other authors have reached identical conclusions (Ferrand & al., 1997). Their results tend to favour a relationship between the frequency effect and the phonological lexicon (Lexemes).

Some authors have tried to determine the focus of this frequency effect (Ferrand et al., 1997 ; Humphreys & al. 1988; Jescheniack & Levelt, 1994), looking at whether the frequency effect is located at the level of the semantic lexicon (activation/recuperation of lemmas), the phonological lexicon (activation/recuperation of lexemes), or at the level of the links between lemmas and lexemes.

- **The frontiers of the frequency effect**

The boundaries remain relative because the frequency effect is a solid and reliable variable for studies of lexical production. Nevertheless, some authors attach greater value to the frequency effect on naming. Variations are observed in particular with subjects aged over 60. The results of many studies on frequency are the consequences of a group analysis, which does not allow inter-individual variations to be taken into account.

Individual variables should also be taken into account: socio-cultural level and age. Howard & al (1984) show that, depending on the frequency effect, scores vary from one aphasic to another; for some subjects, low frequency has no impact on their production. In general, all language tests are normed according to individual criteria. For Caron (2001), individual factors such as socio-professional background reflects a level of education that plays an important role in determining word frequency.

c-Acquisition age

Studies suggest that verbs are acquired later than nouns (Bassano, 2000 ; Bates & al., 1992 ; Nickels & al. 1995).

Zevin & Seidenberg (2004) show that children acquire the most frequent words very early. This is because they are frequently exposed to these words from an early age, which subsequently enables them to acquire them more quickly. Other researchers have put forward the idea that the effect of age on acquisition comes into play in object naming frequency.

d-Familiarity

What strongly links frequency and familiarity Segui & al, (1982) demonstrated through a word frequency judgement task that the subjective frequency given by the subjects most often corresponded to the frequency in use (Babin, 1998). In their study, familiarity corresponds to the subjective frequency linked to the subjects' experience of the words with which they are familiar.

e-Imageability

Recent studies (Bird & al., 2002) show the influence of the factor of imageability of actions in aphasics. Cuetos & al (2005) show that lexical acquisition in children depends on imageability, which has a facilitating effect. In the literature, verbs generally have a lower imageability than nouns, which causes dissociations between nouns and verbs.

Studies by Luzzatti & al (2003) and Jonkers (2007) show that nouns are easier to represent than verbs. This makes it more difficult to name objects.

Imageability emerged when studies looked at the differences in oral noun and verb naming performance in aphasics. It is a variable that is judged on the basis of the ease with which a verbal stimulus is presented, thanks to an image support.

3. Variables specific to verbs

There are other variables that are specific to verbs (Bastiaanse, 2003), such as argumentative structure (Jonkers & Bastiaanse, 1996; Kim & Thompson, 2004), which refers to the notion of transitivity, and thematic roles (Druks, 2002), where each argument fulfils a thematic role whose main

are the agent, the theme and the object.

In our research, we refer to the visual support in oral naming of action and object manipulation, in order to explain the extra-linguistic and semantic relationship in oral naming. We are interested in semantic properties of the verb and instrumental properties that refer to actions involving instruments.

Jonkers and Bastiaanse (2007) have considered two non-grammatical effects that are thought to play a role in oral action naming in aphasics (anomic and Broca): verb morphology (Kiss, 2000) and verb argument structure (Kim & Thompson, 2000 ; Thompson & al., 1998). One of the semantic parameters that can influence verb production is instrumentality. This has been demonstrated by various studies in aphasiology and verbal production in aphasics is affected by a variety of factors.

-Extra-linguistic variables

Using video as a medium, we want to understand the factors that influence the oral production of verbs. We are particularly interested in factors related to the mode of visual presentation: static (images) / dynamic (videos). The extra-linguistic variables include: the mode of presentation (visual, tactile, auditory, etc.), the mode of presentation, the mode of word production (written/oral), and the type of visual material (dynamic/static).

a. The properties of the object in the semantic determination of the action verb
Several studies have been carried out in English on photographs, such as Fiez and Tranel (1997), translated into French by Bonin & al. (2004), Morrison & al. (2003), and Masterson and Druks (1998), based on drawings, translated into French by Schwitter et al. (2004); Szekely et al. (2005).

Research has been carried out by several studies in English on photographs such as Fiez and Tranel (1997) translated into French by Bonin et al. (2004), Morrison et al. (2003), or based on drawings Masterson and Druks (1998) standards in French by Schwitter et al. (2004); Szekely et al. (2005) and in different languages (Alario & Ferrand, 1999 ; Barry et al. 1997 ; Sanfeliu & Fernandez, 1996). With regard to the norms of oral naming material, here again we note a focus on the name, and few normative studies have been carried out on the action.

b.Studies on action and image
Studies have shown that the most familiar actions represent the most frequent verbs. Boyer (2006), presented experimental material to student researchers in order to analyse the results of oral action naming.

In his research, Boyer (2006) compared the oral naming of objects and actions, showing the presence of similar factors between actions and objects: agreement on the appearance of the image, conceptual familiarity and lexical frequency.

Differences were found on important variables: agreement on image name, visual complexity, age of acquisition and imaging value.

Oral naming of actions is slower because of the visual complexity of the stimuli. Conceptual complexity and visual-perceptual processing could have an effect on oral naming.

To understand and name a perceived event, we need to anticipate how it will unfold, predict its outcome and verbalise the action that is taking place by using a verb (Tijus & Zibetti, 2001).

Boyer (2006) has highlighted the importance of creating a database of video sequences of action: "The more the image representation of the object and the action corresponds to the prototypical representation stored in long-term memory, the faster and more effectively this linkage will be made". New psycholinguistic standards have been developed based on Boyer's research (2006).

a. The dynamic image in action recognition
Research by Bonin et al (2009) on 110 action videos has made it possible to establish psycholinguistic norms for the conceptual recognition of actions. This is facilitated by dynamic images (videos).

Bonin et al (2009, p.21) state that "the clips seem to correspond better to the mental representations that the participants form of the actions on the basis of a revocation of their name The perceptive and conceptual identification of the actions can in part be facilitated by presenting them in clip form".

The identification of semantic representations of actions and images is determined by the correlations of the different factors. Research by Bonin § al (2009) confirms that dynamic images provide more accurate responses than static images.

In the same way, dynamic images are higher than static ones. This is based on the modal image-verb ratio. This supports the results of Berndt et al (1997) and allows us to generalise this study.

b.Static and dynamic images: a psychophysical approach

Semantic representation is different from perception of the world (Rensink, O'Reagan & Clark, 1997). This concept was developed by Freyd (1983), who drew on the phenomenon of MR "representational momentum"[6] .

The results of MRI represent characteristics of our perceptual schemas. Freyd & Finke (1984) studied the rotation of a square geometrical shape and found that if the fourth photograph is identical to the third, the square will be distinguished. Semantic knowledge about the physical form allows us to anticipate the future of an action; through assimilation, the mental representation of a scene is made by adapting the semantic information of the scene in question.

The direction of movement and of the action in relation to the action are stored as mental representations in memory.

Thanks to the information we have about the palpable world (objects), which is stored in the form of categories, our brain has the capacity to make logical imaginations about the continuity of a scene and the use of objects (Tranel § al., 2008).

e.Images in aphasiology

Various studies have attempted to evaluate nouns and verbs using a computerised BIMM word miss battery by Gatinol (2008), an object and action naming battery (Drucks & Masterson, 2000).

Our research was based on the aphasiogram "Rendez-moi mes mots" (Give me back my words) developed by S. Kacemi, computerised test software (MTA)[7] adapted and calibrated by Professor Zellal Nacira.

The protocols used in oral action naming assessments are mainly based on an image medium and are therefore static (photos, colour or black and white drawings). They are based on a static action medium.

f.   Aphasiology aids

One of the first studies on the influence of supports in aphasics was by Berndt et al. (1997). Most studies on the verb in cerebral lesions have been based on a static support (Berndt et al., 1997; d'Honincthun, 2008; den Ouden & al., 2009; Jensen,

---

[6] **- Representational momentum: Representational momentum is** a small but reliable error in our visual perception of moving objects. Instead of knowing the exact location of a moving object, we actually think it is a little further along its trajectory. For example, people who see an object suddenly move from left to right and then suddenly disappear say they saw it a little further to the right than where it disappeared. Although not a huge error, it has been seen in a variety of events ranging from simple rotation to camera movement in a scene. The term 'representational moment' originally reflected the idea that forward movement resulted from the perceptual system having interiorised, or evolved, to include the basic principles of Newtonian physics, but now it was about forward movements that: continue a present pattern along a variety of dimensions, not just position or orientation. As in many areas of cognitive psychology, theories can focus on bottom-up or top-down aspects of the task. Bottom-up theories of representational momentum emphasise the role of eye movements and stimulus presentation, while top-down theories emphasise the role of the observer's experience and expectations of the event being presented.

[7] See appendix 5, p294.

2000; Drucks & Shallice, 2000; Pashek, 2002; Tranel et al., 2008).

The results of several studies show that there is no improvement in performance according to the medium. They conclude that oral naming difficulties in aphasics are not due to visual-perceptual difficulties induced by images.

g.   The influence of the substrate

Honincthun & Pillon (2005) demonstrated through a case study of aphasics with frontotemporal disorder that they had inferior verbal competence in oral naming and that the medium used for oral naming could change the results.

However, other results contradict these studies. The naming of actions using a video medium could be more effective than a battery of tests based on static actions (image medium) or at least modify language skills (Honincthun & Pillon, 2005).

The verbal deficit disappears when the support used is dynamic. Drucks & Shallice (2000) and Pashek & Tompkins (2002) claim that videos represent a more suitable and ecological tool for investigating the oral naming of actions.

h.   The influence of support on cerebral structures

Most studies have been based on clinical and neuroantomic observation of lesions in aphasics (Tranel & al., 2008). Those who have tackled this subject have either introduced it into fMRI on healthy subjects through a broader language theme (den Ouden & al., 2009).

Although clinical observations do not allow us to take a clear-cut position, the observation of neuronal structures using imaging techniques can shed light on this subject. Unfortunately, few studies have used imaging tools such as fMRI[3] to observe the cerebral areas active during the oral naming of actions. This is based on action verbs involving manipulable objects.

Manchon et al (2011) speculate that the dynamic nature of the videos engages the mirror neuron system in a fronto-parietal network that allows the dynamic mode to have additional efficiency in observing and comprehending actions.

Research shows that naming actions from a dynamic or static support activates a common left frontal region (pars opercularis) and common activations in basal ganglia.

The static mode calls on greater executive brain resources. The dynamic mode calls on more posterior regions, responsible for verb production, and a majority of activations in the right hemisphere. They conclude that videos are a versatile medium at the visual-language level, as they call on numerous language regions and use the dorsal and ventral visual pathways, which is not the case for images.

An fMRI study (Born & Bradley, 2005; De Jong, 1994; Dumoulin & al., 2000; Malikovic & al., 2007; Riecansky, 2004; Tootell & al, 1995; Tootell, 1995) in healthy volunteers showed the cerebral areas activated during an oral action naming task based on a support presented in static mode (images) and then in dynamic mode (videos) showed that sensory-motor verbal production in the language and visual dimensions function in parallel, based on an oral action naming task.

3. - **FMRI** : Functional Magnetic Resonance Imaging (**fMRI**) **is an** application of magnetic resonance imaging that provides an indirect view of brain activity. It is an imaging technique used to study brain function.

4. The impact of the visual and linguistic process in oral naming of actions on the production of verbs

4.1 Impact on language: observing actions

The observation of 'dynamic' actions activates numerous anatomical structures (Jeannerod, 2006), in particular the visual areas responsible for analysing movement, such as MT/V5 (Born & Bradley, 2005; De Jong, 1994; Dumoulin & al., 2000; Malikovic & al., 2007).

Kable et al (2005) observed the role of cerebral regions to see whether they were sensitive only to the observation of movement (static and dynamic) or whether conceptual information from action words could activate them.

Action words activate posterior temporal regions and manipulable objects activate the posterior middle temporal gyrus (Beauchamp & al., 2002; Grezes & al., 2001; Grossman & Blake, 2002). The observation of movement corresponds to an organisation specific to the nature of the action, which could make the dynamic mode involving the manipulation of tools a variable in its own right.

4.2 Observation of a manipulated object based on dynamic actions

Studies have shown a possible link between the mirror neuron system and language (Arbib, 2005; Binkosfki & Buccino, 2006; for a summary see Rizzolatti & Buccino, 2005).

The role in the recognition of actions would be involved in the comprehension of actions through a linguistic dimension. For Cunnington & al (2006), when participants observe actions (finger movements) on a video medium, they obtain bilateral inferior and superior parietal activations that are much more extensive on the right; activations in the occipital cortex (primary visual areas around the calcarine sulcus) and in the middle occipital regions (area MT). Studies have shown that observing someone handling an object also generates dorsal activations in parietal and temporal regions (Bonda & al., 1996; Decety & al., 1997; Grezes & al., 2001).

Observation of actions performed by others leads to activations in the parietal region along the dorsal visual pathway, for action planning based on spatial representation and visuomotor processes.

Cunnington & al (2006) have demonstrated activation of the premotor cortex and posterior parietal lobe when actions are performed with an object, and mirror neurons promote the ability to recognise actions performed by others. Here they note the presence of mirror neurons.

4.3 From language to visuals in Broca's area

Broca's area is particularly involved in the production of language and the visual representation of objects. Studies have shown that it has a much more versatile role. Naming a verb activates a left frontal cortical network, in particular the frontal operculum (Damasio & al., 2001; Miozzo & al., 1994; Shapiro & Caramazza,

2003; Shapiro & al., 2006; Shapiro & al., 2001).

- The role of Broca's area in action and object observation

At the language level, lesions of the left frontal operculum make it difficult to understand actions that are not performed solely with the hands (Binkofski & al., 1999). This process also provokes dorsal activations in parietal regions (Grezes & al., 1998).

The left inferior frontal gyrus has a primordial role in the observation of actions, more precisely the most dorsal edge of BA 44 is active (Molnar & al., 1998). The manipulation of objects activates the fronto-parietal circuit: the ventral premotor cortex (pars opercularis) and the intraparietal sulcus region.

Buccino & Binkofski (2004) have identified a motor function in Broca's area, in particular the pars opercularis, with sensorimotor integration including complex hand movements (Binkofski & al., 2001; Nishitani & Hari, 2000) and object manipulation (Binkofski & al., 1999; Buccino & al., 2001; Bookheimer, 2002; Gazzola & al., 2007).

Recent neuroimaging studies have shown that area 44 not only plays a role in the production of spoken language, but is also called upon when we observe someone making a movement with their hands (Binkofski & al., 1999).

5. The modular organisation of language: Dissociations in language production

Studies have looked at dissociations in the processing of specific word categories for verbs. Goodglass & al. (1966) postulated dissociation between word classes, supported by aphasiological clinical observations of double dissociations in word processing (Shallice, 1988), whether specific deficits in semantic categories (anime, inanime) or grammatical categories (nouns, verbs) (see Boyer, (2006) for a description of the different types of double dissociations), the verb being studied mainly through this dichotomy. Following the work of Fodor (1986) on the 'modularity of the mind', new methods have been proposed to describe the phenomenon of double dissociation in order to reveal the existence of different cognitive modules. We saw in the previous chapter that the semantic system was governed by the notion of categorisation (Rosch, 1975), and consequently a cerebral lesion could lead to a selective deficit at the level of nouns (Bak & al., 2001).

5.1 Disorders corresponding to a category

These disorders are specific to a semantic category, e.g. animals, tools (Caramazza & Shelton, 1998; Hillis & Caramazza, 1991).

Warrigton & Shallice (1984) observed a deficit in the production and comprehension of living things in two patients suffering from herpetic encephalitis.

From this perspective, other studies have come to support the existence of category-specific disorders in oral naming and comprehension. The most frequently reported specific disorders are those that oppose living concepts (animals, fruit, flowers, etc.) to those that do not.

non-living concepts (tools, furniture, etc.).

5.2 Content words/function words: Grammatical dissociations

Research in aphasiology reveals a (relative) absence of disorders in oral production for function words in anomic aphasics (Biassou & al., 1997). For some grammatical categories in cerebro-lesic patients, there are specific dissociations in cerebro-lesic subjects. The content words determine the meaning of the sentence and the function words its structure, and this is due to the lexical frequency making the content words sensitive and not the function words (Hinojosa & al., 1997). These dissociations are generated between content words (nouns, verbs, adjectives, adverbs, which are open classes of words) and function words (pronouns, determiners, articles, conjunctions, which are closed classes of words).

This dissociation is thought to be influenced by parameters such as imageability, functional words being poorly imageable (Bird & al., 2001). Specific disturbances in the production and comprehension of content words in aphasics are induced by lesions in posterior left regions, whereas specific disturbances in function words are linked to anterior left lesions (Caramazza & Zurif, 1976 ; Schwartz & al., 1980). These results are consistent with an anatomo-functional distinction for these categories, although studies have debated this position. We consider this dissociation to be a distinction between semantics (content words) and syntax (function words) (Friederici & al., 2000; Munte & al., 2001).

5.3 Grammatical breaks: content words/function words

Various dissociations characterising categories have been described in several studies of cerebro-lesional subjects. Function words and content words structure the meaning of the sentence, and imageability plays a relevant role in grammatical rupture (Bird & al., 2002).

fMRI has shown that words with content characterising production and comprehension are related to lesions in the posterior left region, and disorders of function words are related to lesions in the anterior left region.

(Caramazza & Zurif, 1976; Saffran & al., 1980). This break makes the difference between semantics (content words) and syntax (function words) (Friederici & al., 2000; Munte & al., 2001).

5.4 Signs observed in aphasics and in neuroanatomy: The break between nouns and verbs

a. The different double breaks in aphasia

People with aphasia show various breaks between nouns and verbs, and even dissociations. The performance of aphasic subjects varies. Some perform well in the production and/or comprehension of nouns, while for others the performance appears to be in verbs (Bates & al., 1991; Caramazza & Hillis, 1991; Chen & Bates, 1998; Micelli & al., 1984; Zingeser & Berndt, 1990).

Studies by Goodglass et al (1966) show that language disorders in Broca's aphasia are manifested by disturbances in the production of verbs compared with fluent aphasia, which concerns the production of nouns. Experiments (Saffran & al.,

1980) confirmed the presence of agrammatic disorders in the production of verbs and nouns, and it was on the basis of this finding that the hypothesis of a disorder of syntactic origin arose in order to explain the deteriorations in verb production (Zingeser & Berndt, 1990). Based on neurolinguistic research, the different lexical representations (nouns/verbs) are independent of a mental organisation of language constructing the double break or dissociation.

Caramazza and Hillis (1991) assume that there is a grammatical category of words related to lexical organisation and that mental organisation is independent of nouns and verbs.

b.Lesions specific to cerebral areas

Analysis of the results of aphasics shows breaks between the noun and the verb, which has made a neuroanatomical contribution to the neuropsychological sciences. Methods of lesion and imagery analysis have tried to answer the question of whether the double grammatical dissociation (noun/verb) has a specific cerebral relationship.

(N. Zellal, 2011), (Arevalo, 2007; Bastiaanse & Jonkers, 1998 ; Berndt & al., 2002; Bird et al., 2000). Some of these techniques have attributed the production of the verb to the frontal lobe and the noun to the temporal lobe, and the neural organisation of grammatical categories is evidenced by this anatomical-functional phenomenon (Cappa & Perani, 2003; Damasio & Tranel, 1993; Shapiro & Caramazza, 2003; Shapiro & al., 2006).

Research using TMS (transcranial magnetic stimulation) by Shapiro et al (2001) revealed that stimulation of the left prefrontal cortex activated verb production.

Other researchers have used an oral action naming task to demonstrate this categorisation (Bastiaanse & al., 1998; Damasio & al., 2001; Cappa & al, 2002; Matzig & al., 2009; Soros & al., 2003).

Miozo et al (1994) showed the importance of the cerebral parts in the oral naming of actions, finding that the left frontal cortical network and the frontal operculum were active in the oral naming of actions (Damasio & Tranel, 1993; Damasio et al. 2001; Miozzo et al. 1994; Shapiro & Caramazza, 2003; Shapiro et al. 2006). Other research has qualified the concept of double discordance (fission, rupture).

5.5 Methodological and theoretical frontiers

Objections to the dissociation phenomenon have been put forward (Sieroff, 2001), and the mode of oral vs. written presentation (Goodglass & Stuss, 1979), as well as the frequency variable and especially imageability, can modify the noun/verb dissociation.

Luzzati et al. (2006) support this view: the many experiments involving the naming of actions, compared with nouns, have been carried out on the basis of images, since nouns are more easily imageable than verbs. This would explain certain causes, probably at the origin of the double dissociation, which have been attributed by other researchers to linguistic factors inherent in the stimuli, such as frequency of use (Howes, 1964) and length (Howard et al., 1984).

Practical part

Chapter 1 The oral naming of actions with aphasic subjects

1. Experimental protocol

We were inspired by the experimental "semantic approximation" protocol of K. Duvignau, (2004). The first part of this experiment consists of presenting 5 cases of aphasia represented by 3 different types of aphasia: Broca, transcortical and subcortical aphasia, whose medical report showed a cerebrovascular accident (ischemic stroke) 19 action verbs based on the evaluation software intended for cerebral-lesion patients and designed to evaluate oral/written language "Rendez-moi mes mots "[1] concn by

S. Kacemi[8] [9] under the supervision of Pr. N.Zellal[10] . The second part of this experiment is an oral naming task outside the context of the action of objects related to each semantic category of action verbs.

1.1 Experimental material 19 video sequences of actions lasting 45 seconds, which correspond to 3 categories of actions according to the J.M. Meunier § al classification.[11]

Basic activity	Process	Dissociation
Eating Drinking Sleeping Dressing Selaver Maching	Open Write Drive Light Call Stir Park	Cutting Peeling Breaking Destroying Chiseling

Table 1: 19 action videos.

1.2 Tasks: Denomination and reformulation of actions

We put each aphasic in a situation of oral naming and reformulation of action videos.

- Explanatory section

"We'll see short film clips of a lady doing something. When she has finished, you will be asked "What did the lady do? The aphasic describes what she did. Then we ask them to rephrase it (to say it in a different way, using different words).

Denomination stain

Instructions when the result of the action is visible: "What did the lady do?

- Second part of the oral name

Ask the aphasic to name each object on the list: "What is this object? - What is this object used for? What do we do with this object?

The table below shows the objects relating to the three semantic categories mentioned above:

Basic activity	Process	Dissociation
A plate	A Key A Spoon A Car	A knife
A Glass	A Lamp A Pen	A chisel

[8] -Design of a computerised programme for the evaluation of the MTA 2002 test in Broca's aphasia - Comparative study

[9] - S. KACEMI: Researcher, Speech therapist at URNOP Assistant Professor -A- University of Annaba "Badji Mokhtar" Department of Speech Therapy.

[10] -N.ZELLAL: Professor Emeritus, Director of the Language Sciences and Cognitive Neuroscience Laboratory (University of Algiers 2) and President of the Algerian Neuroscience Society.

[11]- Meunier. J.M § al (1998). Semantique cognitive de l'action : Contexte theorique [article], Persee n°132, pp 2847

A Bed		A hammer

Table 2: Representative table of orally named objects

2. Analysis criteria

The responses of aphasics are analysed according to three criteria:

2.1 Valid/invalid criteria

- Valid criteria

If the response is relevant to the target verb, we say that it is a valid response. In other words, the response will have a semantically close relationship with the named action.

For example: producing the verb "aller a" for the target action "conduire - la voiture" is a valid response, because the verbs "aller a" and "conduire" share a common core of meaning/movement or process.

- Invalid criterion

If the response obtained by the aphasic is not relevant to the verb of the target action to be named, it is an invalid response.

Example:

- No answer
- A description of the action, such as "he gets into the car" for the action "Driving the car" is an invalid answer.
- A gesture is considered invalid. Even when the gesture correctly mimics the action.
- A phoneme paraphasia is considered invalid because the response cannot be identified. Even if the response includes letters from the target verb "contuig pour conduire".
- Verbs that have nothing to do with the target action, e.g. "he's going home".
- The production of the object that is part of the "steering wheel" action for the "driving a car" action.
- Answer with a drawing or "ca", with or without the gesture designating the action, or accompanied by a verb "faire ?a".

2.2 Conceptual criterion / verbal semantic approximation

Conceptual responses and semantic approximations are considered valid responses.

-Conceptual criteria

If the verb obtained by the aphasic retains the same lexical-conceptual field as the noun of the object performing the action, it is a conceptual verb. There is no semantic or pragmatic break between the response and the target verb.

For example: "Cut" for "peel".

-Semantic approximation criterion

If the resulting verb creates a discrepancy, a tension with the target action, then this response will be reconsidered as a semantic approximation.

For example: "Steer the car" for "drive the car".

2.3 Intra-concept approximation/inter-concept approximation -Intra-concept approximation

If the valid response is characterised by a difference in semantic potential between the verb and the reality being described, it is an approximate Intraconcept response. The object/noun relating to the action in the video belongs to the same semantic domain as the intra-concept approximant verb. Example for the action: (write a letter) the object related to the action is the "pen", we will get the answer "draw" or "colour": these are intra-concept approximations to the question proposed to the aphasic: "What did the lady do? The use of this verb (draw, colour) in relation to the action presented is inaccurate and causes a difference in semantic-pragmatic potential.

In the video presented / writing a letter / it is incorrect to use the verb "to draw, to colour" which could be used conventionally for another action - video: context where he has drawn a tree for example.

-The inter-concept approximation

Is a valid response characterised by a potential difference between the verb and the object/noun. In this case, there is a semantic break between the verb and the noun in question. The verb does not belong to the same semantic domain as the object/noun in play in the video. Examples: for the video-action "peel the banana": "the lady undressed the banana" - "she separated, ?a" are cross-domain approximations to the set question proposed to the participants: "What did the lady do?".

2.4 General verbs / specific verbs criterion

The verbal productions of aphasics include general verbs and specific verbs which are linked by the hyperonymy -hyponymy relationship[12] **-Specific verb:** it includes in its morphology the object to which it refers, or the instrument, or the result implied in the action concerned, as in the case of scier which includes the instrument scie.

-Verb generique a verb that refers to the many fields and objects, such as cutting, that apply to paper, fabric, etc.

3. The role of the frequency of referent verbs in the lexical production of affected subjects

Verbal frequency plays a relevant role in verb production. On the other hand, frequency has been shown to be a strong factor influencing the acquisition and production of verbal morphology in L1 and L2 (see Ellis, 2002 for a review).

Verb production can be influenced by lexical frequency. We will take into account

---

[12] See : Chapter III.

the lexical frequency of verbs produced by aphasics. Verb frequency was measured using the free lexical database (a site created by Boris New & Christophe Pallier and hosted by RISC).

4. Representative sample: adults with aphasia

The subjects chosen were bilingual and were interviewed by speech therapist S. Kacemi. The aphasics were selected on the basis of the following criteria: 5 aphasics who had been undergoing rehabilitation for six months and had different brain lesions in the posterior part of the third left frontal convolution f3 and neighbouring brain regions, an interruption in the connection between the frontal cortex and a lesion in the basal ganglia due to an ischemic stroke[13] . All had lexicalisation disorders. The aphasics selected had the skills required to perform the experimental task (sufficient expression and comprehension of instructions, absence of visual or gnostic disorders, absence of attention disorders).

- **.1 Inclusion criteria**

We have chosen all types of aphasia presenting verbal paraphasia in order to show semantic approximations with a verbal pivot. The etiology of the aphasia must be of vascular origin, i.e. cerebrovascular accident (CVA). In fact, the cognitive disorders present during a cranial trauma or a vascular dementia can make the interpretation of the results more difficult, given that they generally interfere with the aphasia.

- **.2 Exclusion criteria**

We excluded aphasics with :
- A previous mental impairment.
- Severe visual and perceptual problems.
- Neurodegenerative disorders.
- Hearing problems.
- Comprehension difficulties - Significant praxis difficulties.

5. Oral naming of action/object verbs (dynamic vs. static) in 5 aphasic cases

5.1 Case study : M.B

Age: 60.

Professional activity: retirement (IT engineer)

Type of aphasia at the time of the test: Non-fluent aphasia (Broca-type aphasia).

Aetiology and lesion location: Ischemic stroke in the left frontal lobe (at the foot of the 3^e frontal convolution-foot of F3) (left inferior frontal gyrus).

Observation :

M.B's comprehension is preserved, and his expression is as follows: he is able to name and describe the objects in front of him. Language is interrupted by pauses due to a lack of words or phonetic disintegration syndrome, resulting in

---

[13] - This is a sudden destabilisation of blood flow to the brain, i.e. of the blood supply that provides it with oxygen. In 80% of cases, a cerebrovascular accident (CVA) is the result of a blood vessel being blocked by a clot (ischemic CVA).

aspontaneity.

From the oral naming of objects, we note phonemic paraphasias that often follow the syllabic pattern and are close to the target word "fourchette -▶ rouchette". Semantic paraphasias, in which a word is replaced by another word with a more or less close relation in meaning or semantic field: "cup "▶ "glass" or "saucer". and responses represented by gestures.

In the case of agrammatism, the aphasic chooses a few words to enunciate one by one with articulatory difficulties, but is unable to link them together in the context of the sentence. He therefore expresses himself with a greatly reduced flow of speech.

By analysing the production of the aphasic M.B., we note that he omits everything that serves to construct the context of the sentence, i.e. words belonging to the major grammatical categories, with a clear preeminence of the noun, are likely to be emitted, unlike words from the minor categories, mainly the functional ones, which disappear, so the deficit is morphosyntactic.

In M.B., agrammatism manifests itself in "reduction"; the aphasic is sparing with his words, seeking to convey meaningful information in a few words, as in the example "Aller midi Orthophoniste" (Go to the speech therapist at noon), a style of production similar to the telegraphic style.

Qualitative analysis

We obtained the results below from the responses obtained when we examined the "Give me back my words" aphasiogram.

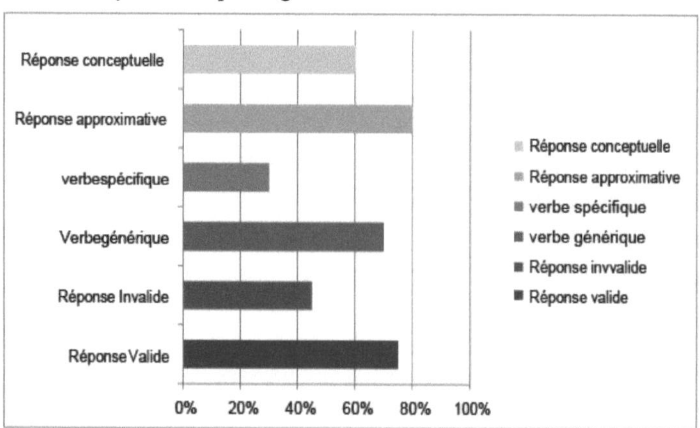

Types of answers obtained after the oral examination from the aphasiogram

In the course of our analysis we note inter-syntagmatic disruptions represented by the absence of functional monemes, the omission of connector words resulting in 45% agrammatism, e.g. "here ... fall ... and here ... the hospital ... here ... the anaesthetic ... and here ... the void ... it's awake". The word of

M.B is marred by 50% semantic paraphrases; hence 50% aspontaneity, e.g. "ehhhh it's a glass ehhhhhh no I know we're eating, it's a meal".
an ehhhh ehhhh assie.. ..tte.". As a result, the inability to evoke the objects to be named results in a 75% lack of words, which sometimes translates into a 25% gestural response (mime of the object present).

Quantitative analysis :

In relation to the objects to be named

For a quantitative analysis of valid and invalid responses, we will present a list of objects to the aphasics. In the first stage, the objects will be presented out of context (i.e. we will present the object to the aphasic - the object is not represented in the context in which the action takes place - the image -) and we will present the object as it is by asking the aphasic to feel it. The second stage of our analysis consists of presenting images of objects represented in their context of use.

We will represent valid responses by the number 1 and invalid responses by the number 0.

The answers considered valid are :

- The answers correspond exactly to the target word,
- Acceptable synonyms,
- Incorrect but self-correcting answers,
- Answers with semantic approximation,

Responses considered invalid include :

-Absence of answers,

-Gestural responses,

-Unrelated verbal phonemic paraphasia,

-Phonemic sketches,

-Periphrases,

-Neologisms.

The percentage obtained was calculated using the aphasiogram "Give me back my words".

\ List Object 'X	Out of context (palpable object present outside the context of the action)		In context (static image of the object in the action situation)	
	Answer Valid	**Invalides answers**	**Answer Valid**	**Answers Disabled**
Plate		0	1	
Glass	1			0
Bed		0	1	
Key		0	1	
Culiere	1		1	
Car		0	1	
Lamp		0	1	
Pen	1		1	

		0	1	
Knife		0	1	
Hammer	1	0	1	
Number of Answers	4	7	9	1

Table 2: Valid/invalid responses to the oral object name

The responses are represented by the following graphs:

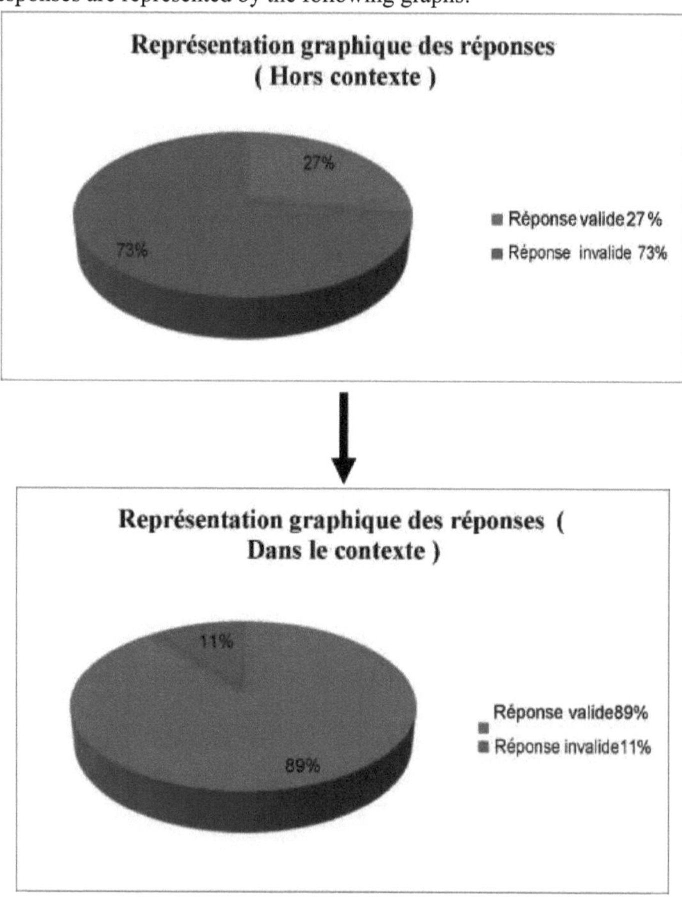

Graphical representation of valid/invalid responses.

This table shows that M.B. has more difficulty naming objects that are presented out of context (that are not represented in a situation of use).

We found 73% invalid responses compared with 11% invalid responses when naming objects orally in the context (situation of use) represented on a static image. M.B's poor lexical performance suggests the presence of a contextually influenced apragmatic disorder.

Analysis of verbal representations of actions using a dynamic medium (video)
In this second stage of our experiment, we will present the aphasic with videos lasting 2 min -3 min in which the action is represented in the use of the previously named object.

Video presented to 1'aphasique	Responses by category		
	Basic activity	**Process**	**Dissociation**
1- The lady is **eating** chips from a plate.	1- Dine		
2- The child takes a glass to **drink**	2-Valve		
3- The lady **sleeps** on a white bed	3- Snore		
4- The lady **dresses** her child	4- Cover		
5- The child **chews gum** 6-The lady takes the keys to **open** her door	5- Eat		
7- The man **writes** a letter		6- Close	
8- The man **drives** a red car		7- Draw	
		8-Directing	
9- The lady **lights** the lampshade		9- illuminates	
10- The gentleman **calls** his friend telephone.		10- Talk	
11- The lady **parks his car** in the garage. 12-The lady **stirs** the soup		11- Preserve	
13-The lady **cut** a apple in two 14-		12- Shake	13- Divide
She **peels** a mandarin orange			14- Deshabille
15- The lady **breaks** the glass in the window			15-Breaking

16- The gentleman **to** the newspaper 17- The cook **chops** the onion			16 - Detruit 17- Cup

Table 3: Representation of responses to the oral naming of actions

In oral naming of actions, M.B. clearly shows that he recognises the action; he provides knowledge of each action presented. The context surrounding the action helps him respond by keeping the verbal category of the original verb (e.g. for action 7 "The man is writing a letter (the object used is the pencil), M.B. responded "to draw", we note here that the verb "to write" and "to draw" are part of the same semantic field.

We note that M.B. infers from the physical characteristics of objects (for action no. 3 "The lady sleeps on a white bed" the object "bed": "it's for resting" or "the knife" in action no. 17 is for cutting.

M.B. refers to the descriptive elements, the functional characteristics that are mostly congruent with the action and the object used in the action (for the car in action no. 8, "to get around", he also refers to the context in which the object is presented (for car: "I think it's on the road"). Based on his descriptions of the actions presented, we note that 93% of the action verbs are identified, although he cannot give the exact verb.

At the level of semantic field categorisation, we observe no effect of semantic category variables on M.B.'s performance. Note that at the level of close semantic field categorisation, M.B. shows no difference on semantic category variables.

b. Results obtained when naming 1 share using a dynamic medium (video)

^\Actions Answers	List 1	List 2	List 3	Total
R- Approximately valid IntraConcept	50%	60%	40%	50%
R- Approximative valid Inter - Concept	30%	40%	35%	35%

Table 4: Approximate intra- and inter-concept responses to the "give me back my words" aphasiogram

Before analysing the results obtained during the oral designation of action, let's recall the evaluation criteria;

To define an action, the aphasic will use verbs that have a relationship with the object of the action without having a synonymous relationship. We therefore consider **these approximate responses to be valid intra-conceptually,** for example: the verbs chisel and cut are two verbs that refer to the knife object in the action "cut the onion", the action of which is different.

Verbs that do not relate to the object of the action represent **approximate inter-concept** responses, for example: between "start and take off", the verb take off does not relate to the car object for the action "start the car".

Concerning general and specific verbs which are linked by the hyperonymy-hyponymy relationship. **A specific verb** refers to the object involved in the action concerned, as in the case of scier, which refers to the instrument saw.

A generic verb is a verb that refers to several semantic fields and objects, e.g. the verb deplacer, which refers to several objects: car, bicycle, etc.

We note that valid intra-concept responses in the three verbal categories are higher (50%) than valid inter-concept responses (35%). Numerous expansions appear in the oral naming of actions: M.B. uses the verb "to speak" instead of "to call" in action no. 10 and the verb "to direct" instead of "to lead" in action no. 8. As a result, M.B retains the semantic field of the verbal category. By referring to supra-ordered or sub-ordered categories, the differentiating features of each verbal category are preserved in M.B.

The results obtained are represented in the form of bars based on the criteria considered (valid/invalid; generic/specific; approximate/conceptual):

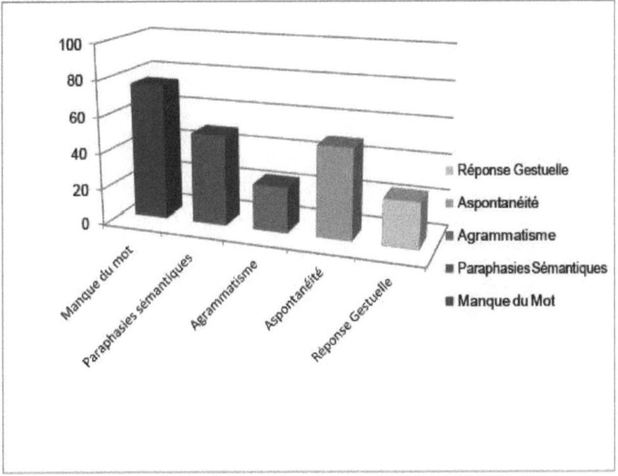

Graphic representations of evaluation criteria

Contextual influence governs this verbal diversity, and M.B., aware of his mistakes, tries to repair his inability to control each of the verbs he uses to describe each action.

An analysis of M.B.'s performance on lexical and semantic tasks involving the oral naming of actions shows that he produces 75% of valid responses that are relevant to the target verb. In other words, the verb is semantically close to the named action.

For example: in action no. 17 "the cook **chisels** the onion", the response obtained is "cut", so dissociation is a semantic category common to the verbs "chisel" and "cut". Most of M.B's answers are valid by preserving the semantic category of the original verb (Mange   к-Dine/ Ecrire   ▶   Dessiner / BriserkCasser).

Invalid responses are represented by gestures, descriptions of the action "he separates the onion" or phonetic paraphrases and account for 45% of responses. We note that the rate of valid responses is higher than that of invalid responses, resulting in a high rate of general verbs (65%) compared to 25% of specific verbs.

The fact that the semantic fields have been preserved throughout the responses can be explained by MB's conscious struggle against this pragmatic disorder.

The analysis is preserved in M.B., because he retains the differentiating features of each semantic category of verbs but is unable to synthesise them. This illustrates the high percentage of semantic approximations (80%) versus conceptual responses (60%).

5.2 Case study : J.K

Age: 53.

Professional activity: French teacher in a private school.

Type of aphasia at the time of the test: Non-fluent aphasia (transcortical motor aphasia).

Aetiology and lesion location: Ischemic stroke in the left frontal lobe (at the foot of the 3^{e} frontal convolution-foot of F3) (left inferior frontal gyrus).

Observation :

J.K. is able to express himself fairly well when asked in a dialogue. His comprehension is normal. He is able to answer questions in short sentences, but his verbal behaviour is characterised by distortions in the form of semantic paraphasias. To externalise his own speech, he relies heavily on the words of his interlocutor, seizing on his questions. The disorder is evident in spontaneous expression. JK's sentences are generally short, incomplete and lacking in syntactic elements.

People with aphasia are unable to generate a sentence and formulate it in its entirety: "here it ... falls, but er ... falls out of the water ... plate".

. ,.euh....c'est bon....a pied jambe.... " We note an agrammatism in this statement. Sometimes, J.K. is unable to answer the questions posed by relying on repetition through echolalia of the question. Semantic paraphrases are present but less pronounced than in the first case.

J.K.'s oral comprehension was preserved overall, with the effects of sequential and syntactic complexity. The preservation of J.K.'s oral comprehension enables him to perform palliatively in the absence of words. It is therefore an expressive aphasia derived from Broca, but less severe.

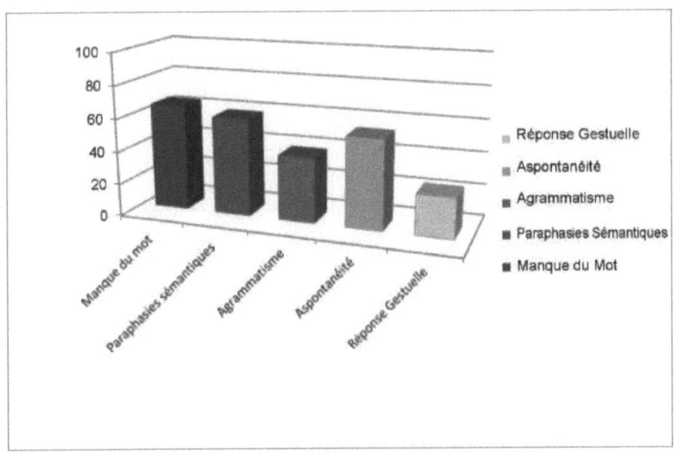

**Types of answers obtained after the oral test using
the "give me back my words" aphasiogram**

An analysis of J.K.'s verbal production reveals an a-dynamism manifested by an absence of charnel words, justifying 40% agrammatic speech.

The aphasic's vocabulary is poor, which explains 60% of the lack of words. J.K.'s linguistic code is defined by a literal analysis, manifested by semantic confusion, resulting in 65% of semantic paraphasias, and a partial grasp of signifiers, resulting in 25% of gestural responses, which represents the difficulty J.K. experiences in projecting himself into his language and using it as a palliative strategy.

Quantitative analysis

In relation to the objects to be named

We will represent valid responses by the number 1 and invalid responses by the number 0.

\ List X' objects	Out of context (palpable object present outside the context of the action)		In context (static image of the object in an action situation)	
	Answers Valid	Answers Invalides	Answers Valid	Answers Invalides
Plate		0	1	
Glass	1		1	
Bed		0	1	
Key		0	1	
Culiere	1		1	
Car		0	1	
Lamp	1		1	
Pen		0	1	
Knife		0	1	

Hammer	1	0		1	
Number of Answers	4	7		10	0

Table 6: Valid/invalid responses to the oral object name

The responses are represented by the following graphs:

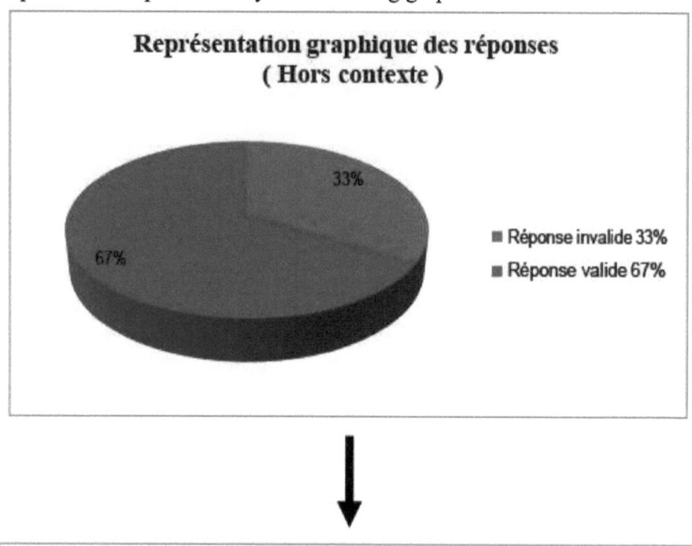

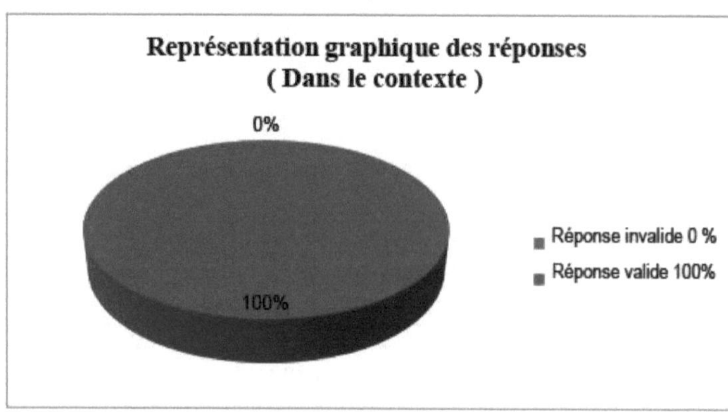

Graphical representation of valid/invalid responses.

We found that J.K presented a valid response rate of 100% when the objects were presented in their contexts. Note that the image naming task is preserved, and only the lexical comprehension tasks are altered.

J.K does not seem to have any lexical problems in oral production, which can be explained by the transcortical motor aphasia. The errors made in naming images are semantic in nature (visual-semantic paraphasias).

In addition, the errors made occur on semantically related items or categories, but the majority of them are self-corrected.

Analysis of verbal representations of actions using a dynamic medium (video)

As in the first case, this second task consists of showing the aphasic videos lasting 2 min -3 min in which the action is represented in the use of the previously named object.

Video presented to the aphasic	Responses by category		
	Basic activity	Process	Dissociation
1- The lady is **eating** chips from a plate.	1- Deguste		
	2- Thirst		
2- The child takes a glass to **drink.**	3- Resting		
	4- Protects		
3- The lady **sleeps on the sofa 4-** The lady **dresses** her child	5- Eat		
5- The child **chews** gum			
6-The lady takes the keys to		6- Spread	
open your door		7- Redige	
7- The Mister **writes** a letter		8-Start	
8- The gentleman **leads** a red car		9- Works	
9- The lady **light** the shade day		10-Discute	
10- The gentleman **calls** her friend on the phone. 11- The lady is **parking her car (garage).**		11- Protector	
12-The lady **stirs** the rice cream with a wooden spoon.		12- Shake	
13-The lady **cuts** an apple in half 14- She **peels** a mandarin orange			13- Separe 14- Tear off
15-The lady **breaks** the glass in the			15-Loving

window 16- The Mister **to** the newspaper			16- Detruit
17-The lady **chops** the onion			17-Divide

Table 3: Representation of responses to the oral naming of actions

Context through use has made it easier for J.K to recognise the action, and he qualifies the action using a unit from the same semantic field "Se reposer pour Dormir". We note that J.K. does not have a total loss of lexicon; he does not manage to master useless semantic associations.

J.K presents a disorder, not at the level of the production or integration of signifiers, but at the level of the organisation of semantic fields. Thus, J.K behaves as if he could only focus on one of the semantic components of the proposed verb: (In action no. 2 "Soif" for "boire", in action no. 12 "agite" for "remuer" and "divise" for "cisele" in action no. 17) and the selection of this component seems to be linked to the event experienced at the time, on the one hand, and on the other, to the most frequent available stock in his semantic taxonomy.

By observing the physical characteristics of objects as they were used, J.K. was able to project himself into verbal approximations, from which the verbs Rediger, agiter, abimer were deduced by J.K. with reference to the objects: Stylo, cuillere and marteau.

.b. Results obtained when naming the share using a dynamic medium (video)

^\Actions Reponses^\	List 1	List 2	List3	Total
R- Approximate valid Intra Concept	70%	80%	65%	72%
R- Approximatively valid Inter - Concept	40%	50%	35%	%42

Table 7: Results of approximate intra- and inter-concept responses to the "give me back my words" aphasiogram

When naming the action using a dynamic medium (video), we obtained a higher percentage of valid intra-concept responses (72%) than valid inter-concept responses (42%).

J.K exhibits vocabulary unavailability which is reflected in disruptions organised according to a hierarchy which, moreover, proves that word integration is not totally lost. The intra-concept approximation behaviours are reflected in the following responses: "rediger" in action no. 7, "abimer" in action no. 15 and the verb "se reposer" in action no. 3. We also note that the majority of the verbs obtained by J.K. are generic verbs expressing a reference to several semantic fields and objects.

The results obtained are represented in the form of bars based on the criteria considered (valid/invalid; general/specific; approximate/conceptual):

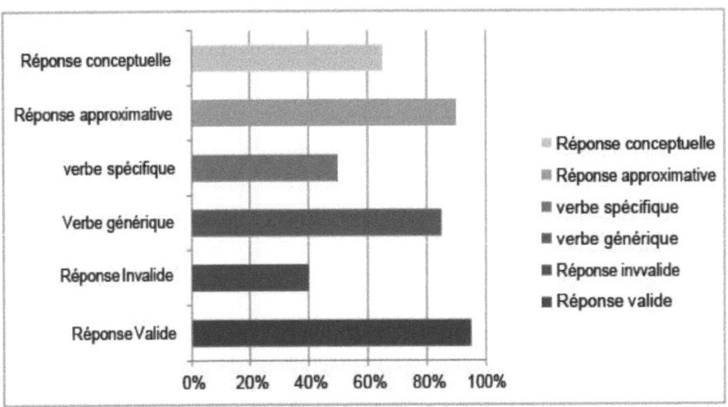

Graphic representations of evaluation criteria

Observation of the results of the oral action naming tests verifies all the findings we have just made:

In view of the results obtained, we can deduce that the disorder exhibited by J.K is of semantic-lexical origin; we observe from this diagram 95% valid responses, which proves that J.K's comprehension is preserved. The naming of images reveals substitutions between semantically related words: "Deguster" for "eat" in action no. 1, "rediger" for "ecrire" in action no. 8 and "proteger" for "garer" in action no. 11.

In studying J.K.'s responses, we found that he exhibits adynamism or aspontaneity. The incentive to speak, the programming of the discourse, is lacking mainly when J.K has to initiate the description of the image or action on his own. What's more, J.K. makes up for his lack of words by looking for more or less correct formulas, with a constant concern to tighten the links between words as much as possible, in order to maintain the unity of the encoded whole. Hence the 85% of generic verbs resulting from a reference to several semantic fields and objects, for example the verbs "to guide", "to function" and "to cut", which refer to different objects.

We observe a new organisation in J.K., which is not arbitrary, and which represents the active and conscious struggle, led by this aphasic, against the weakening of coexisting control over his productions, resulting in a rate of 95% approximate responses.

5.3 Case study : T.S

Age: 59.

Professional activity: Executive at Air Algerie

Type of aphasia at the time of the test: Fluent aphasia (subcortical aphasia).

Aetiology and lesion location: Ischemic stroke in the basal ganglia (thalamus, putamen, pallidum, caudate nucleus).

Observation :

T.S's oral production is characterised by fluency, logopenic spontaneous language (pauses, hesitations), verbal incoherence and altered speech execution. The oral naming of objects shows a significant production of verbal paraphasias " train к une plaque d'electricite qui ne parle pas". His

Speech appears disorganised (spatio-temporal disorder), with a particular richness in the descriptions of actions or items reflecting a preserved comprehension.

The aphasic has the ability to link the words he has spoken *(the speech therapist: "How have you been since we last saw you?", the aphasic: "Well, I can't comment on that").*

As a result, we did not notice any significant disorder linked to agrammatism.

Qualitative analysis

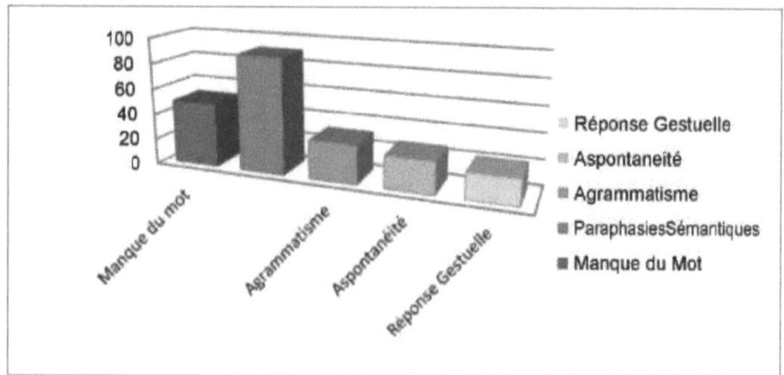

Types of answers obtained after the oral examination from the aphasiogram

On the basis of the oral examination of the aphasiogram, we note that the most significant disorder in T.S. is semantic paraphasia with a verbal focus, with a rate of 95% reflecting fluency. T.S.'s oral production was not totally disrupted, resulting in 30% agrammatism. The oral naming task reflects descriptions of each item, with 50% word failure representing 25% aspontaneity and 20% gestural response.

Quantitative analysis

In relation to the objects to be named

\ List Object	Out of context (palpable object present outside the context of the action)		In context (static image of the object in the action situation)	
	Valid answers	**Invalides answers**	**Answers Valid**	**Invalid answers**
Plate	1	0	1	
Glass	1		1	0
Bed		0	1	0

Key		0	1	
Culiere	1		1	0
Car		0	1	
Lamp	1		1	
Pen	1	0	1	
Knife				
Hammer	1			
Number of Answers	6	4	7	3

Table 9: Valid/invalid responses to the oral object name
based on the aphasiogram

The responses obtained are represented by the following graphs:

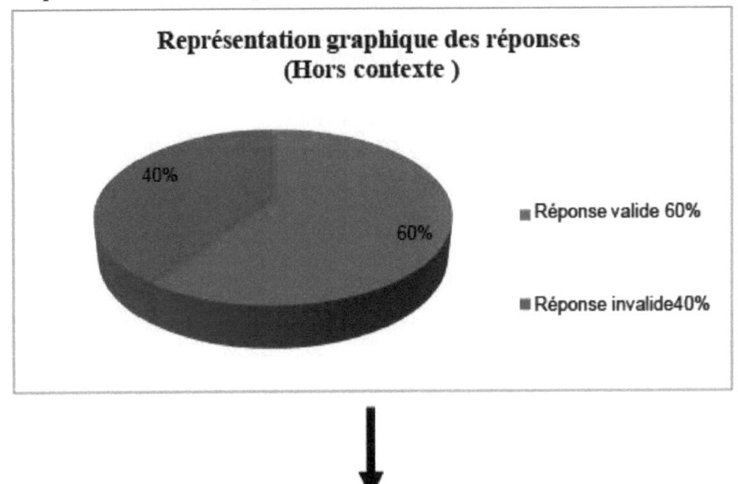

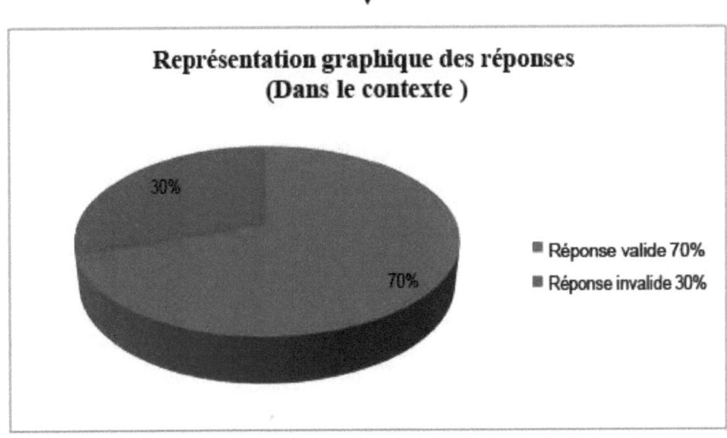

Graphical representation of valid/invalid responses.

Analysis of these results shows that T.S. performs well in both the lexical production and comprehension tests, which indicates that T.S. refers to the context in order to compensate for his disorder without affecting the semantic system. The errors observed between the auditory modalities and between the expressive and receptive sides would suggest a storage deficit, in which the semantic representations are degraded.

On average, T.S produced 70% valid responses close to the target word, and 30% invalid responses. The number of valid responses increased after presenting the object in its context of use.

Analysis of verbal representations of actions using a dynamic medium (video)

Video presented to the aphasic	Responses by category		
	Activity of Base	Process	Dissociation
1- The lady **eats** chips from a plate square.	1-Kitchen	6- Push	
2- The child takes a glass to **drink**	2-Deguster	7- Drawing	
3- The lady **sleeps**	3- Sleep	8- Ordering	
4- The lady **dresses** her child	4- Recover		
5- The child is **chewing** gum 6- The lady is taking the keys to **open** her door	5- Mord		
7- The gentleman is **writing** a letter 8- The gentleman is **driving** a red car			
9- The lady **lights** l'abat day		9- Declenche 10-Telephone 11-Etincele	
10- The gentleman **calls** her friend on the phone. 11- The lady is **parking her car** in the garage.		12- Melange	13- Breaking 14- Separate 15-Break
12-The lady is **stirring** the soup			16- Breaking 17- Breaking

13-The lady is **cutting** an apple in half 14-The lady is **peeling** a mandarin orange 15-The lady is **breaking** the window pane 16- The gentleman **tears up** the newspaper 17-The butcher **slices** the meat			

Table 10: Representation of responses to the oral naming of shares

To maintain the unity of the code set, T.S. compensates for his disorder by producing verbs that are semantically close to the target word. T.S's language is deconstructed by semantic paraphasias.

Analysis of verbal representations of actions using a dynamic support shows that T.S.'s interpretation of action verbs is disorganised, preventing the production of words that are appropriate to the context of the action. T.S substitutes each verb while being perfectly aware of it. Furthermore, we note that T.S.'s perception of the action shows an oral production of semantic approximations. Referring to the characteristics of the action, the aphasic represents action 1 "The lady is **eating** chips from a square plate" by the word "kitchen", which corresponds to the semantic field of the verb "to eat". For actions 15, 16 and 17, we see that T.S attributes the same verb "to break" to three different actions. Hence, T.S refers to the same verbal category (dissociation) of the objects hammer, knife and cut in order to produce the verb "to break".

Results obtained when naming 1 share using a dynamic medium (video)

^\Actions Answers	List 1	List 2	List3	Total
R- Approximative valid Intra Concept	73%	65%	77%	72%
R- Approximately valid Inter- Concept	47%	35%	45%	%42

Table 11: Results of approximate intra- and inter-concept responses to the "give me back my words"

When naming the action from a dynamic medium (video), we obtained a higher percentage of valid intra-concept responses (72%) than valid inter-concept responses (42%).

T.S exhibits vocabulary unavailability, which is reflected in disruptions organised according to a hierarchy that also proves that word integration is not totally lost.

The intra-concept approximation behaviours are reflected in the responses obtained: "rediger" in action no. 7, "abimer" in action no. 15 and the verb "se reposer" in action no. 3. We also note that the majority of the verbs obtained by J.K. are generic verbs reflecting a reference to several semantic fields and objects.

The results obtained are represented in the form of bars based on the criteria considered: (valid/invalid general/specific; approximate/conceptual):

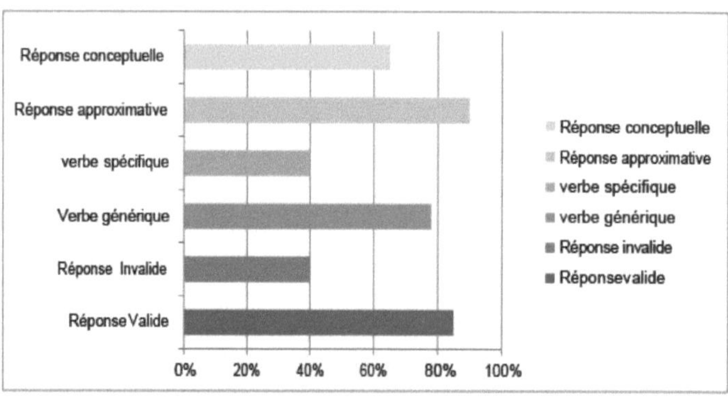

Graphic representations of evaluation criteria

We note that T.S produces a high percentage of valid general verbs and approximations. We note a significant use of the verb "to break".

In fact, most of the participants use this verb in an approximate way for several actions. The use is not considered conventional because there is a discrepancy between the verb and the objects of the action or the reference situation.

Nevertheless, the responses are valid since the verb quoted has features in common with those of the expected verb. We mentioned earlier that when two semantic domains are involved, these are extra-concept approximations, and when there is a mismatch between the verb and the reference situation, these are intra-concept approximations.

5.4 Case study: A.R

Age: 59.

Professional activity: Executive at Sonatrach

Type of aphasia at the time of the test: Fluent aphasia (transcortical motor aphasia).

Aetiology and lesion location: Ischemic stroke in the basal ganglia (thalamus, putamen, pallidum, caudate nucleus).

Observation :

A.R. shows preserved comprehension, spontaneous verbal prompting and initiation, even verbal aspontaneity, and a quantitative reduction in words, which reflects his lack of words.

We note that the sentences produced by A.R. are short, incomplete and lacking in syntactic elements, hence the agrammatism: *"here the grave. But euuuuuuh...plate...euh it's good on foot..".*

His expression is as follows: he is able to name and describe the objects in front of him. Language is interrupted with pauses due to a lack of words or phonetic disintegration syndrome, resulting in aspontaneity. From the oral naming of objects, we note phonemic paraphasias which often follow the syllabic pattern and are close to the target word.

These include "fork rouchette", semantic paraphrases in which a word is replaced by another word in the language with a more or less close relationship in meaning or semantic field "cup" -▶ "glass" or "saucer" and responses represented by gestures.

Qualitative analysis

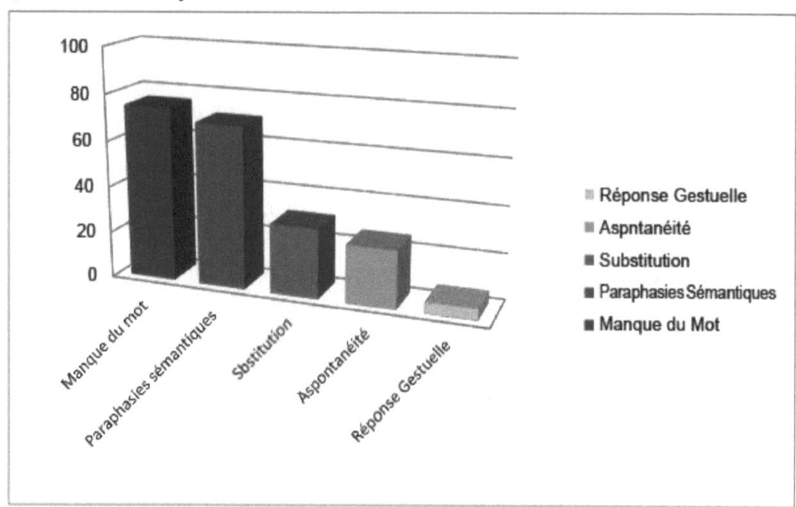

Types of answers obtained after the oral examination from the aphasiogram

A.R showed a very low percentage of gestural responses (5%) followed by substitutions and spontaneity (20%). These results demonstrate the fluency of language in this type of aphasic who seeks to compensate for his lexical disorder through semantic paraphasias with a verbal pivot of 75%.

Quantitative analysis :

In relation to the objects to be named

\ List D'objet	Out of context (palpable object present outside the context of the action)		In context (static image of the object in the action situation)	
	Answers Valid	Invalides answers	Answers Valid	Invalides answers
Plate		0	1	
Glass	1		1	0
Bed		0	1	0
Key		0	1	
Spoon	1		1	
Car		0	1	
Lamp	1	0	1	
Pen		0	1	
Knife	1			
Hammer				0
Number of Answers	4	6	7	3

Table 12: Valid/invalid responses for the oral object name a

From the aphasiogram

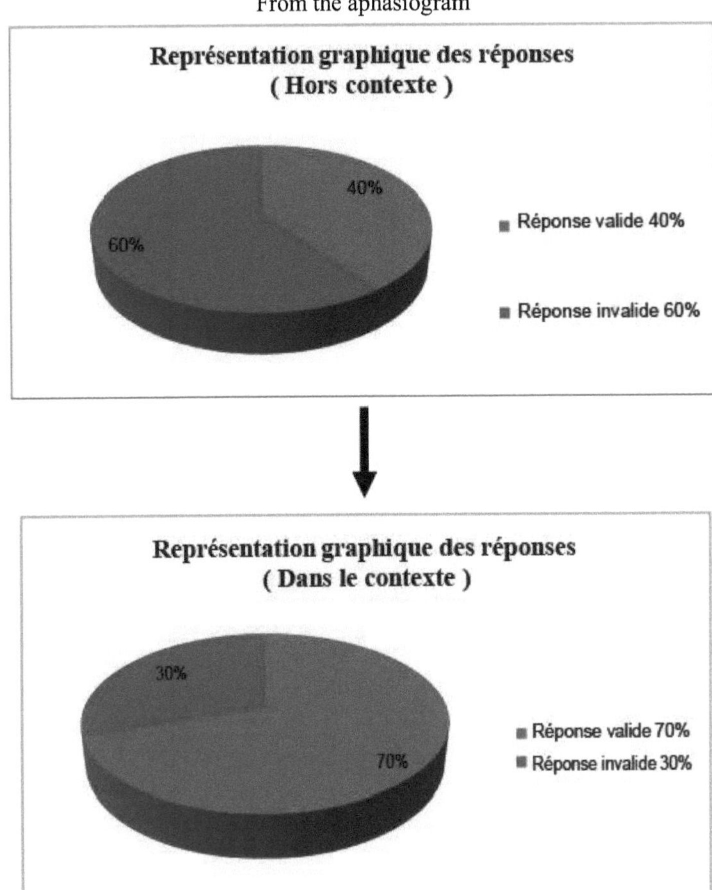

Graphical representation of valid/invalid responses.

This analysis shows that the number of valid responses (70%) increased after presenting the object in its context (action-object video).
This result highlights A.R.'s ability to analyse the action in order to categorise the object to be named.

Analysis of verbal representations of actions in relation to the video shown

Video presented to 1'aphasique	Responses by category		
	Activity of base	Process	Dissociation
1- The lady is **eating** chips from a square plate.	1-Dinner 2-Swallowing 3- Resting	6- push 7- Drawing 8-Vehiculer	

2- The child takes a glass to **drink** 3- The lady **sleeps** 4- The lady **dresses** her Child 5- The child **chews** chewing gum 6-The lady takes the keys to **open** her door 7- The gentleman **writes** a letter 8- The gentleman **drives** a red car 9- The lady **lights** the lampshade 10- The gentleman **calls** his friend on the phone. 11- The lady	4- Wrap 5- Bite	9- Press 10-Telephone	
park your car (garage). 12-The lady **stirs** the cream 13-The lady **cuts** an apple in half. 14- She **peels** a mandarin orange 15-The lady **breaks** the glass in the window 16- The gentleman **tears up** the newspaper 17-The cook **chops** the onion		11-etincele 12-turn	13- Separate 14- remove the skin 15- cut 16- destroy 17- separate

Table 13: Representation of responses to the oral naming of actions

A.R qualifies the action on the basis of the context of the action, referring to units in the same semantic fields in order to name the action "diner pour manger". Based on this analysis, we have observed that A.R does not present useless semantic associations, hence its preservation of the lexicon. Consequently, A.R. is experiencing a disorder at the level of the semantic field and not at the level of signifier integration.

This is why A.R. uses a palliative strategy, focusing on just one of the semantic components of the proposed verb: in action no. 2 "Avaler" for "boire", in action no. 13 "separer" for "couper en deux" and "dessiner" for "ecrire" in action no. 7, this choice is made on the basis of the event experienced at the time, on the one hand, and the most frequent available stock in his semantic taxonomy, on the other.

A.R. projects himself into verbal approximations from which the verbs: "Rediger", "agiter", "abimer" have been deduced by observing the physical characteristics of the objects: pen, spoon and hammer and from their uses.

Results obtained when naming 1 share using a dynamic medium (video)

^""■"-Actions Answers	List 1	List 2	List3	Total
R-Approximately valid IntraConcept	70%	60%	75%	68,33%
R-Approximatively valid Inter - Concept	45%	30%	40%	38, 33 %

Table 14: Approximate intra- and inter-concept response results
from the "give me back my words"
aphasiogram

We observe a high production of generic verbs, which represent the approximate intra-concept responses (68.33% for the three semantic categories).

With regard to valid inter-concept approximate responses, the percentage is not as high, which can be explained by the ability to bring together objects that belong to distinct categories on the basis of shared physical or functional properties.

A.R reveals an unavailability of vocabulary which is reflected in disturbances organised according to a hierarchy which proves, moreover, that the integration of words is not totally lost. The intra-conceptual approximation behaviours are reflected in the responses obtained: "rediger" in action no. 7, "abimer" in action no. 15 and the verb "se reposer" in action no. 3. We also note that the majority of the verbs used by A.R. are general verbs, reflecting a reference to several semantic fields and objects.

When naming the action from a dynamic medium (video), we obtained a higher percentage of valid intra-concept responses (72%) than valid inter-concept responses (42%).

The results obtained are represented in the form of bars based on the criteria considered: (valid/invalid; generic/specific;
approximate/conceptual) :

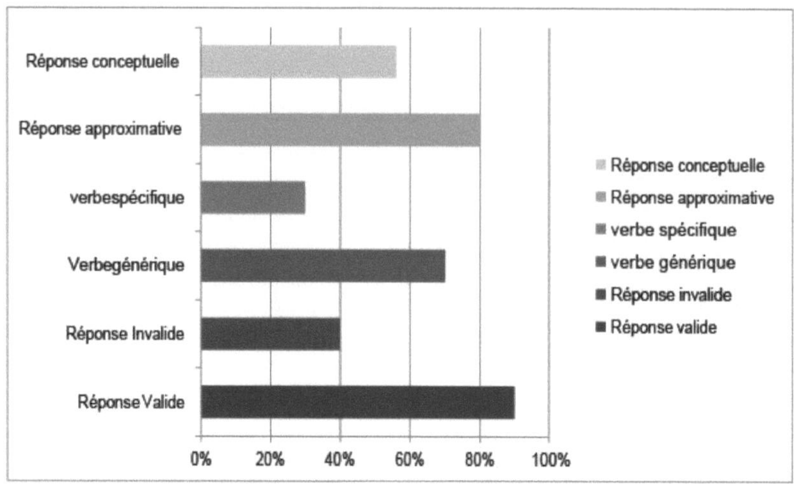

Graphic representations of evaluation criteria

We found that A.R produced a high 75%-80% percentage of general verbs and approximations that represented valid responses (85%). We can conclude from this that language in subcortical aphasia is characterised by a greater quantity of generic verbs and approximations than in other profiles of subjects undergoing language reacquisition.

5.5 Case study: R . F

Age: 65.

Professional activity: General Practitioner

Type of aphasia at the time of the test: Fluent aphasia (subcortical aphasia).

Aetiology and lesion location: Ischemic vascular accident in the basal ganglia (thalamus, putamen, pallidum, caudate nucleus).

Observation

R.F's oral language is characterised by fluency and hypophonia (a transient correction). During oral naming, we observed verbal semantic paraphasias, preservation of comprehension, and his speech appeared disorganised (disturbance of chronology). On the other hand, oral production is characterised by a loss of verbal meaning, reflecting an alteration in semantic representations. R.F has difficulty articulating sounds.

The aphasic has the ability to link the words he has spoken *(the speech therapist: "How have you been since we last saw each other?", the aphasic: "Well, I can't pronounce on that").*

As a result, we did not notice any significant agrammatism.

R.F exhibits echolalia, reflecting an inability to respond to the questions posed, and we observed the presence of semantic paraphasia, albeit of minor importance. R.F's performance was palliative to the lack of words, due to the preservation of oral comprehension.

Qualitative analysis

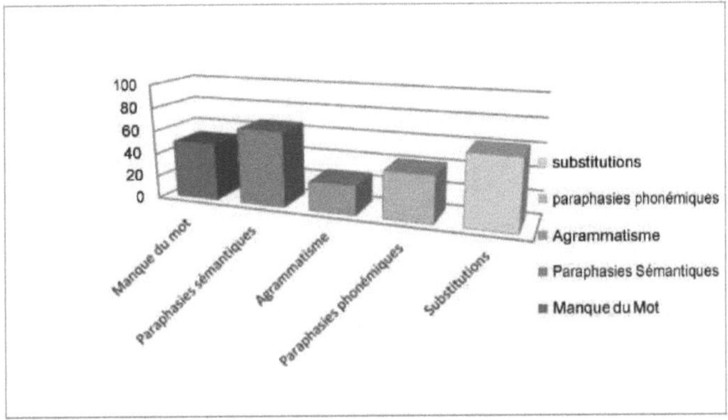

Types of answers obtained after the oral examination from the aphasiogram

The aphasiogram shows 50% lexical poverty, and 25% absence of logical connectors, justifying agrammatic discourse. The oral naming test reveals a rate of 65% semantic paraphasia, which explains the 60% lexical substitutions; we note a confusion of phonemes in R.F. translating into 40% phonemic paraphasia.

Quantitative analysis

In relation to the objects to be named

\ List Object	Out of context (palpable object present outside the context of the action)		In context (static image of the object in the action situation)	
	Answers Valid	Answers Invalides	Answers Valid	Answers Invalides
Plate	1			0
Glass	1		1	
Bed		0	1	
Key		0	1	
Culiere	1		1	
Car		0	1	
Lamp	1		1	
Pen		0	1	
Knife	1			0
Hammer	1			0
Number of Answers	6	4	7	3

Table 16: Valid/invalid responses to the oral object name

based on the aphasiogram

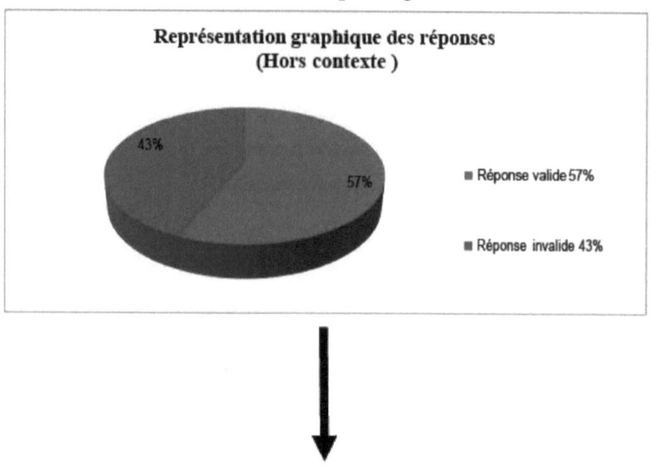

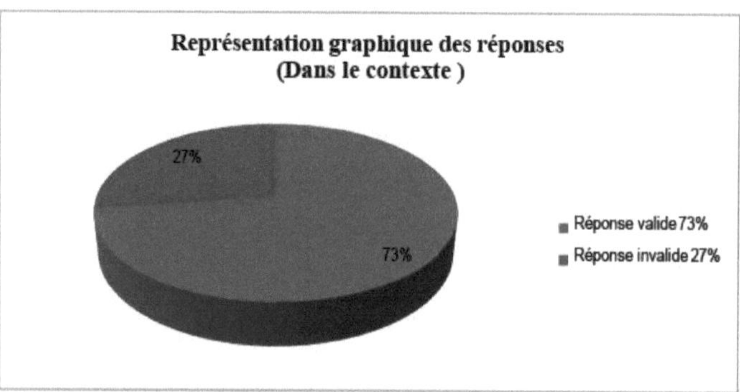

Graphical representation of valid/invalid responses.

Only 43% of items were identified as objects presented out of context. R.F. clearly showed that he did not recognise the use of objects outside their context of use: "9a ne me dit plus rien du tout... je ne sais pas... j'en ai jamais vu". He provides little knowledge about the items presented to him.

After presenting the object in its context, it turns out that this context helps him a great deal in answering and deducing many of the physical characteristics of objects (for the plate: "it's for eating" or the pen: "it's not for knowing"). The elements he provides are not always congruent with the characteristics of the object presented (for the car: "to carry sick people", for the knife: "to eat with", etc.).

These results show that R.F. refers to the context of the image in order to name the items presented and performs well, which leads us to conclude that R.F. does not have a semantic system disorder.

R.F. provides rich and detailed descriptive elements. These are mostly congruent with the image and concern the functional properties of the object shown in the image, as well as physical characteristics such as the colour of the car:

104

"They are not always coloured, they can be white or red", the size (always evaluated appropriately, either verbally or using a gesture), and the functional characteristics (for the car, "it's for going to work"). He also refers to the context in which the item is presented (for the plate: "9a tends to be put on the kitchen table"), its familiarity and frequency (for the key: "9a is also known").

Referring to the descriptions he gives of the images (objects present in their context), we note a performance of73% valid responses, which proves that the objects are identified, although he cannot give the exact name of the object.

Analysis of verbal representations of actions in relation to the video shown

Video presented to the aphasic	Responses by category		
	Activity of Base	Process	Dissociation
1-The lady is **eating** chips from a square plate.	1-Kitchen		
2-The child takes a glass to **Drink**	2-Deguster		
3- The lady **sleeps** on a white bed	3- Sommeille		
4- The lady **dresses** her Child	4- Cover		
5- The child is **chewing gum** 6- The lady is taking the keys to **open** her door 7-The gentleman is **writing** a letter 8- The lady **parks her** car (station) 9- The lady **turns on** l'abat Jour	5- Bite	6- Space	
10- The gentleman **calls** his friend on the phone.		7- Trace	
11- The lady **lights** l'a Bajour 12-The lady **stirs** the cream		8-Control 9- Declenche 10-Speaking 11-etincele 12- Melange	13-Breaking
13-The lady **cuts** an apple in half 14- She **peels** a mandarin orange		14-arach 17-slice	15- Breaking 16- Breaking

15- The lady **breaks** the window pane 16- The gentleman **tears up** the newspaper 17-The cook **chops** the onion			

Analysis of R.F.'s semantic representations reveals a verbal disorganisation that prevents him from producing the appropriate verbs in relation to the contexts of the action. R.F. clearly shows that he recognises the action; he provides knowledge of each action presented. We note that R.F keeps the verbal category of the original verb by referring to the context of the action (e.g. for action n°2 "The lady is eating chips from a plate (the object used is the plate), R.F replied "to cook", we note here that the verb "to cook" and "to eat" are in the same semantic field.

Aware of his mistakes, R.F presents an oral production characterised by semantic approximations.

R.F analyses the physical properties of the objects (for the object "knife" in action no. 17 "The cook **chisels** the onion", he replies: "it's for slicing" or in action no. 10 it's for (for the object "telephone": it's for "talking").

The functional characteristics mainly help R.F. to produce valid responses that are approximately congruent with the action and the object used in the action (for the car in action no. 8 "to go to work", he also evokes the context in which the object is present (for car: "I think it's on the road").

Results obtained when naming 1 share using a dynamic medium (video)

""\Actions Answers """"""\	List 1	List 2	List3	Total
R- Approximate validIntra Concept	65%	70%	85%	73.33%
R- Approximatively valid Inter - Concept	30%	45%	35%	36.66%

When naming the action from a dynamic medium (video), we obtained a higher percentage of valid intra-concept responses (73.33%) than valid inter-concept responses (36.66%). The intra-concept approximation behaviours are reflected in the responses obtained: "rediger" in action no. 17, "ciseler" in action no. 15 and the verb "se reposer" in action no. 3, we note that R.F. refers to the functional properties of the objects to get closer to the object to be named.

These results show that R.F obtains better scores when the action is presented using a dynamic medium. This highlights the relevance of the context when naming the action.

The results obtained are represented in the form of bars based on the criteria considered: (valid/invalid; general/specific; approximate/conceptual):

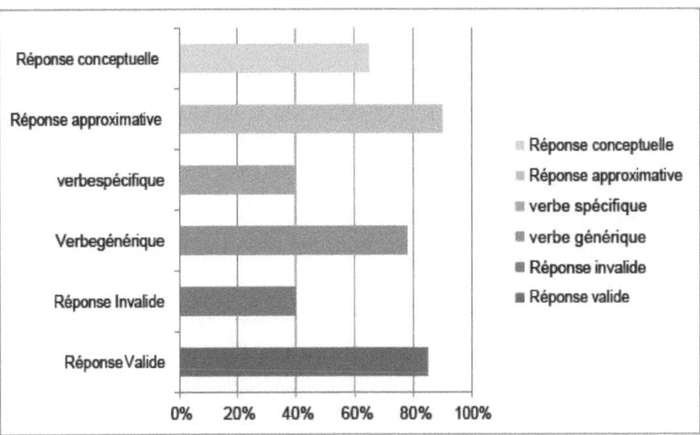

By analysing R.F.'s performance on lexical and semantic tasks in the oral naming of actions, we find that it produces 85% of valid responses that are relevant to the target verb, which represents a semantically close relationship to the original verb (the action to be named).

For example: in action no. 17 "the cook **chops** the onion", the response obtained is "slice", so the dissociation is a common semantic category between the verbs "chop" and "cut".

Overall, R.F.'s responses are valid, preserving the semantic category of the action presented. Invalid responses are descriptions or phonemic paraphrases and represent 40% of responses.

The rate of valid responses is higher than that of invalid responses, which explains the high rate of general verbs (67%) compared with 40% of specific verbs. This pragmatic disorganisation can be explained by the analysis of the action by R.F., hence the conservation of semantic fields. This illustrates the high percentage of semantic approximations 87% against 62% of conceptual responses.

6. Discussion of the results

From a psycholinguistic point of view, the results obtained highlight the observation of language components in their interaction. From a semantic point of view, the results corroborate our initial hypotheses on the predominant role of context (dynamic image) in the determination of action, which manifests itself in semantic approximations.

With regard to semantic categorisation, this case study enabled us to determine the relationship between the oral naming of objects and actions.

These results confirm our hypothesis of the existence of a semantic categorisation preserved in aphasics during the oral naming of actions. The results show that aphasics have the ability to name actions based on their knowledge of object properties.

These results are related to the ability to verbalise, as the capacity to express aspects of knowledge explicitly, through metalinguistic processing.

In this respect, it would seem that certain aspects of language are more easily explicable, in particular semantic knowledge.

Concerning the analysis of general verbs and specific verbs, aphasics produce specific verbs when the object is present in the context of the action. Aphasics recover and produce general verbs more easily, because of the strong semantic representation that characterises them.

The oral naming of actions enabled us to analyse the semantic representation of action verbs in aphasics. During the action, the object can be manipulated, which activates the semantic system that allows the aphasic to recognise the semantic category of the action verb. Therefore, naming action verbs with object manipulation will activate a frontal region that participates in the naming process, as well as in the comprehension of the action. These observations coincide with the results of Lebrun & Buyssens (1982).

We were able to distinguish between the concrete and abstract concept, i.e. the object named outside its context of use and in its context of use (from an image), reflecting the processes involved in accessing the semantic representations of the words that refer to it and the functional properties of the objects.

In a semantic categorisation task comparing approximate valid responses with approximate invalid responses that could be ambiguous (several possible meanings), abstract words were associated with a more diffuse brain activation profile than concrete words (Pexman, Hargreaves, Edwards, Henry, & Goodyear, 2007).

Thus, the results of this case study in aphasics provide evidence in favour of the involvement of motor control regions and circuits in the semantic processing of action words. The semantic representations of these words describing actions would partly include the premotor and motor areas, so that these areas would be activated to facilitate access to the lexico-semantic representations of the words. These results are congruent with some studies showing a deficit in the processing of action concepts in motor pathology (aphasia) (Lebrun & Buyssens, 1982), (Van Elk, Van Schie & Bekkering, 2009).

Analysis of the responses based on the oral naming of actions leads us to deduce that recognition of the specific semantic field of the action verb refers to analysis of the functional properties of objects by aphasics, i.e. oral production of a sensory-motor nature.

As a result, the intact processing of the meaning of action words following motor lesions explains why damage to motor control regions would not lead to a global deficit in words describing actions and in the processes for retrieving these words from memory. The neural networks involved in the semantic processing of action words would therefore include pre-motor and motor areas, as these regions contribute to facilitating the retrieval of these words.

Chapter 2 Cognitive interpretation of results

1. Comprehension disorders

The phonetic-phonological analysis of the linguistic message (decoding of the sounds of language) is not disrupted. As a result, the 5 cases of aphasia do not present with verbal deafness. The tests assessing comprehension levels (naming of images, oral naming of actions) were passed, hence the semantically close palliative strategies.

The tasks exploring the phonological level (lexical decision) were successful. A frequency effect characterised the naming tests. Categorical classification and judgement of synonymy are performed successfully, hence the absence of deafness to the meaning of words. Aphasics automatically activate representations similar to those of the target words. The oral comprehension of the 5 aphasics was therefore preserved, and we did not observe a central semantic deficit that would cause any disturbance whatever the input or output modality   .

Comprehension and/or production of verbs is less poor than that of nouns and functional words (prepositions, determiners).

translating the telegraphic style in aphasics and their agrammatism.

As a result, the effect of grammatical class in the oral production of aphasics is very significant. In the diagram below, we represent the disorders of comprehension:

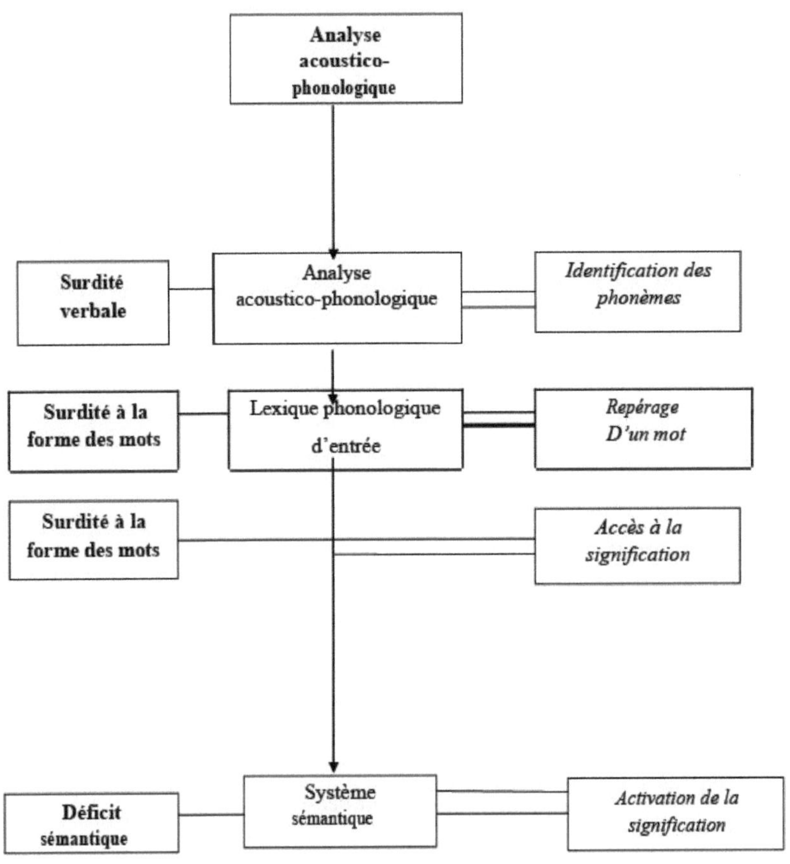

Representation of people with comprehension disorders

2. Central disorders of oral production

2.1 Lexico-semantic disorganisation

Analysis of the oral productions of the 5 aphasics revealed lexico-semantic disturbances caused by the lack of words, indicating an inability to communicate effectively, or even not at all.

In an oral naming task, the aphasic goes through various processes: Visual analysis is a stage in which the object is identified as familiar in order to perceive structural forms;

-At the level of the semantic system, the different representations corresponding to objects are activated in the form of the various features that characterise them;

- Phonological encoding, or the phonological lexicon, and the planning and assembly of phonemes are activated in order to retrieve phonological representations (articulatory gestures).

2.2 Damage to the lexical system

Semantic properties are degraded by disturbance

semantic representations. Aphasics present an oral naming disorder, reflecting damage to the lexical system manifested by semantic paraphasias or absence of response. Observations of clinical cases show that nouns are less affected than verbs in the 5 aphasics.

We have noticed a difference in responses between objects in context and out of context (oral naming of objects and oral naming of actions - animated and inanimated items). Recalling some aspects characterising the functional properties of the object has an effect on access to the semantic representations of the items (Warrington & Shallice, 1980).

2.3 Impairment of lexico-phonological production

At this level the semantic system is intact, so there is no comprehension deficit. Aphasics understand the speech therapist's instructions but cannot name the object or action, based on analysis of the approximate valid responses obtained.

3. Lack of access to phonological form

Analysis of the oral productions reveals a dissociation between grammatical classes: verbs are better evoked than nouns.

During oral naming, aphasics produce verbs that are semantically close, the explanation being that the correct representations of target items and neighbouring items with common semantic features are active in the semantic system.

The item sharing common semantic features is activated instead of the target item when the phonological and semantic representation of the latter is no longer accessible: the action "draw" is produced instead of the action "write". According to Ellis and Franklin (1992), the phonological deficiency of the lexicon generates semantic paraphrases or semantic approximations.

4. Syntax disorders

We found ^{that alllest} aphasics have relevant agrammatism, linked to lexical access without associated semantic difficulties.

This has resulted in a different representation in the mental lexicon of nouns and verbs (Miceli & al., 1984; Caramazza & Hillis, 1991). The deficit in verb processing is caused by syntactic disorganisation, resulting in agrammatism (Zingezer & Berndt, 1990).

5. Semantic system or long-term semantic memory

The action verbs produced by aphasics correspond to a basic level where the target items of a category have the greatest number of attributes in common: the action "cut"; the superordinate level: "dissociate"; and the subordinate level containing the different variants of a class: "chisel, slice, separate, divide".

Aphasics show confusion, on the one hand, between the relations of inclusion (dissociate-▶   cut ->■ chisel) and, on the other hand, between the words of the

same level (coordinated terms: eat dinner).

The categorial conception of concepts is confirmed by the presence of categorial anomies in aphasics. As a result, information diffuses from one concept to another within a semantic network in order to construct modalities. From the quantitative and qualitative analysis of the case study, we noted that the notion of concept accessibility operates from the most general to the most specific level (Warrington, 1987).

The results obtained during oral action naming confirm that aphasics refer to the use of the object by analysing the action in order to associate the concepts of each object with the target action.

This explains why the semantic proximity of two action verbs will be greater the more relevant the number of features they share. Consequently, the intensity of the activation process varies according to the strength of the link between the source unit and the neighbouring units generating the transmission of activation from one concept to another.

The architecture of the lexical system is a major factor in the interpretation of lexico-semantic disorders in aphasics.

Cognitive interpretation has therefore enabled us to deduce that the lack of words is not limited to an absence of response or to semantic errors, and to understand the role of semantic categorisation in the construction of semantic approximations by the aphasic.

6. Moderation of production and oral names

In the production of language, we pass through three cognitive stages: conceptualisation, formulation and articulation (Segui & Ferrand, 2000).

By referring to the responses of aphasics, we deduce that the communicative intention is determined by the messages corresponding to the conceptual structures, so that they express themselves verbally - this is *the conceptualisation stage*, which represents the "preverbal".

The semantic approximation observed in the 5 aphasics proves that the formulation translating conceptual structures into a linguistic message is disorganised. Two stages are necessary to select the mental lexicon:

-When we retrieved words that were semantically appropriate to the message concept, we noticed a higher rate of approximate intra-concept responses.

To select the target word, the aphasic goes through a process of semantic categorisation, in order to choose between several semantically related words (from the same semantic field), which explains the confusion in aphasics and the production of semantic verbal paraphasias; this stage represents **semantic and syntactic encoding.**

-Finding the correct phonological form of the word relating to the concept of the object represents the "formulation" stage, which is **phonological encoding or articulation.**

-Nature of the dissociations between semantic categories

The responses from the 3 types of aphasia suggest that their knowledge is rooted in sensorimotor experiences analysed during interaction with the action.

These semantic approximations reflect the fact that knowledge about objects is not dissociated from the episodes in which aphasics interacted during the oral naming of actions. Several arguments effectively support the theory of sensorimotor experiences in the formation of and access to object concepts. **7 Categorisation and over-extension** Observation of the verbal behaviour of aphasics when faced with functional categories explains the construction of verbal categories. This proves the role of context in the construction of new verbal categories adapted to particular situations.

During the second stage of our study (presentation of the object in its context using dynamic support), we observed the role of interaction with the context and the interactional properties of the objects.

These results show that the way in which aphasics interact with the context of action is a key factor in the structuring of verbal categories. The disturbances in categorisation observed in aphasics are structural (conceptual organisation).

In terms of lexical access, we found that items were easier to access when they were presented in their context of use during oral naming.

The 5 aphasic subjects tend to "contextualise" their responses based on the task of orally naming actions (Hilaire. A 2000).

During the oral object naming task, we observed that: -Aphasic subjects will use "contextualisation" strategies similar to those observed in action.

-    The presence of a contextual effect in the 3 types of a p h a si e s

(the instruction) and category on the criteria used to carry out the categorical inclusion task.

-    The relationship between the functional properties of objects is reflected in the semantic approximations, by the production of generic verbs.

This interpretation is based on categorisation work (Caramazza, A. & Hillis, A.E. 1991). The relationship between actions and objects is reflected in the discourse, during a categorial inclusion task, by a different use of verbal markers compared to the original verbs, and in particular by a marked difference between responses.

- Over-extensions and cognitive flexibility

By analysing the linguistic characteristics of over-extensions, we observe that this phenomenon sometimes results from an analogy of the action performed "the lady protects her son" for the action "the lady dresses her son" or "he draws a letter" for the action "he writes a letter".

This lexical construction is the result of cognitive flexibility due to the analogy skills that aphasics possess. The aphasic does not have the exact term to describe an action (action A), e.g. "to tear up the newspaper", but he does have the cognitive ability to draw an analogy between action A and another action B, e.g. "to break a window", by appropriating the verb "to break" while preserving the same semantic category.

8. The influence of action on the processing of manipulable object concepts

Comparison of the data from the stages of our study based on oral naming of objects confirms that simply seeing a manipulable object reactivates the motor information associated with it.

In this study, aphasics categorise manipulable objects by analysing the action, while aphasics produce more approximate valid responses while preserving the semantic category of the verb.

We found that the performance of valid responses differed during the oral naming of actions, which proves that in order to categorise objects, the aphasic degrades the action performed by the object.

Aphasics perform a lexical decision task on the target verb. The same target object can activate several action verbs in aphasics.

The results show that the lexical choice of aphasics is faster when the action is observed and the object is presented in its context of use, thus confirming the impact of the reactivation of motor information on access to the concept.

In addition, the oral object naming results obtained show that motor skills and conceptual processing of manipulable objects are constructed on the basis of static or dynamic representations of actions.

When naming actions based on objects, we observed that all five participants used the same verbal categories.

The responses concerning the objects to be named are associated with the action observed by the aphasic. Participants categorise objects more quickly when they induce an input compatible with the use of the object presented.

In our study, we noted that these semantic approximations are associated with dynamic representations of actions which are used to interpret the actions. Hence, when the word is missing, aphasics mime the use of manipulable objects.

The oral naming of target objects was categorised by the aphasic speakers on the basis of the actions observed. Indeed, the facilitation effect was observed in the second part of our experiment: associated targets were identified and categorised more quickly than unassociated targets, particularly when naming the action from a dynamic support.

It should also be noted that the recognition of action by aphasics is less marked in the first experiment (oral naming of object) than in the second experiment (oral naming of action).

As a result, the influence of the reactivation of motor experiences on the conceptual processing of manipulable objects has been demonstrated in aphasics on the basis of verbal productions.

Indeed, the target object is clearly identifiable during the oral naming of action (video), since the mime corresponds to a specific object (for example, a person sawing). The alternative interpretation according to which the effect of the functional properties is due to a pre-activation of the object itself rather than of the action cannot be rejected. The results obtained did, however, attempt to demonstrate the influence of action on access to object concepts in aphasics.

Taken together, these verbal results show that objects and action representations automatically induce the reactivation of the motor experiences associated with them. The processing of manipulable object concepts is influenced by action-related information.

This translates into the construction of specific verbs. This leads us to project this phenomenon onto all manipulable objects. These arguments support the crucial role of action with objects in the formation and processing of concepts of manipulable objects. When naming objects orally in their 'no action' context, aphasics observe how the speech therapist moves the object.

In the second part of our experiment, "naming objects without action or movement", the speech therapist simply presented the object to the aphasic in order to name it. We found that the aphasics named the objects by explaining the actions and referring to each object.

These results reveal a clear recovery of language for the test objects congruent with the action performed during the familiarisation phase in the 'action' condition. On the other hand, no difference between the choices for the two test objects was observed in the 'no action' and 'no action, no movement' conditions. The results obtained show that the sensorimotor experience of the aphasic influences the formation of object categories.

We can therefore suggest that contextual and functional knowledge play a crucial role in the retrieval of action verbs in aphasics. When the use of manipulated objects is analyzed by the aphasic, contextual and functional knowledge is more easily accessible for these objects. Consequently, this reflects the links between motor experience and knowledge about the context of use and the function of the objects.

8.1 The interaction between contextual and functional knowledge By analysing verbal association norms for the functional properties of objects in adults with aphasia, we found that aphasics retained a hyperonymous relationship with the target action.

Other generic attributes are common to the majority of the categories concerned, for example, "has wheels" for "vehicle" in the production of generic verbs.

At the same time, other semantic features of the category are present, for example, "plane" for "vehicle", which group together the same semantic field "means of transport". Referring to these results, we confirm that processing an over-ordered concept would amount to processing functional categories of objects. This will in turn activate the sensorimotor information associated with them.

Contextual information is transmitted by the reactivation of sub-ordinate concepts (hyponyms). In this case, aphasics create sensorimotor interactions in order to link them to the meaning of the contextual information, thus facilitating access to the sub-ordinate concepts.

For example, the context of the kitchen shown in the image would make it possible to link together various objects (e.g. glass, fork, colander, plate, spoon) that different motor experiences would not make it possible to group together directly.

When aphasics determine whether the object in the image belongs to the category mentioned, several factors are manipulated: the category may be at the basic level, e.g. for the object "hammer" which represents an over-ordered level in the category "tools" corresponding to the under-ordered level, the image may correspond to an isolated object or to a scene (i.e. several objects in a context), and the index object may or may not belong to the category mentioned.

The results of the approximate responses show an interaction between the level of the concept and the type of image: the production of generic verbs at the basic level is significantly observed when the object is presented in its context compared with a presentation of the object in isolation. Moreover, when the object to be categorised is presented in an inappropriate image, the categorial performance of aphasics regresses, producing more invalid responses.

Aphasics make a categorical choice about the object, either at the basic level, for example, "a kind of plate", or at the superordinate level, "a kind of utensil".

As a result, the effect of context interacts with the level of categorisation required. Action-related information is more likely to help the aphasic access basic-level concepts, while contextual information is more likely to facilitate access to superordinate concepts.

These results are consistent with the variations in results observed between the inter-concept and intra-concept approximate responses. Taken together, these results suggest that the grouping of varied actions performed with objects is facilitated by the context in which the objects are encountered, in particular the scenes in which the interactions with the objects take place and, consequently, this helps the aphasic to access the ordered concepts of the objects present. These semantic approximations represent strategies centred on the use of contextual information, and could therefore be considered to facilitate the comprehension of over-ordered concepts (hyperonymy) in cerebro-lesioned adults.

The relationships between action and object function reflect the approximate inter-conceptual responses when naming objects on the basis of action. We have observed that aphasics' knowledge of the function of objects emerges from the analysed actions of these objects.

Aphasics show a confusion of action verbs which proves the presence of a double neuropsychological dissociation between the naming of actions and the function of objects.

When naming objects from a dynamic support (action) to assess the knowledge of aphasics, the instruction was to determine the object from the action video. The approximate responses obtained in the form of general and specific verbs in relation to the target action belong to the same context of the semantic category of the objects presented. As a result, aphasic subjects are better able to analyse items related to manipulation.

Aphasics' observations of manipulation and object function activate similar semantic categories, although some of these categories appear more strongly activated when knowledge about manipulation is preserved in the aphasic. We compared the retrieval of knowledge about object function using an action matching task. We observed that all semantic categories of action referring to the target object are active in both conditions, 'object function' and 'object manipulation'.

However, the approximate inter-concept responses (see Chapter 6) are not activated during the oral naming of objects out of context.

This means that the retrieval of action verbs in aphasics will depend on "manipulation" and "function", and that the retrieval of knowledge about function does not seem to be underpinned by a specific semantic network (Canessa et al, 2008).

Knowledge of the function is recuperated from knowledge of the object's properties when the verbal association is made with the action appropriate to the target object. This explains the production of generic verbs.

This activation classically represents information about object handling.

This analysis is sometimes interpreted by gestures corresponding to the use of the target object, or by a description of the action (e.g. hammer - whole hand grasping gesture). These results are interpreted by activation of the aphasic's semantic system, and demonstrate the ability of aphasics to analyse the use of different objects.

8.2 Conceptual processing of objects

The results of oral object naming in the context of adults with aphasia represent action-related information, which influenced access to the concepts of manipulable objects, such as the tools and utensils we use every day. These verbal results are consistent with the activation of regions of the visuomotor system during conceptual processing of these objects (Barde., § al 2007).

In the aphasics we studied, we saw that access to functional knowledge of objects was preserved by the presence of approximate inter- and intra-conceptual responses ("what's it for?"), whereas knowledge about objects is largely impaired.

These neuropsychological data suggest that the recruitment of motor information is concomitant with, but not necessary for, access to object function.

However, this interpretation merits some reflection. First of all, we know that functional knowledge of objects is relatively preserved in aphasics because of their ability to describe the actions presented. This can be explained by functional disorganisation at the cerebral level and in terms of the compensatory strategies used.

Following the recovery and/or relearning phase, the 5 aphasics carry out a matching task between videos depicting actions and objects. From the semantic representations of the objects, they selected the object that corresponded to the action. We found that the aphasics' overall performance was inferior when naming an object orally out of context compared with when naming an object from a static image representing the context of the object.

Cerebrospinal cells are much better at recognising objects in static images by means of structural and functional descriptions than they are at recognising objects when they are presented out of context. This means that they have the skills to analyse the potential of conceptual processing of objects, reactivating new approximate strategies.

These strategies enable them to represent action verbs. In our study, we were able to understand how aphasics analyse the context of objects in order to reactivate their conceptual knowledge.

We can therefore compare these approximate strategies to the re-acquisition of new knowledge about functional objects.

This conceptual knowledge about objects brings together different types of information, not all of which are systematically determined by semantic categories. This leads the aphasic to distinguish between specific and general functional knowledge, resulting in the production of general and specific action verbs. The specific functional properties of objects play a crucial role in identifying actions.

For example, the fact of cutting and having a blade would be fundamental to the "knife" concept. These specific functional attributes would also be very close to motor information, such as the action of cutting.

In addition, the knowledge relating to objects during out-of-context oral naming would be more general, such as the fact that a knife is used to cut food in the kitchen, which could be assimilated to contextual knowledge. However, we have seen that the specific and general functions of objects are rarely dissociated when functional knowledge (the oral naming of actions) is assessed.

It is possible to imagine that action-specific functional knowledge is closer to contextual information about objects. It therefore seems important to distinguish between these two types of functional knowledge when assessing aphasics.

The motor experiences of aphasics play a crucial role in the comprehension of actions. Aphasics reactivate their information about manipulable objects by referring to other forms of knowledge about familiar objects, which are associated with other forms of sensorimotor information, including visual and structural information, in order to access knowledge about the use of the object (Barde., § al 2007). This multifunctional information is closely linked to the approximate language of aphasics.

Chapter 3 Lexico-semantic interpretation of the results

1. Recovering the lexicon

From a linguistic point of view, during language recovery, the aphasic creates new strategies in order to name the target word in context very quickly and implicitly.

To establish a new referent and a corresponding mental representation, aphasics use a variety of contextual cues, from the moment they are confronted with a task to name actions based on the object in question. In order to recreate a lexical network, they associate these new words with words already stored in semantic memory. The aphasic will refine his semantic representations, by associating the words in his lexical network more and better to create these semantic approximations. This improves their ability to retrieve stored words.

- **Access to glossaries and organisation**

The results obtained by aphasics show the presence of several models of lexical access in adults. In order to account for the processes involved in speech production and word identification, we have distinguished models that are consistent with three types of representations involved in lexical access and word retrieval: semantic, syntactic and phonological representations. As a result, lexical access involves two stages, and activation of one stage results in activation of another;

-The selection of abstract entities which bring together the syntactic properties of words, representing lemmas. To select the target lemma, a lexical set is activated to retrieve the lexicon. This creates relationships between words.

- After this stage, the phonological forms appropriate to the target lemma *(lexemes)* are activated and selected, in order to activate phonological encoding.

The selection of the target lemma enables phonological encoding by assigning appropriate lexemes to the target lemma, leading to the naming of the item, translating a serial process from lemma to lexeme.

These types of processes lead to the production of speech, which has been proven in Levelt's (1989) work in psycholinguistics. The production of a word or oral noun involves various stages: recognition of the object, activation of the noun and articulation of the word. This refers to the cognitive interpretation of semantic approximations in the aphasic translating the production of words which goes through conceptualisation (the concept of the action in relation to the object to be named); a formulation stage (retrieval of lexical information in accordance with the concept of the object and appropriate to the syntactic and phonological encoding of the lemma).

2. The lack of a word

The spontaneity, periphrases, circumlocution, delay in evoking the word and approach behaviours observed in the 5 aphasics reflect the lack of the word.

Apart from the consequences of pathophysiological mechanisms, cognitive disorders (visual recognition of the different objects presented to the five aphasia cases shows that they do not have visual agnosia), may reflect a lack of words in the aphasic. Echolalia (uncontrolled repetition of words or phrases) could be the result in some aphasics of a behavioural approach to the lack of words. From a linguistic point of view, the alteration of the lexical process is at the origin of the lack of words, which has been proven in the research of Caramazza & Hillis (1990) ; Hillis *et al. (*1990).

Two types of alteration can be distinguished depending on the linguistic level affected:

-Difficulty in retrieving semantic information ("spoon" for "plate", "door" for "key", "scissors" for "knife"), in which case we observe an alteration in semantic encoding or lemmas. Hence the aphasic's difficulty in storing or accessing words, reflecting a semantic difficulty.

-We observe a phonological encoding disorder, if the lexemic level is affected, resulting in difficulty in accessing the phonological form of the word, which may go as far as paraphasia or no response at all, without any comprehension disorder.

3. Knowledge preserved in aphasics

Analysis of the cases shows that word retrieval is based on the aphasics' preserved linguistic information. They will use denominative strategies that are more or less effective, depending on their preserved lexical knowledge.

We distinguish three types of strategy:

-Strategies based on the phonological and morphological form of the target word.

- Strategies that relate to the semantics of the target word, based on the context in which the object is presented.

-We have observed that people with aphasia use non-verbal strategies (gestures, mimicry, onomatopoeia) to compensate for their difficulties.

The responses obtained by the aphasics enabled us to distinguish between *linguistic* and non-linguistic strategies in relation to the knowledge possessed by the aphasic.

Models of lexical access can be used to explain purely linguistic strategies.

The results show that the naming of objects in aphasics depends on their experience. The aphasic's relationship with the objects to be named is a relevant criterion in the correct naming of the item presented, as demonstrated in Tran's research (2007).

In semantic paraphrases, we deduced interesting aspects in semantic strategies, reflecting the evaluation of the deficit in lexical access processes and lexical selection.

The problem lies in lexical selection, particularly at lexeme level, when the recovered form is phonologically and articulatively correct at lexeme level.

Let's take the example of the lexical representation of "car": several features make up its semantic representation (four wheels, means of transport, travel, means of getting around,   etc.). As a result, if one of the sub -

If the set of features is not active, this will lead to an erroneous lexical selection by the aphasic (motorbike instead of car), which will explain the deficit at this level of selection. This type of paraphasia reflects a compositional structure of lexico-semantic representations.

4. Representing the processing of the semantic system

In terms of semantic knowledge processing, we observed strategies used by aphasics to refer to conceptual notions, enabling them to understand language and our environment (objects, actions, faces, sounds, etc.). The context in which the objects presented to the aphasics are used, as well as their shape, colour and the purpose of the actions, allow them to reach the sequence of actions within which they fit, explaining the semantic approximations produced by the aphasics.

The naming disorders we have analysed refer to problems in identifying and attributing meaning to stimuli in the environment, whether these take the form of words, objects, actions or events.

The results of semantic approximations in aphasics have shown us that there is a distinction between 'semantic' and 'conceptual' disorders, and that this difference reflects a different conception of the representation of meaning.

At the "semantic" level, aphasics retain the meaning, borrowed from linguistics, "meaning of linguistic units and their combination". Studies by (Bierwisch & Schreuder, 199, Malt, Sloman, Gennari, Shi, & Wang, 1999, Tranel, Kemmerer, Adolphs, Damasio, & Damasio, 2003 ; Vigliocco, Vinson, Lewis, & Garrett, 2004) show that the "lexico-semantic" system thus represents the meaning of lexical units in long-term memory; it therefore does not only concern language production and comprehension activities.

We observed that aphasics analysed each object, action and their dimensions semantically, which would represent all the non-verbal concepts of the "conceptual system". This explains the direct relationship between the "lexico-semantic" system and the "conceptual system".

From this same perspective, we have been able to distinguish between the "verbal semantic system" and the "visual system" in terms of inter- and intra-concept responses, as developed by Paivio (1978), who distinguishes between a "verbal" system, translating the meaning of words, and an "image" semantic system concerning the visual properties of imageable objects and actions.

We found that the responses obtained showed a relationship between the different semantic features of the semantic/conceptual system. In this perspective, each semantic property is represented by a "node" (Hillis & Caramazza, 1995; Jackendoff, 1987; Masson, 1995; Miller, & Johnson-Laird, 1976) and the activation of a different set of "nodes" would correspond to each concept. For example, the conceptual representation of "car" would activate the set of nreud-traits (is an object) , (has four wheels) , (is made of metal) , (is used as a means of transport).

5. Assessment and nature of semantic disorders

The aphasics who produced approximate responses in the oral naming of objects and actions did not present semantic disorders. The presentation of a naming task based on an image made it possible to establish a relationship between difficulties in naming objects orally out of context and difficulties in recovering lexical form. The aphasic had naming difficulties and deficits in object naming, and this was observed when naming orally out of context.

We have seen that when naming objects in context, aphasics produce circumlocutions or periphrases, verbal paraphrases (especially semantic paraphrases), or even no response at all. In the task of oral naming of objects out of context, aphasics may refrain from responding or may describe the use of another object which has a semantic relationship with the test word.

By referring to the results for the oral naming of actions, we will understand that these inferior results are also linked to a pre-semantic performance affecting the component of structural representations of objects.

Similarly, deficits in naming or verifying the recognition of objects in the image (in context) could be due to a deficit in semantic representation in the aphasic.

Evaluation of our results will confirm the preservation of semantic processing in the aphasics we studied. As a result, the presentation of objects by oral naming (out of context/in context) is an auditory or visual lexical decision task (words/action).

Deficit results in these oral naming tasks (invalid responses) may be useful for understanding the pathological language profile of the aphasic and/or for testing earlier perceptual levels, i.e. acoustic/phonological levels in the types of aphasia we have studied.

6. Over-extension: a compensatory phenomenon for the lack of words in aphasics

The language phenomenon observed in adults with aphasia, "semantic paraphasia with a verbal pivot", involves the production of lexical substitutions between items linked by a semantic concept. The lack of a word in the aphasic is compensated for by a substitution of a word (verb) with a semantic proximity relationship (approximate valid response) to the action to be named, and constitutes categorial over-extensions (approximate valid intra-concept responses) or analogical over-extensions (approximate valid inter-concept responses).

-On category extension

Analysis of our results in this study, based on the naming of dynamic vs static images, reveals that the word substitutions (verbs) obtained are of the same semantic concept: "swallow" for "eat", "destroy" for "tear", "snore" for "sleep". We note that in the 3 forms of aphasia, the verbs obtained retain the same category as the action to be named.

-Analogue over-extensions

The ability to extend words also concerns verbs that share a semantic relationship but do not refer to the same semantic concept, as described by R. Jakbson (1963, p. 58): "his approached identifications are of a metaphorical nature". These analogical over-extensions concern approximate inter-concept responses: "undress - the mandarin" for "peel - the mandarin", the aphasic makes an analogy of the action observed from the video and attributes a specific verb "undress".

From the above, we have deduced that the lack of words in aphasia is due to a difficulty in accessing the lexicon, linked to the limited number of words available to the aphasic.

This lexical disorder is compensated for by these over-extensions, and it is in this conception that Nespoulous (1996) introduces the notion of "palliative strategy" to replace the status of error: "Yes, the cerebral lesion which gives rise to aphasia also gives rise to a deficit and creates a communicative handicap in everyday life. But yes, the aphasic - in the presence of his handicap - will try, and in many cases succeed, in deploying a panoply of strategies to adapt to his deficit and try to bypass it in order to satisfy his daily communicative needs" (Nespoulous, 1996, p. 423).

This concept operates at a pragmatic level, to which other factors of a lexico-semantic and cognitive nature are added. Thus, over-extensions represent a palliative concept in the aphasic's communicative process to replace the status of error.

6.1 The lexico-semantic relationship between sur -extensions

Linguistic analysis of over-extensions shows that these productions make it possible to enrich syntactic embodiments and are most often based on a lexico-semantic relationship of inter-concept co-hyponymy between verbs (Duvignau, 2003; Duvignau & al., 2004).

For example, the verb "to swallow" is in an inter-conceptual co-hyponymic relationship with the verb a denommer "to eat".

We find that aphasics produce semantic paraphasias by bringing into play this type of lexico-semantic relationship, which represents one of the modes of organisation of the lexicon.

These categorial over-extensions have an inter-concept co-hyponymy or hyperonymy-hyponymy relationship.

Here we distinguish between :

* "Swallowing to drink

▶ Intra-domain co-hyponymy between "Drink" and "Swallow" (hyperonym = Eat) for the basic activity category.

* "Break" for "Break

▶ Intra-domain co-hyponymy between "Break" and "Break" (hyperonym = Deteriorate) in the dissociation category.

* "Parler" for "Telephoner

▶ Intra-domain co-hyponymy between "Talk" and "Telephoner" (hyperonym = Call) in the "basic activity category".

* "cover" for "dress

▶ Cross-domain co-hyponymy between "cover" and "dress" (hyperonym = "protect oneself") in the "basic activity" category.

* "Drawing to write

Cross-domain co-hyponymy between "Write" and "Draw" (hyperonym = Create) in the "process" category.

*   "Directing" for "Driving

▶ Cross-domain co-hyponymy between "Direct" and "Drive" (hyperonym = "to move") in the "process" category.

*   "cut" for "slice

▶ Cross-domain co-hyponymy between "Cut" and "Slice" (hyperonym = "divide") in the category "process".

We note that all the over-extensions are in the form of cohyponymy or hyperonymy-hyponymy, which means that the lexical productions of aphasics are part of the same categorical linguistic system.

Faced with this lack of a word, the aphasic does not develop random strategies; on the contrary, he creates a kind of para-synonymy in relation to the object he is using; the result of this over-extension is what we will call semantic approximation (Duvignau, 2003).

As Duvignau shows in his research, the status of error is called into question by the lexico-semantic approach to over-extensions.

6.2 Macro-lexical structuring strategy

The semantic categories of discourse are preserved overall in our five aphasics, and even over-employed in spontaneous discourse production. We conclude that the use of semantic approximations made it possible to compensate, at the level of lexical macro-structure, for the lack of elaboration at the level of verbal micro-structure. When semantic representations are no longer as easily accessible, approximate semantic categories are preferentially used, in order to have a link with palliative pragmatico-discursive organisation strategies. This hypothesis was tested by means of qualitative analyses during the task of oral naming of actions.

7.   Valid answers

The study of the valid response variable corroborates the trends described for the overall category of action verbs. From a qualitative point of view, the very partial analysis of the different types of valid responses used and of semantic substitutions illustrates palliative strategies specific to the category of verb to be named during the oral naming of actions, such as the frequent recourse to descriptions of the use of the objects present.

As regards approximate responses, we observed that they were fairly common in aphasic corpora, but in neutral or weak forms (semantic paraphrases).

On the other hand, reference to the objects present is made more by lexical means than by action verbs. This is in line with the trends already mentioned in relation to categorisation.

Detailed examination of the valid responses confirms, once again, that recourse to the context of the objects presented is rather a characteristic of spontaneous production. We found that after observing the actions during the second oral naming task, aphasics showed greater lexical precision.

7.1 General verbs and specific verbs

From the qualitative analysis, we observed that certain verbs are used preferentially, such as "to be" in descriptions of actions, and elementary constructions with a copula verb or a presentative. On the other hand, some cases of aphasia (Broca's aphasia) tend to use a verb by default, with a general value (such as to do or to take) instead of the specific verb required. This palliative choice makes it possible to improve the semantic structuring of the action around a verbal predicate, which may not be semantically precise, but which is very present and thus serves as a pivot.

In particular, we found that overall, the five cases of aphasia we studied manifest a dysfunction affecting verbal inflection mechanisms, and use forms that are less specific to encode and insert into the lexico-semantic matrix (object-action), such as non-finite or basic forms of the infinitive. This simplification of verbal morphology is a characteristic of the approximative style as defined by Duvignau (2002).

In addition, we observed variability in the approximate inter-concept responses: in general, when the object to be named is presented outside its context of use, the verbs are used in a generic form, i.e. approximate inter-concept responses.

And vice versa: the more spontaneous the speech, the less specific the verbs, i.e. the more frequently they appear in a basic non-finite or finite form (non-finite, often in the infinitive, alongside finite verb forms in the present simple which are relatively less frequent).

7.2 Palliative strategies and reformulation procedures

The reduction in capacity dedicated to the encoding processes between the action verbs and the object to be used during encoding in context has consequences for the quality of the semantics.

From this point of view, the variability of the approximate inter-concept and intra-concept responses, for each of the lexico-semantic variables studied, reveals the existence of the underlying dysfunction and the analysis of the various functional properties of the objects.

The quantitative and qualitative aspects that characterise semantics are largely the result of strategies for formatting the constructs to be produced.

The variability of approximate responses clearly reflects the adaptation procedures used by aphasic subjects to improve the lexico-semantic quality of their utterances.

Indeed, we have observed that, overall, the lexical structuring of action verbs in aphasic productions gains in semantic correction when verbal representations are analysed using a dynamic support.

And vice versa: in freer production, the oral production of aphasics is characterised by interspersed constructions (in terms of quantity), in other words the lack of words and non-canonical forms (in terms of quality).

In our opinion, this is probably due to the fact that the aphasic creates a less precise formulation, which is very clear in spontaneous production.

Morpho-lexical palliative strategies

Palliative strategies, which rely on convenient morphemes that are preferably used, significantly improve the quality of the syntax (such as constructions around the pivots "to take" and "for" or the use of the presentative "it is" or minimal syntactic constructions (c;i va or c'est bien).

In this way, the quality of syntax is improved by morpho-syntactic palliatives which can be systematised so that their mobilisation becomes routine. It should be added that other palliative strategies of this type could certainly be described through more in-depth qualitative analyses.

- Self-correction and reformulation procedure

The reformulation and self-correction procedures seemed to us to be more characteristic of the oral naming of action verbs, reflecting the ability to distinguish between the different functional properties of the objects referring to each action. They make it possible to improve the quality of the lexico-semantic construction of action verbs.

As a result, verbal elocution becomes more fluent, leading to an acceleration in verbal rate. On the other hand, in spontaneous production (oral naming of objects out of context), reformulation processes are less characteristic.

To be precise, this semantic approximation of aphasic utterances improves as the task gains in conceptual precision induced by the action and targeted by the aphasic speaker. Subjects prefer to use non-adaptive structuring strategies in spontaneous production (i.e. preventive adaptations). On the other hand, when naming objects orally from a static support referring to the context, they tend to use self-corrective or even reflexive strategies (i.e. explicit or silent corrective adaptations).

- Verbal precision and palliative strategies

Based on conceptual and functional analyses of the objects presented to aphasics, we observed an improvement in verbal fluency. This was achieved by means of approximate semantic simplifications.

So in oral naming of objects in the context of use from a static image:

There is less recourse to the telegraphic style, which reflects the lack of words, the utterances are longer and more elaborate, and the lexico-semantic quality improves at the cost of a slower verbal flow (i.e. less fluency);

The lexical construction relies in particular on appropriate morphemes to express the functional use of objects (such as the preposition pour) and pivotal structures (such as "Take object X for Z" for example). In oral naming of objects in their functional contexts, we observed an overall improvement in verbal fluency and/or the lexico-semantic quality of verbal productions.

7.3 Adapting action verbs and reformulation strategies

In situations involving the oral naming of actions based on a dynamic medium (video), the formulations are of "better lexico-semantic and morphosyntactic quality", in favour of metalinguistic strategies:

To achieve the semantic accuracy of action verbs, the use of self-correction or reformulation procedures is more characteristic of oral action naming tasks than conceptual analysis of the functional properties of the objects of each action;

This performance of self-correction observed in the 5 aphasics (or semantic approximation), occurs in relation to a slowdown in verbal flow (verbal fluency) reflecting the lexico-semantic processing of the actions to be named.

In other words, verbal fluency is inversely targeted because of the extra processing time probably devoted to reflective procedures on what is produced. The empty or filled pauses, which lengthen and multiply, are probably necessary for corrective adaptations, which in fact slows down the verbal flow.

7.4 The relationship between action verbs and categorisation

In various categorisation tasks, the results we obtained from the oral naming of actions allow us to investigate the relationship between explicit verbalisable knowledge. They confirm the close relationship between categorisation ability and verbalisation performance.

The results for aphasic subjects show that the responses obtained correspond to the semantic fields of the categories created and are preserved. Furthermore, the results of the analysis of the oral productions show the presence of a relationship between the semantic components, but not for the prosodic and syntactic components. Thus, aphasic subjects verbally express their responses concerning semantic categories.

These results are interesting in relation to the observations on the preceding pages. These results reinforce our hypothesis of a language hierarchy, with semantics constituting, in ascending order, the first level of difficulty for subjects with aphasia. As a result, the successes of the oral naming of actions are supported by similar patterns that we observe between the aphasics' comments and the rate of semantic representation obtained. Thus, we observe a semantic approximation effect in the aphasic responses.

Thus, we observe a clear improvement in the retrieval of action verbs in aphasics by referring to the context of each action presented. These results also confirm the three-level difficulty hierarchy for language pathology: the success of comments is clearly better for the semantic component, less good for the prosodic component and very deficient for syntax, which reflects the high percentage of agrammatism in the 5 aphasics.

We found that verbalisation is related to the processing of metalinguistic knowledge. As a result, semantic knowledge about objects in aphasics is more preserved than other aspects of language. Consequently, aphasic subjects have more difficulty producing the semantic categories of language than the formal aspects.

Chapitre 4   Pragmatic interpretation of the results

1. Approximation from a conceptual point of view

Cognitive-semantic interaction enabled us to establish a clear distinction between meaning and signification, between pragmatics and semantics, which was observed in practically all the oral productions of the aphasics we studied. These palliative linguistic means serve to blur the categorial boundaries of the linguistic element they modify. Aphasics often compensate for their lack of words with gestures or descriptions of manipulable objects. These palliative strategies represent conversational implicatures Grice (1979) which translate unconventional expressions or metaphors, because they are not produced in relation to the context. For example: in action no. 14 "She **peels** a mandarin" the aphasic responds "**to tear off** the skin of the mandarin" this action verb is not in its given context of enunciation, produced by the unconventional form of the linguistic expression.

The aim of this study is to distinguish between meaning and signification, pragmatics and semantics, using a sample of lexical approximation markers. We will identify the communicative strategies and semantic reinterpretation processes that lead to the emergence of approximation markers in the oral naming of action verbs.

The oral production of aphasic speakers is characterised by a range of palliative strategies, which makes their utterances unclear.

The results obtained in the five aphasia cases show a more specific function of lexical approximation at the level of action verbs, which must be distinguished from the similar functions of semantic approximation at the level of the utterance (action verbs vs. object).

The approximators we observed operate at the level of action verbs, whereas when naming objects out of context, we found that the number of valid responses decreased.

In the case of intra-concept approximative responses, the semantic relevance of action verbs is reduced. Furthermore, in the case of inter-concept approximative responses, the semantic load of action verbs is reduced. When naming an object orally from a static support, we observed a lexical approximation, reflecting the contextual influence in the semantic representation.

In this way, the context of the objects represents a catalyst for the attenuation of the lack of words and the illocutionary force of the object. This will enable the aphasic to transport the idea to a lexical approximation.

The results obtained have enabled us to distinguish between means of approximation which serve to indicate a flexible use of a lexeme and means of semantic approximation such as ("diner" and "cuisiner" for the action "manger").

We shall confine ourselves to analysing a few central means of linguistic adaptation, i.e. lexical approximators. Lexical approximation at the level of the oral naming of objects (in their contexts of use) is not explicit and is constructed on the basis of extralinguistic information.

In this case, the aphasias we have analysed make no conceptual distinction between pragmatics and semantics.

The meaning of the object presented can thus acquire a more specific, more general, metaphorical or approximate meaning.

Similarly, approximate interpretation can be triggered by para-verbal means such as the shape of the object or the colour of the image presented. These pragmatic effects are not part of the semantics of lexemes.

However, the approximate function tends to be anchored in the meaning of certain expressions that blur the meaning of the word produced and which they modify, such as "roughly", or "stuff like that", like, "To use".

2.   From pragmatics to semantics

The process by which the literal meaning of the words produced by aphasics is modified (or linguistically specified) by the use of the objects present.

We observed three phenomena that converge in the approximation of meaning in the 5 aphasics: specification, approximation and extension, reflecting the results of a process that adapts to most words, hence the pragmatics.

The concept of objects corresponds to the mental representations of actions, thus translating action verbs as elements that encode meaning. When naming the action using a dynamic medium (video), we observed a high percentage of intra-concept approximate responses. These results show that the concept communicated by the use of an object differs from that encoded in words. In other words, the linguistic denotation of words is specified by these concepts (context).

With regard to general verbs, most verbs obtained by aphasics are cases of semantic broadening, in which a word is used to convey a more general meaning, thus leading to a semantic extension of the linguistic denotation. This explains the metaphorical transfer of meaning, hence the semantic approximation.

From the responses obtained during oral naming of actions, we found a variety of semantic approximations reflecting an extension of meaning. This extension of meaning is relatively applicable to an action by aphasics and represents a categorial linguistic denotation.

We note that the responses obtained by the aphasics in action no. 1 ("to eat chips") are as follows: "dine", "cuisine" and "deguste". We see that these verbs retain the semantic field of the verbal category in relation to the original verb.

These expansions refer to supra-ordinate or sub-ordinate categories, and the distinguishing features of each verbal category are preserved by aphasics. This observation is valid for each action presented.

There are different degrees of semantic approximation, as in the case of actions 16 and 17, where the responses obtained were "break", "cut" and "separate" instead of the verbs "tear" and "chisel".

We note that some verbs correspond to a more general level, reflecting a hyperonymic relationship (supra-ordinate categories) and form the most inclusive category; for example, the verb "to break" represents a categorial extension formed from the aphasic's analysis of the action "to tear up the newspaper" by relating the object of the action "scissors".

3.   The pragmatics of action verbs

The pragmatic (lexical) explanation is why such a process might occur. In other words, what would be the result, for cognition and communication, of having a plastic repertoire of approximate expressions? The function of generic verbs would be to create preferred semantic paths in aphasics: the more the generic verb is used, the more the path is marked out and known, and therefore the more accessible its meaning. The fact that semantic approximations translate metaphors, the use of which, and therefore the meaning of which, has become widespread, is not crucial here. What is crucial is the idea of a preferred path. This idea must be related to the procedure for understanding Relevance (Wilson & Sperber, 2004, p. 613). Aphasic speakers produce metaphorical action verbs such as "undress", "tear off" for "peel off", which demonstrate their ability to bring together objects that belong to distinct categories on the basis of shared physical or functional properties (Winner, 1995; Gelman & al, 1998; Bassano, 2000).

With regard to the development of the verbal lexicon, we have observed that aphasics have an analogical competence based on the oral naming of actions, which consists of comparing different actions, which is essential for the recovery of language and cognitive development.

The results obtained show that these aphasic speakers have a semantic-cognitive flexibility that enables them to compensate for the lack of words.

By analysing the semantic approximations produced by the five aphasics, we found that they displayed erroneous over-extensions based on verbs, adjectives and object nouns. These semantic approximations are also created by referring to an analogy competence that reflects their cognitive flexibility. For example, we obtained the verb "divide" for the action of "cutting an apple" thanks to the identification of an analogy of the type "Divide an apple".

These semantic approximations reflect linguistic manifestations of this cognitive competence, which can be defined as the stressing of a lexical term, either in relation to its linguistic context, or in relation to its pragmatic context, thus giving rise to two types of approximation (Duvignau, 2002):

-Inter-concept semantic approximations in the action "peel a mandarin", the aphasic responds with the following sentence: "she peels the skin off a mandarin". This is a description of the action verb "peel" which mobilises a discrepancy between the semantic concept "dissociation" associated with the approximative lexeme "peel the skin off a mandarin" and the semantic concept "skin" associated with the action "peel a mandarin".

The relationship between the approximate lexeme 'arracher' and a conventional lexeme 'peler' is then one of inter-concept co-hyponymy in which the co-hyponyms are in a synonymous relationship even though they do not belong to the same semantic field: 'dissociation ^ corporel' (Duvignau, 2003; Duvignau et al. 2007).

This relationship of inter-concept co-hyponymy (as between 'eplucher' and 'arracher') is the linguistic core of what Gentner (Gentner et al. 2001) calls, at the conceptual level, the relationship of partial identity between relational predicates (as between eplucher and arracher) from distinct conceptual domains.

-The intra-conceptual semantic approximations in the action "the lady protects her car (garage)" is produced to describe "the action of parking her car in a garage", which refers to the difference between the concept "the lady protects her car (garage)" and "the lady protects her car (garage)".

"In this case, the approximate lexeme produced, "proteger", is in a co-hyponymic relationship with the expected item "garer", although it may belong to the same semantic concept. Here, the approximate lexeme produced, "proteger", is in a co-hyponymic relationship with the expected item "garer", although it may belong to the same semantic concept. It is therefore no longer a synonymy relationship but rather an intra-concept troponymy relationship that causes pragmatic tension.

This is due to the unsuitability of the troponymic verb to designate the action concerned. The semantic approximations observed in aphasics therefore reflect a lexical manifestation of conceptual analogy (Lakoff, 1992; Gibbs, 1994; Glucksberg and Keyzar, 1990).

4. Paradigmatic projection on the syntagmatic axis

During lexical access, semantic approximations arise which are within the cognitive capacity of aphasics. Aphasics project the structure of a conceptual domain onto the structure and functional characteristics of the object of action. This projection leads to metaphors in the form of semantic approximations, called the metaphorical process by Lakoff and Johnson (1980), based on the identification of structural similarities between the object of action and the conceptual domain.

The aphasic speaker, wishing to communicate the action of "peeling a mandarin", produces a metaphorical statement using the verb "to tear off the skin of the mandarin", thus expressing a semantic dissociation of verbal category.

Aphasics make an analogy by comparing the observed action of "peeling a mandarin", in which they have lost the verbal category by referring to a previously memorised action, with the lexical entry "peeling the skin off the mandarin".

To exploit these semantic approximations at a lexical level, we distinguish two types of relationship between lexemes:

- The syntagmatic relationship between the verb and the object: the verb V1 is in a syntagmatic relationship with the object if the term V1 can appear in a greater or lesser number of syntactic contexts of V2; Example: the verb "eplucher" is in a syntagmatic relationship with the term "mandarine". The paradigmatic relationship between verbs: the term t1 is in a paradigmatic relationship with the term t2 if the term t1 can be substituted for the term t2, without any fundamental change in meaning, in a greater or lesser number of syntactic contexts; Example: the term "peler" is in a paradigmatic relationship with the term "eplucher".

On the basis of this analysis, we observe a relationship of similarity at the conceptual level between "peel a mandarin" and "tear off the mandarin", which has enabled aphasic speakers to resolve the linguistic level by means of semantic approximations in metaphorical form.

The conceptual level allows aphasics to elaborate the analogical input to the action "Peel a mandarin" as "Remove the mandarin". In order to understand this lack of representation of the conceptual level, we refer to the semantic crossing of the paradigmatic axis of semantic approximation (e.g. "devetir").

With the syntagmatic axis of the object used in the action and the term used by the aphasic creating a semantic tension.

On the paradigmatic axis, the aphasic relies on similarity between lexical entities. On the syntagmatic axis, the aphasic presents a disorganisation between the linguistic elements of the sentence, which explains his agrammatism. The verb "Devetir, arracher" creates a semantic tension in relation to the context of the object used.

5. Semantic approximation to pragmatics

The evolution of new functions can then lead to purely procedural functions as meta-discursive markers which signal the use of figures or other marks or the work of formulation, and to attenuating functions at the level of illocution. We have observed from this research that the language of the aphasic presents a dissociation between the locutionary act (phonetic, phatic, syntactic, semantic; linguistic) and the illocutionary act (pragmatics) through the perlocutionary act (the act of informing, describing, etc.) (Austin, 1962).

According to Olson's research (1970), the meaning of words in verbal utterances is determined by the objects they denote; the object, space and time constitute the context.

From this point of view, the process of categorical assignment (including action) is the result of the physical properties of the objects, followed by those of a cognitive nature, which play a key role in the information gathered in order to interpret the utterance in terms of action in the aphasic.

Approximators operate on several linguistic levels, the starting point for the emergence of the approximation markers described lies in communicative and cognitive strategies (choice of a provisional response similar to the concept of the target object by analogy, categorisation, comparison), typical for pragmaticalisation phenomena. Thus, approximations represent hybrid linguistic elements.

It is clear that the changes which produce the majority of approximants analysed in this research represent at least the beginnings of pragmaticalisation. The structure of aphasic discourse is characterised by an evolution in the approximant functions of action verbs

At the syntactic level, both semantic approximators and their use are relatively fixed and limited in scope, because they modify lexical categories, even though they often belong to the same linguistic category.

Semantic approximations then resemble grammatical morphemes, just like determiners, which operate at the level of the proposition and have a fixed, reduced scope.

At the same time, they serve to guide the interpretation of a statement and reflect the work involved in formulating it, so they also have a procedural element that represents the conceptual meaning of another element in the discourse.

Chapitre 5   Nature   of   semantic   dissociations   and conceptualisation

1. Suggested explanations

To show categorial dissociations, we used the naming or categorisation of objects on the basis of a visual presentation of the object itself, or of an action of the object; naming on verbal presentation, which proceeds in the manner of a riddle; the naming of a presented object; verbal questioning about the properties of an object [and we then distinguish between questions relating to taxonomy, such as "is this a car? "or "functional questions" such as "does this object roll?", and finally "sensory" or "perceptual" questions such as "does it have one of the wheels?]

To identify objects and test semantic association, we used multimodal matching (e.g. linking the object to its possible action).

In general, the performance of aphasics on the tasks of oral naming, action naming and answering questions is correct, at least in a given mode of presentation, and it is these tasks that are best used to diagnose category impairment.

We have observed that the phenomenon most frequently observed in aphasics with categorial deficits is selective impairment of the category of objects.

The construction of semantic dissociations in aphasics is defined on the basis of the semantic features of objects. This explains the general dedifferentiation of semantic representations that occurs in categorial deficits.

The effects of such dedifferentiation would be intensive in tasks involving, for example, category objects that are more difficult to separate from the point of view of their functional characteristics.

As a result, the concept of the object and the semantic representation of the action are closely related, i.e. the semantic approximations are due to the concept of the object in relation to its action.

The responses obtained from the aphasia cases show that the visual analogy of the functional descriptions of the objects present would disrupt the semantic processing of the semantic categories, without a selection of the semantic features from the structural descriptions.

The dominant idea is therefore that the categorical organisation of semantic memory derives from the respective roles played by information from different sensory channels in the formation of representations used in semantic tasks.

We identified two categorisation behaviours in particular in the aphasics we studied: taxonomic categorisation and thematic categorisation.

Semantic paraphasia can arise from taxonomy. This is the case if the aphasic groups together different objects (or images) on the basis of common characteristics that can be designated by a common term (for example, a chisel can be associated with a knife because they both have the characteristics common to specimens of the taxonomic category of sharp objects).

Oral action naming enabled us to identify the different elements of a thematic category that are linked together by spatial or temporal analogy relations (for example, the object 'plate' can be associated with a 'spoon' if the theme is cooking). Most of the semantic crosstalk we have observed is characterised by pluriapportion (i.e. choosing several associates instantiating different categorial relations for the same target).

The results we obtained highlight the presence of difficulties in justifying choices or a lack of coherence in word choices when naming objects orally. Aphasics could therefore produce several responses corresponding to the same categorisation class (taxonomic, for example), without however being aware of the common link between these different associations.

We therefore distinguish two forms of variability in the responses of aphasics. The first, assessed by the out-of-context oral object naming test, is a spontaneous variability that we call pluripairing, guided by object characteristics.

The second corresponds to categorial flexibility (Maintenant & Blaye, 2008) and would require top-down control and therefore more precise representations of categorial relations. In fact, in an object-action pairing situation, aphasics can allow themselves to be directed by the semantic primers constituted by the actions in relation to the objects presented: responses are therefore produced on a case-by-case basis, on the basis of specific associations.

Maintaining the use of a categorisation behaviour is therefore not required, either by the instructions or by the structure of the test we have proposed. The aphasic who associates a car with a garage and with the action of "parking" is considered to have produced a thematic pairing and a taxonomic pairing for the same object, and therefore to have demonstrated a form of response flexibility.

However, the context of the action involved in no way requires the nature of the relationship (thematic/taxonomic) that we observe through a particular pairing.

We studied categorial flexibility through action in order to analyse the different semantic approximations in categorisation.

Our results show that aphasics are capable of demonstrating taxonomic and thematic choice during the task of orally naming actions in relation to objects. We can therefore deduce that they have the ability to construct categorial relations in a controlled manner.

In addition, an asymmetry between these two relations, in the sense of access to understanding of the thematic relation, has been demonstrated on the basis of the oral naming of static objects in their contexts.

Thus, in our study, we observed a development of categorial flexibility in aphasics and an effect of the type of relationship, in favour of the thematic relationship.

When naming objects orally out of context, aphasics maintain the use of a semantic relation (thematic or taxonomic) between the object and its context of use. Then, in the second phase (oral naming of objects in their context of use), the task is the same, but an interference is introduced by the presence of an associate instantiating another semantic relation than the one expected, and finally, in the third phase of our oral action naming experiment. This involves switching to an analysis of the object based on its action in order to denominate the verb. Their results show that categorial flexibility develops with an effect of the relation in favour of the thematic relation. We were also able to show that maintenance abilities in aphasics develop more during oral action naming at an earlier stage. We therefore observed a relationship between the concept of action and semantic dissociation in relation to categorial flexibility performance.

2. Influence of association strengths on matching choices in aphasia

We observed that the association between objects and action would depend on the concept of object use "[...] on the co-occurrence of objects in the real world and therefore on each individual's experience with objects" (Scheuner, 2003, p. 205). Association strengths can thus vary from one aphasic to another for the same object, depending on the context of use of each object in question. For example, an aphasic who has a car and uses it regularly to get around will give greater weight to the association between these two elements (car and getting around) than an aphasic who does not have a car.

The study of 5 cases of aphasia revealed the influence of categorisation on the evolution of the recovery of action verbs.

Thus, the results obtained from this study enabled us to show the relevant role of association forces in aphasics' oral object naming choices. When the dissociations produced by the aphasic correspond to the same categorical relation (thematic or taxonomic), the aphasic's choices are guided by the forces of association, and the approximate responses are the item judged to be strongly associated with the objects present. The greater frequency of thematic choices compared with taxonomic choices is observed in these aphasics only in cases where the object themes are judged to be more strongly related to the object present than the taxonomic associates. We observed categorical flexibility when naming objects presented in their contexts of use, making it necessary to maintain the use of a first categorisation behaviour (thematic). In addition, when the oral naming of actions leads to the use of another (taxonomic) behaviour. This is a form of "relational conceptualisation".

-Developing the conceptualisation of relationships

The creation of semantic approximations by the aphasic implies a development of categorisation, which would be constituted by access to different categorisation behaviours (taxonomic or thematic), represented by the observation of the action and its object, i.e. the conceptualisation of these relations.

At the level of categorical relationships, we observe the conceptualisation of the objects that unite the elements of different taxonomic categories (such as kitchen utensils and sharp objects, for example), so the conceptualisation of the relationship reflects the spatio-temporal analogy that unites the elements of the same thematic category. Our research has shown us that in order to use flexible categorisation behaviours, it is necessary to have conceptualised the relationships involved (thematic and taxonomic).

We have shown a synchrony in the development of these two abilities, based on the semantic approximations produced by aphasics and the relationships that can be used flexibly.

We therefore used a correlational approach to evaluate the categorial flexibility performance of the 5 aphasia cases, as well as their level of conceptualisation of relations based on the oral naming of actions, in order to identify the associations used (inter-concept and intra-concept response).

Through our results, we were able to determine whether conceptualisation would allow us to account for the performance of aphasics in a categorial flexibility test, by excluding association performance. To sum up, we analysed the development of categorial flexibility in aphasics, to show the taxonomic and thematic relationships. On the basis of the previous results, we observed the effect of the concept and the functional characteristics of the object in distinguishing thematic relations. We were able to identify a predictor of this development of categorial flexibility. The categorial choices of aphasics in verbal retrieval are influenced by association strengths. This factor is less involved in their categorial flexibility performance, as the conceptualisation of the semantic relations studied (thematic and taxonomic) available to aphasics may be a good predictor of their categorial flexibility abilities. The concept of an object during its manipulation plays a relevant role in the conceptualisation that will be carried out and used. The conceptualisation process involves an explicit representation of the properties and functioning of a class of objects, an activity or a phenomenon.

The development of categorial flexibility and the ability to conceptualise semantic relations are two important factors in the creation of categorisation behaviours.

Concerning the development of categorial flexibility, our results confirm that aphasics possess a capacity for the development of categorial flexibility. They also showed a significant improvement in performance in creating semantic relations during naming. On the other hand, we observed particular difficulties in the controlled and flexible use of the taxonomic relation during the oral naming of objects out of context.

More specifically, the five cases of aphasia we studied managed to maintain the use of the two semantic relations in a situation without interference, thus confirming access to associations.

The aphasic maintains a semantic relation in oral naming out of context, and adopts a taxonomic relation, which is no longer a source of error. The results obtained show the presence of cognitive flexibility in the use of semantic relations in aphasics. The test we chose for oral action and object naming required the aphasic to make two consecutive choices of associates (taxonomic and thematic) for the same target, but did not involve maintaining the use of one type of (semantic) relation. The study of these aphasia cases showed that aphasics globally consider two thematically related images to be more strongly associated than two taxonomically related images.

This result confirms that thematic criteria are analysed more easily than taxonomic criteria by aphasics. This means that lexico-semantic dissociation (verb-object) affects the taxonomic level, since aphasics create semantic paraphrases when naming actions orally.

The controlled use of thematic and taxonomic categorisation represents a dissociation.

Categorial flexibility involves several levels of discordance and conceptualisation, which are required respectively by the forced-choice matching tasks and our categorial flexibility test. Aphasics require two levels of variability in their responses: multi-matching requiring little control and low conceptualisation, and categorial flexibility requiring top-down control and therefore sufficient conceptualisation of relations.

Our results show that association forces do not significantly influence flexibility performance.

We were able to distinguish the performance of categorial flexibility in aphasia on the basis of the conceptualisation of semantic relations, by analysing inter- and intra-concept responses, with reference to the taxonomic relation or the thematic relation towards the taxonomic relation. Conceptualisation would enable the development of categorial flexibility and optimise or promote the development of verbal lexical retrieval in aphasics.

In fact, during the test of oral naming of actions with categorial flexibility, the aphasic maintains the use of the taxonomic relation. In oral naming of objects in their contexts, the proposed stimuli (concept of the object) involve specific verbs and represent the presence of conceptual flexibility. This situation may be more difficult for aphasics, as they have difficulty making thematic associations compared with taxonomic associations.

Through their approximate responses, the aphasics switch from using the thematic relationship, which is better conceptualised by the plus, to using the taxonomic relationship, which is less accessible.

Categorial flexibility can and does facilitate the retrieval of action verbs in aphasics and the generalisation of categories through the selection of information and the strengthening of feature-category associations.

In this study, we found that aphasics had to reactivate a new theory concerning the use of a manipulable object. The

In the first case, the aphasic speaker presents a particular interpretation of the object when naming an object orally out of context, and in the second case another interpretation of the same object when naming an action orally. Both interpretations focus on a different part of the object. During retrieval, the functional characteristics of the objects represented by the transfer stimuli are presented to the aphasics, who must analyse the category11 membership of each object. Among the transfer stimuli, one item was consistent with one of the interpretations of the object, a second item was consistent with the other interpretation, and a third item was inconsistent with both interpretations. The results show that aphasics project the same category as the object to be named.

These semantic approximations are evidence of linguistic readaptation in aphasia and show that the actions of objects facilitate the retrieval of action verbs and the generalisation of categories through the selection of information and the strengthening of feature-category associations. It is essential to study the contribution of the concept to oral naming in aphasia. This is in order to understand the influence of the knowledge that the aphasic possesses in the formation of concepts, as well as the process of updating theories as a function of categorisation. In general, aphasia presents a difficulty in associating the opposition between analytical processing and lexical naming, due to the possible interdependence between these two modes. The more two objects have a functional analogy, the greater the probability that they share many properties, and the greater the probability that some of these shared properties will be used for analytical processing. Thus the aphasic will analyse the structural and functional dimensions of stimuli that represent the structural and functional properties of the objects present, both of which possess emergent characteristics that are no less than dimensions of the stimuli processed by the semantic memory.

3. Nature of dissociations

We observed in our five cases of aphasia a difficulty in finding the word corresponding to a given (iconographic) referent, despite their ability to recognise the object presented to them. "I know it but I can't say it", they often say, miming the object or its action while making the gesture of using the object in question (a knife, for example). The result is a double dissociation between the management of extra-linguistic referents and that of linguistic signs **-Dissociations in the analysis of the two sides of the linguistic sign** We find that aphasics analyse and perfectly understand the content they wish to convey (the signifier), while at the same time experiencing difficulty in accessing the lexical items in their mental lexicon (the signifier) - a pragmatic disorganisation between the two sides of the linguistic sign. This phenomenon can be explained by the differentiation of lexico-semantic disorders in aphasics (Jl. Nespoulous, 2016). In other words, they have a problem of access to the language, without semantic disturbances.

When aphasics realise that the word they have produced does not correspond to the meaning they wish to convey to others, they launch into successive self-corrections, with varying degrees of success, which reflect/ betray full awareness of their lexicalisation problem, resulting in the production of semantic approximations.

4. Cognitive factors and category structure in language recovery in aphasics

From the oral denomination of action, we have observed that the concept of an object is a mental representation of a category whose multiple functions are to categorise, understand the world, draw inferences, explain and reason, learn, communicate and combine.

Through our results, we observed the analysis of the concept of action by the aphasic, according to the selection capacity for the categorisation of the multidimensional stimuli to be categorised.

From the conceptual representation the aphasic attempts to create relevant features of the object and its use in order to compensate for the lack of words, which results in semantic approximations. When naming an object orally out of context, the aphasic identifies the dimensions of the object in order to categorise them, filtering them and, if the characteristics are not relevant, generalising the responses (general verb).

For example, if the stimuli are features related to the object's form or its function, examples of each of these two categories can be presented in terms of size, colour, and the relationship between form and function. The conceptual aspects generally reflect stimuli that do not represent everyday entities but rather simple forms made up of elementary dimensions (shape, colour, position, orientation, etc.). In most of these studies, a series of stimuli is presented to the aphasic, who must learn to group them into classes predefined by the speech therapist.

We were able to distinguish the relationship between concept, categorisation and cognitive flexibility on the basis of the various responses representing semantic approximations. The development of concepts in aphasia is essentially considered through the conceptual contents associated with the real world (object categories or biological categories), the relations that unite them (how a chisel or a knife are sharp objects), and the structural characteristics that unify the categories.

In our research, we have focused on semantic approximations, essentially on the factors that explain the search for and discovery of relevant classification dimensions.

Summary of the case study

Analysis of the results of disturbances accompanied by compensatory strategies implemented by aphasics shows that analysis of procedural data is a remarkable tool for accounting for compensatory behaviour in aphasics. The study of these strategies is the subject of research into language comprehension and production. They therefore concern a metalinguistic domain of interest to us.

The preserved linguistic-cognitive abilities of aphasics are used to compensate for the presence of linguistic deficits and to increase their cognitive flexibility. In clinical therapy, understanding these spontaneous strategies is vital in order to focus recovery efforts on the aphasic's preserved linguistic-cognitive abilities.

The analysis of the production of the aphasics we studied enabled us to arrive at very varied results. On the one hand, it confirms the existence of paraphasias, which represent a sign of a lack of words. This was expected in line with the literature on motor aphasia. On the other hand, we showed that the categorisation phenomenon was linked to oral action naming tests.

In this type of test (oral naming of objects), the results showed a phenomenon of analysis on the part of aphasics. When looking at the action established by the object, the aphasic's lexical repertoire is active, making it difficult to find the corresponding word, which creates semantic approximations.

In aphasiology, speakers produce metaphorical statements: "a moon is a balloon", "a cat is a lion", reflecting their ability to bring together objects that belong to distinct categories on the basis of shared physical or functional properties.

This type of utterance shows that speakers with lexical disorders (aphasics) have a flexible lexical system in which verbs are linked by inter-concept and intra-concept synonymy, a structure which helps to guarantee their communication despite the lexical limitations they suffer.

We found from this study that aphasics whose lexical production is disorganised present a profile similar to that of children in the process of acquiring language as well as foreign language learners (Duvignau, 2003). They produce a relevant number of semantic approximations with a verbal pivot, such as: "la dame mache le pain" (for action-video-Manger_pain), "Elle casse le journal" (for actionvideo Dechirer le journal).

The results obtained show that semantic approximations with a verbal pivot have a pragmatic status. To determine the disorder of pragmatic use through semantic approximation, we retain that the phenomena of rejection and modalisation as markers of condition and metaphor are a (de)categorisation of words into distinct categories (Duvignau, 2003).

Interconceptual approximations in aphasics represent terms that are unusual but semantically close to the habitually used word that refers to a categorical lexicon, which implies a process of "deconceptualisation" (Kleiber, 1999; Prandi, 2002).

In aphasic speakers, this process of "de-conceptualisation" is often involuntary and is caused by the problem of access to a conventional item. With this in mind, we plan to study the reformulation used by aphasic speakers to compensate for the lack of a word, as well as their metalinguistic representation of reformulation: "She broke the newspaper". In this way, we hope to contribute to the articulation of paraphrastic reformulation and speech acts (Giry-Schneider, 1994), (Austin 1962).

The use of generic verbs in different contexts by aphasics demonstrates the semantic flexibility of the verb lexicon. They are able to substitute one verb for another to produce intelligible utterances.

For example, *"dechirer"* is extended semantically to various actions, and is open to various contexts. Aphasics extend the action verb even further, in relation to their lack of the word. The concepts mastered by aphasics determine their choice of words: they choose a verb that corresponds to the concept, that is included in it, just as 'dechirer' is included in the concept of deterioration.

Aphasics take account of or neglect certain semes (Le Ny, 1987), which is the case in the choice of verbs containing the seme of "deterioration". The verb used translates a vast context of functional manipulation, which makes it possible to use it for actions for which it is not a priori appropriate.

Gentner (1978) states that through the use of verbs, children demonstrate an ability to make analogies and creative extensions. This ability can also be observed in learners of a foreign language (Duvignau, 2003). They extend the verb to different situations and decide to choose a verb when only part of its meaning applies. They would thus base the meaning of a new word on the conceptual data they possess; these conceptual data would be linked to their culture and their learning within a particular society, each language having its own concepts.

The verbs chosen turn out to be co-hyponyms of the expected verbs. Thus "couper", used for the action "déchirer le journal" is an extra-conceptual co-hyponym of *"de dissocier"*: they share the hyperonym "deteriorer".

We propose a structuring of the verbal lexicon based on semantic proximity, which could be used in foreign language learning.

Semantic approximations represent a palliative strategy for the lack of words. The use of a generic verb in a conventional or unconventional way calls on cognitive categorisation processes that are important in the acquisition and structuring of the verbal lexicon in a foreign language (Duvignau, 2003).

As a result, the aphasic presents semantic approximations with a generic verbal pivot and represents a phase of language re-acquisition.

Conclusion

The aim of the present study is to explore compensatory strategies in aphasia, namely semantic approximations of categorisation. This is a first attempt to analyse linguistic-cognitive functioning in language pathology.

For this reason, it would be very presumptuous to draw precise conclusions at this stage, as we are only at the beginning of the study of categorisation in aphasia. For this reason, this work only reflects the fruit of initial observations in the vast field of cognitive-linguistic categorisation, in particular semantic paraphasia with a verbal focus.

From the above, we have observed that aphasics are capable of creating in-conceptual meaning through semantic approximations despite their communicative handicap. We have tried to understand how these categorial over-extensions and adaptations favour their success in approximating meaning arise.

The research of K. Duvignau (2003) and M. Manchon (2011) has been useful in analysing the semantic organisation of action verbs in aphasics.

Based on analyses of the oral naming of objects and actions (static image vs. dynamic image), we found that the oral production of aphasics is favoured by semantic over-extensions linked by hyperonymy and hyponymy relationships and by cerebral elasticity.

As a result, the overall result of the criterion analysis for the five cases of aphasia reflects the cognitive flexibility of aphasics, which is a fundamental function for the structure of the mental lexicon. The production and retrieval of action verbs is easier in aphasics, due to their strong semantic representation.

Through this study we have seen that semantic approximations characterise the oral language of aphasics, since they have managed to analyse and decode messages and instructions.

Our aim is to master the main parameters inherent in the task of orally naming an action. The diagnosis of categorial over-extensions is based on the oral naming of the action verb lexicon, in order to analyse the different relationships between hyponymy, hyperonymy and co-hyperonymy. None of the linguistic criteria studied produced significant results as a function of fluency. From a semantic point of view, we found that all three types of aphasia produced semantic paraphasia. This was due to the significant production of specific verbs compared with general verbs.

The neuropsychological models focus on the object and the norms established for the oral naming of actions using a static support. No significant differences were found according to the type of aphasia studied.

The presence of the object makes it possible, through its function, to infer what the object is going to be used for and to infer its purpose, because by designing a state of the object to be performed we will make it possible to find the necessary functional category. We see that in the interpretation of 1 action the object and the verb have different roles.

By presenting the object "knife" to the aphasic, when he sees the action of taking the knife to cut he gains access to the networks of categories constituted by the properties of the object in question; "it's a sharp instrument for cutting" this access is ascending. We access subordinate categories by starting from the goal associated with a category. Access is descending with the object "spoon": the aphasic searches the over-ordered categories for the different kinds of action using a spoon; eating, mixing, stirring. Performing these inferential processes requires two different modes of access to the categories.

The results we have obtained are compatible with this method of accessing categories in a hierarchical network. Top-down access provides many alternatives. This is what we find when we ask aphasic subjects to provide action sentences based on a verb. Bottom-up access provides few alternatives (providing action sentences from a noun).

These semantic approximations relate physical properties to cognitive properties in order to understand the mechanisms underlying interpretation. The physical properties of objects and then the cognitive properties inferred from the process of categorical assignment (including action) play a central role as a source of information for the interpretation of events in terms of actions. The results of our research show that knowledge about objects, including knowledge acquired during the course of the situation, plays a key role in the interpretation of action. They also indicate the importance of the temporal and spatial context in the construction of action representations (Zibetti, Hamilton, & Tijus, 1999).

The context is constituted by the objects present in the action, based on changes in the time and space of these objects (N. Zellal, 2011). Mental representations of an object depend on what we call 'the context'.

In fact, as soon as we represent an object in our minds, we create reality. Studies in cognitive neuroscience show that our brain has a neuro-activator, a system that enables us to represent everything around us. We can compare it to an operating system; a cerebral Google that filters our knowledge and the information we receive.

We have been able to affirm that the aphasic will recover the verbal class more easily by referring to the observation and analysis of the object of the action (object vs action). This is based on the theory of the construction and representation of action demonstrated by Heider and Simmel (1944), whose results showed that when the characteristics of objects are modified, we observe great differences in the interpretation of the same action.

To compensate for their lack of words and to structure their utterances, aphasics produce verbal paraphasias of semantic approximation; we have supported this hypothesis by the invalid responses to action verbs, which are a sign of lexical disorders. And through analysis of the criterion in terms of general verbs/specific verbs. The results we obtained correspond to the study of semantic approximation and palliative strategies in young children and aphasics by K. Duvignau (2002), which shows the presence of semantic approximations with a verbal pivot in children in the acquisition phase and in recovering aphasics.

Our results are in line with research by N. Zellal (1986), who redefined aphasia as a linguistic disorder that is both plural and unique in cognitive terms.

During the oral naming of actions, we observed a large number of responses of an approximate nature within the concept. Aphasics show their ability to create analogies despite their lexical disorders. The aphasic presents a disorder in the pragmatic use of language; the constative statement in the aphasic depends on the action he observes. This enabled us to validate the hypothesis of cognitive elasticity in aphasia, which represents a fundamental strategy used for the structure of the mental lexicon. This was done with reference to the semantic approximations in the oral naming of action verbs.

We therefore deduce that semantic approximations reflect cognitive-semantic elasticity in the aphasic, a fundamental strategy for the structure of the mental lexicon.

Bibliography

• Abdullaev, Y.G., Bechtereva, N.P., § Melnichuk, K.V. (1998). *Neuronal activity of human caudate nucleus and prefrontal cortex in cognitive tasks.* Behavioral Brain Research, 97(1-2), pp. 159- 77.

• Adolph, R.J. (1995). *Langage et communication: chez les handicape mentaux,* ed: Pierre Mardaga Bruxelles, p 163.

• Aljouane, T., (1968) *l'Aphasie et le langage pathologique,* Paris.

• Alario, X., & Ferrand, L. (1999). *A set of 400 pictures standardized for French: Norms for name agreement, image agreement, familiarity, visual complexity, image variability, and age of acquisition.* Behavior Research Methods, Instruments, & Computers, pp. 531-560.

• Alexander, M.P. (1996). *Aphasia: Clinical and anatomic aspects.* In T.E. Feinberg & M.J. Farah (Eds), Behavioral Neurology and Neuropsychiatry, New York, pp.140-149.

• Alexander, M.P., Hiltbronner, B., & Fischer, R. (1989). *The distributed anatomy of transcorticalsensory aphasia.* Archives of Neurology, pp. 888892.

• Andler, D. (1992). *Introduction aux sciences cognitives,* Paris, Gallimard, 2004.

• Arbib, M.A. (2005). *From monkey-like action recognition to human language: an evolutionary framework for neurolinguistics.* Behavioral Brain Science, pp. 105-124.

• Arevalo, A., Perani, D., Cappa, S. F., Butler, A., Bates, E., & Dronkers N. (2007). *Action and object processing in aphasia: from nouns and verbs to the effect of manipulability.* Brain and Language, pp. 75-100.

• Baddeley, A. (1990). *La memoire humaine: theorie et pratique,* Grenoble, Presses universitaires de Grenoble, 1993.

• Bak, TH., & Hodges, J.R. (1999). *Cognition, language and behaviour in motor neurone disease: evidence of fronto temporal dysfunction. Dement Geriatr Cogn Disord* 10 (1), pp. 39-42.

• Bak, T.H., O'Donovan, D.G., Xuereb, J.H., Boniface S., Hodges J.R. (2001). Selective impairment of verb processing associated with pathological.

• Bard, C., &Vezina, J.L. (1996). *Neuroradiological evaluation.* In. Neuropsychologie clinique et neurologie du comportement. Sous la direction de Botez M. I. 2eme Ed. Les Presses de lUniversite de Montreal. Masson.

• Barde, L.H.F., Schwartz, M.F. & Boronat, C.B. (2006). *Semantic weight and verb retrieval in aphasia.* Brain and Language, pp. 267-280.

• Bassano, D. (2000). *La constitution du lexique: le developpement lexical precoce.* In Kail, M. and Fayol, M., L'acquisition du langage, le langage en emergence, de la naissance a trois ans, tome 1, Puf, pp. 140-169.

• Bastiaanse, R., & Jonkers, R. (1998). *Verb retrieval in action naming and spontaneous speech in agrammatic and anomic patients,* Aphasiology, pp. 960-

979.

• Bechtel, W., & Abrahamsen, A. (1991). *Le connexionnisme et l'esprit*, Paris, La Decouverte, 1993.

• Blayo, F., & Verleysen, M. (1996), *Les reseaux de neurones artificiels*, Paris, PUF. changes in Brodmann areas 44 and 45 in the motor neurone disease-dementia-aphasia syndrome. *Brain 124* (Pt 1), pp. 103- 120.

• Bottela, C., & Botella, S. (1996). *La figurabilite psychique*, Lausanne/Paris, Delachaux & Niestle.

• Bastiaanse, R., Hugen J., Kos, & M., van Zonneveld, R. (2002). *Lexical, morphological, and syntactic aspects of verb production in agrammatic aphasics.* Brain and Language 80(2), pp. 142-59.

• Bastiaanse, R., Rispens, J., Ruigendijk, E., Rabadan, O. J., & Thompson, C. K. (2002). *Verbs: some properties and their consequences for agrammatic Broca's aphasia.* Journal of Neurolinguistics 15(3-5), pp. 240-265.

• Bastiaanse, R. (2003). *Verb retrieval problems at the word and sentence level Localisation of the functional impairments and clinical implications.* In Papathanasiou I. & De Bleser R. (eds), The Science of Aphasia: From Therapy to Theory. Amsterdam, Pergamon.

• Baylon, C., & Favre P. (1978). *La semantique,* Paris, Nathan.

• Beauchamp, M.S., Lee, K.E., Haxby, J.V., & Martin, A. (2002). *Parallel visual motion processing streams for manipulable objects and human movements.* Neuron, 34(1), pp. 150-161.

• Berndt, R.S., Mitchum, C.C., Haendiges, A.N., & Sandson, J. (1997). *Verb retrieval in aphasia.* 1. Characterizing single word impairments. Brain and Language, 56(1), pp. 68-106.

• Berndt, R. S., Haendiges, A. N., Mitchum, & C. C., Sandson, J. (1997). *Verb retrieval in aphasia.* 2. Relationship to sentence processing. Brain and Language, 56(1), pp. 107-37.

• Bertier, J.L, Brost G, al. (2018). *Les neurosciences cognitives dans la classe : Guide pour expérimenter et adapter ses pratiques pedagogiques.* Paris: Edition Amazon.

• Bertrand, A., Epelbaum .S . (2012): *Neurologie,* Elsevier Masson, 62, Rue Camille Desmoulin.

• Bonin, P. (2002). *Les niveaux de traitement dans la production verbale orale et ecrite de mots isoles a partir d'images.* Chapter in M. Fayol (Ed.), Production du langage (pp. 89 105). *Traite des Sciences Cognitives.* Paris: Editions Hermes.

• Bonin, P. (2003). *Verbal word production: A cognitive approach.* Editions De Boeck Universite, Brussels.

• Boyer, B. (2006). *La denomination orale et ecrite d'actions: Comparaison avec la denomination d'objets.* These de Doctorat, Universite Blaise Pascal, under the supervision of Bonin, P. and Fayol, M.

• Biassou N., Obler, L. K., Nespoulous, J., Dordain, M., & Harris, K. S. (1997).

Brain and Language, 57, pp. 365-3775.

• Bierwisch, M. & Schreuder, R. (1992). *From concepts to lexical items.* *Cognition*, pp. 25- 67.

• Binder, J.R. & Rao, S.M. (1994). *Brain mapping with functional magnetic resonance imaging. In: Localization   andneuroimaging.* in neuropsychology, ed. A. Kertesz, Orlando , pp. 192-215.

• Binder,J.R., Frost A., Hammeke, T.A., Cox, R.W., Rao S.M. & Prieto, T. (1997). *Human brain language area identified by functional magnetic resonance imaging.* Journal of Neurosciences, 17(1), pp. 355-362.

• Binkofski, F., Buccino, G., Stephan, K.M., Rizzolatti, G., Seitz, R.J., & Freund, H.J. (1999). *A parieto-premotor network for object manipulation: evidence from neuroimaging.* Experimental Brain Research, 128(1-2), pp. 212213.

• Binkofski, F.,& Buccino, G. (2006). *The role of ventral premotor cortex in action execution and action understanding. Journal of Physiology Paris*, 99(4-6), pp. 395-405.

• Bird, H., Howard, D., & Franklin, S. (2000) *Why is a verb like an inanimate object? Grammatical category and semantic category deficits.* Brain and Language, 72(3), pp. 250-309.

• Bird, H., Franklin, S., & Howard, D. (2002). *'little words' - not really: function and content words in normal and aphasic speech.* Journal of Neurolinguistics, 15, pp. 212-240.

• Bird, H., Howard, D.,& Franklin, S. (2003). *Verbs and nouns: The importance of being imageable.* Journal of Neurolinguistics, 16, pp. 115150.

• Black, M. & Chiat, S. (2003). *Noun-verb dissociations: a multi-faced phenomenon, Journal of Neurolinguistics,* 16, pp. 231-250.

• Blake, R.,& Shiffrar, M. (2007). *Annual Review of Psychology*, 58, pp. 50-78.

• Blanche-Benveniste, C. (1987). *Syntaxe, choix de lexique et lieu de bafouillage, DRLAV36- 37 (Dialogues : du marivaudage a la machine),* pp. 124-160.

• Bloem, I., Van den Boogaard, S., & La Heij, W. (2004). *Semantic facilitation and semantic interference in language production: Further evidence for the conceptual selection model of lexical access.* Journal of Memory and Language, 51, pp. 310-323.

• Broca, P. (1861). *Sur le principe des localisations cerebrales.* Bulletin de laSociete d'Anthropologie, pp. 180-204.

• Broca, P. (1861). *Loss of speech, chronic softening and partial destruction of the left anterior lobe.* Bulletin de la Societe d'Anthropologie, 1861b 2, pp. 240-255.

• Broca, P. (1861). *Nouvelle observation d'aphemie produite par une lesion de la moitie posterieure des deuxiemes et troisiemes circonvolutions frontales gauches.* Bulletin de la Societe Anatomique, 1861d 36, pp. 399-415.

• Brunner, R., Kornhuber, H., Seemuller, E., Suger, G., & Wallesch, C.W. (1982). *Basal ganglia participation in language pathology.* Brain and Language,

16, pp. 281-299.

• Buccino, G., Binkofski, F., Fink, G.R., Fadiga, L., Fogassi, L., Gallese, V., Seitz, R.J., Zilles, K., Rizzolatti, G., & Freund, H.J. (2001). *Action observation activates premotor and parietal areas in a somatotopic manner: an fMRI study.* European Journal of Neurosciences, 13(2), pp400-404.

• Cnac, C. (2008). *La double dissociation noms-verbes dans l'aphasie: Apport des observations cliniques a la modelisation du langage ordinaire.* These de doctorat, Universite Toulouse Le- Mirail sous la direction de Nespoulous, J.L.

• Cappa, S., Cavalotti, G., Guidotti, M., Papagno C., & Vignolo, L. (1983). *Subcortical aphasia: two clinical-CT correlation studies. Cortex,* 19, pp. 230-241.

• Cappa, S.F., Perani, D., Schnur, T., Tettamanti, M., & Fazio, F. (1998). *The effectsof semantic category and knowledge type on lexical-semantic access: a PET study.* pp. 350-359.

• Cappa, S. F., Sandrini, M., Rossini, P. M., Sosta K.,& Miniussi, C. (2002). *The role of the left frontal lobe in action naming: rTMS evidence. Neurology 59(5),* pp. 720-723.

• Cappa, S.F., & Perani, D. (2003). *The neural correlates of noun and verb processing.* Journal of Neurolinguistics, 16, pp. 183-189.

• Caramazza, A., & Zurif, E. B. (1976). *Dissociation of algorithmic and heuristic processes in language comprehension: evidence from aphasia.* Brain and Language, 3, pp. 575-588.

• Caramazza, A., & Hillis, A. E. (1990). Where do semantic errors come from? *Cortex,* 26, pp 97- 128.

• Caramazza, A.,& Hillis A.E. (1991). *Lexical organization of nouns and verbsin the brain.*Nature, pp. 788-90.

• Caramazza, A. (1997). *How many levels of processing are there in lexical access?* Cognitive Neuropsychology, pp. 179-208.

• Caramazza, A., & Shelton, J. R. (1998). *Domain-specific knowledge systems in the brain: The animate-inanimate distinction.* Journal of Cognitive Neuroscience, 10, pp. 1-34.

• Caron, J. (2001). *Precis de psycholinguistique,* Quadrige, PUF.

• Carroll, J. B., & White, M. N. (1973). *Word frequency and age-of- acquisition as determiners of picture-naming latency.* Quarterly Journal of Experimental Psychology, 25, pp. 87-98.

• Caselli, M.C., Bates, E., Casadio, P., Fenson, J., Fenson, L., Sanderl, L. & Weir, J. (1995). *A cross-linguistic study of early lexical development. Cognitive* Development, 10, pp. 165-199.

• Caselli, M.C., Casadio, P., & Bates, E. (1999). *A comparison of the translation from the first words to grammar in English and Italian.* Journal of Child Language, 26, pp. 70- 115.

• Chibout, K., & Vilnat A. (1999). *Semantic primitives, verb classification and polysemy.* In Organisation des connaissances en vue de leur intégration dans les systemes de representation et de recherche d'information, Ed. Jacques Maniez. Widad Mustafa Elhadi. Universite Lille 3, pp. 160-173.

* Chomsky, N. (1957). *Syntactic structures*. The Hague Paris: Mouton.
* Chomsky, N. (1965). *Aspects of the Theory of Syntax*. Cambridge, MA: MIT Press.
* Chomsky, N. (1969), *Le langage et la pensee*, Paris, Payot.
* Chomsky, N. (1980), *Regies et representations*, Paris, Flammarion, 1985.
* Clark, E. V. (1993). *The lexicon in acquisition,* Cambridge Studies in Linguistics Series, 65, Cambridge University Press.
* Cohen, D., & Gautier, M. (1965) Persee: *Aspects linguistiques de I'Aphasie -tome 5 n°2.*
* Collins, A.M., & Quillian, M. R. (1969). *Retrieval time from semantic memory.* Journal of Verbal Learning and Verbal Behavior, 8, pp. 242-248.
* Collins, A.M., & Quillian, M.R. (1970). *Facilitating retrieval from semantic Memory: the effect of repeating part of an inference.* Acta Psychologica, 33, pp. 306-320.
* Collins, A.M., & Loftus, E. (1975). *A spreading activation theory of semantic processing.* Psychological Review. 82(6), pp. 410-428.
* Calrpaldi, CD., Aggujaro, S., Arduino, L., Zonca G., Ghirardi, G., Inzaghi, M.G., Colombo, M., Cherchia G.,& Luzzati, C. (2006). *Noun-verb dissociation in aphasia: The role of imageability and functional locus of the lesion.* Neuropsychologia, 44(1), pp. 76-90.
* Crepaldi, D., Berlingeri, M., Paulesu, E., & Luzzatti, C. (2011). *A place for nouns and a place for verbs? A critical review of neurocognitive data on grammatical-class effects.* Brain & Language, 116(1), pp. 40-49.
* Damasio, A.R., McKee, J., & Damasio, H. (1979). *Determinants of performance in color anomia,* Brain and Language, 7, pp. 77-85.
* Damasio, A.R., Damasio, H., Rizzo, M., Varney, N., & Gersh, F. (1982). *Aphasia with nonhemorrhagic lesions in the basal ganglia and the internal capsule.* Archives of Neurology, 39, pp. 18-20.
* De, Boissezon X., Marie, N., Castel-Lacanal, E., Marque, P., Bezy, C., Gros, H., Lotterie, J. A., Cardebat, D., Puel, M., & Demonet, J. F. (2009). *Good recovery from aphasia is also supported by right basal ganglia: a longitudinal controlled PET study.* EJPRM-ESPRM 2008 award winner. European Journal of Physical and Rehabilitation Medecine, 45(4), pp. 550558.
* Deleval, J., & Leonard, A. (1985). *Marginal aphasic syndromes.* Questions de Logopedie, 6, pp. 23-48.
* Dell, G.S. (1986). *A spreading activation theory of retrieval in language production,* Psychological Review, 93, pp. 284-323.
* Deloche, G., Hannequin, D., Dordain, M., Perrier, D., Pichard, B., Quint, S., Metz-Lutz, M.N., Kremin, H., & Cardebat, D. (1996). *Picture confrontation oral naming: performance difference between aphasics and normals.* Brain and

Language, 53, pp. 107-125.

• Demonet, J.F., & Puel, M. (1994). *Aphasia and cerebral correlates of linguistic functions. In X. Seron, et M. Jeannerod,* Neuropsychologie humaine, pp. 336-359. Liege : Mardaga.

• Denes, G., & DallaBarba, G.G.B. (1998). *Vico: Precursor of cognitive neuropsychology? The first reported case of noun-verb dissociation following brain-damage.* Brain and Language, 62, pp. 25-37.

• Denis, M. (1976). *Dissociated naming and locating of body parts after left anterior temporal lobe resection: an experimental case study*, Brain and Language, 3, pp.149-167.

• De Partz, M.P., & Pillon, A. (1999). *Aphasias. In J.-A. Rondal and X. Seron, Troubles du langage.* Bases theoriques, diagnostic et reeducation. pp. 659699. Liege: Mardaga.

• De Partz, M.P. (2000). *Revalidation des troubles du langage ecrit.* In X. Seron and M. Van Der Linden, Traite de neuropsychologie clinique, Tome II (pp.131-146). Marseille : Solal.

• Demonet, J.-F., Cardebat, D., Bonafe, A., Gazounaud, Y., & Guiraud-Chaumeil, B. (1984). *Aphasies sous-corticales : etude neuro- linguistique* avec scanner X de 25 cas. Revue Neurologique, 140, pp. 695-710.

• D'Honincthun, P., & Pillon, A. (2005). *Why verbs could be more demanding of executive resources than nouns: Insight from a case study of a fv-FTD patient.* Brain and Language 95(1), pp. 38-40.

• D'Honincthun, P., & Pillon, A. (2008). *Verb comprehension and naming in frontotemporal degeneration: The role of the static depiction of actions.* Cortex 44(7), pp. 837-849.

• Didierjean, A., & Marmeche, E. (2005). *Anticipatory representation of visual basketball scenes by novice and expert players.* Visual Cognition, 12, pp. 265-283.

• Druks, J., & Masterson, J. (2000). *An object and action naming battery. Hove,* Psychology Press.

• Druks, J., & Shallice, T. (2000). *Selective Preservation of Naming from Description and the "Restricted Preverbal Message".* Brain and Language, 72(2), pp. 105-128.

• Duvignau, K. (2003). *Verbal metaphor and approximation.* In Regards croisessur l'analogie.

• Duvignau, K. (2005). *Pour un apprentissage-enseignement du lexique verbal calque sur l'acquisition: revisite et apport des " metaphores / erreurs " des enfants de 2- 4 ans.* In Grossmann, F., Paveau, M.-A., Petit, G. (Eds.). Didactique du lexique : langue, cognition, discours. ELLUG, Grenoble: 37- 49.

• Duvignau, K. " L'analogie pour 1 apprentissage des verbes ", Ministere de la Recherche & Projet 2004- 2007 : JC n° 6010 *: " Approx : Architecture structurale et fonctionnelle du lexique verbal : La flexibilite semantique comme principe fondamental de la cognition humaine et artificielle ".* ACI Jeunes Chercheurs,

Fonds National pour la Science.

• Duvignau, K., Gardes-Tamine, J., & Gaume B. (2004). *Approximations semantiques enfantines et distance inter-verbes : pour une organisation proxemique du lexique verbal. Le langage et l 'homme,* De Boeck, Belgique, V 39-2, Decembre, pp. 100-141.

• Duvignau, K., Gaume, B. (2001, 2004). *Project 2001-2004, School & Cognitive Sciences*

• Dubois, J., & al (2002). *Dictionary of linguistics and language sciences.* Larousse.

• Dumoulin, S.O., Bittar, R.G., Kabani, N.J., Baker, C.L.Jr., Le Goualher, G., Bruce Pike, G.,& Evans, A.C. (2000). *A new anatomical landmark for reliable identification of human area V5/MT: a quantitative analysis of sulcal patterning.* Cerebral Cortex,10(5), pp. 460-467.

• Duvignau, K. (2002). La metaphore, cerceau et enfant de la langue. These Sciences du Langage, Universite Toulouse Le-Mirail, November 2002.

• Duvignau, K., Fossard, M., Gaume, B., Pimenta, M. A., & Elie, J. (2007). *Semantic approximations and flexibility in the dynamic construction and "deconstruction" of meaning.* Linguagem em Discurso, 7(3) (H. Moura,J. Viera & M.I.A. Nardi (eds)) Metaphor and Context, pp.382-392.

• Duvignau, K., Gaume, B., Tran M., Manchon, M., Martinot, C., & Panissal, N. (2008). *Flexibilite semantique du systeme verbal chez I'enfant et l'aphasique : contre l'" erreur " et pour l'" approximation semantique ", Actes du Congres Mondial de Linguistique Franqaise* (CMLF- 08), Paris, 12 juillet 2008.

• Elie, J. (2005). *Le metalinguistique chez les enfants atteints du syndrome d'Asperger et de l'autisme de haut niveau.* DEA dissertation, Toulouse Le-Mirail University, August 2005.

• Elie, J. (2009). *Structuration du lexique, enonces non conventionnels et flexibilite semantique : etude exploratoire dans les Troubles Envahissants du Developpement.* These de Doctorat, Universite de Toulouse Le Mirail, sous la direction de Nespoulous J.-L. et Duvignau K.

• Evangeliou, M.N., Raos, V., Galletti, & C., Savaki H.E. (2009). *Functional imaging of the parietal cortex during action execution and observation.* Cerebral Cortex 19(3), pp. 650-669.

• Fellbaum, C. (1999). *The representation of verbs in the WordNet semantic network.* In Langages, Semantique lexicale et grammaticale, p.136.

• Ferrand, L. (1994). *Acces au lexique et production de la parole: un survol.* L'annee Psychologique, 94 (2), pp. 260-312.

• Ferrand, L., Grainger, J.,& Segui, J. (1994). *A study of masked form priming in picture and word naming. Memory and cognition,* 22, pp. 433-441.

• Ferrand, L. (1995). *Repeated prime-target presentations do not eliminate repetition and phonological priming in naming digits.* Acta Psychologica, 89, pp. 218-227.

• Ferrand, L., Segui, J.,& Grainger, J. (1995). *Amorqage phonologique masque et denomination.* L'Annee psychologique, 95 (4), pp. 679-659.

• Ferrand, L. (1997). *La denomination d'objets: Theories et données.* L'Annee Psychologique, 97, pp. 115-146.

• Ferrand, L., Humphreys, G.W., & Segui, J. (1998). *Masked repetition and phonological priming in picture naming.* Perception & Psychophysics, 60, pp. 266-274.

• Ferrand, L. (2001). *Language production: An overview.* Psychologie Fran^aise, 94, 3-15.

• Fiez, J.A., & Tranel, D. (1997). *Standardized stimuli and procedures for investigating the retrieval of lexical and conceptual knowledge for actions.* Memory & Cognition, pp. 545- 569.

• Fiez, J.A. (2001). *Neuroimaging studies of speech. An overview of techniques and methodological approaches.* Journal of Communication *Disorders,* 34, pp. 449-454.

• Fodor, J.A. (1986). *La modularite de l'esprit, Essai sur la psychologie des facultes.* Paris, Les Editions de Minuit.

• Folstein, M., Folstein, S., & McHugh P. R. (1975). *Mini-mentalstate", A practical method for grading the cognitive state of patients for the clinician.* Journal of Psychiatric Research, 12(3), pp. 190-198.

• Foygel, D., & Dell, G.S. (2000). *Model oh impaired lexical access in speech production.* Journal of Memory and Language, 43, pp. 190-216.

• Freyd, J.J. (1983). *The mental representation of movement when static stimuli are viewed.*Percept Psychophys, 33(6), pp. 575-581.

• Foygel, D., & Dell, G.S. (2000). *Model oh impaired lexical access in speech production.* Journal of Memory and Language, 43, pp. 190-216.

• Freyd, J.J., & Finke, R. A. (1985). *A velocity effect of representational momentum.* Bulletin of the Psychonomic Society, 23(6), pp. 443-446.

• Friston, K.J., Frith, C.D., Turner, R., & Frackowiak, R.S. (1995). *Characterizing evoked hemodynamics with fMRI.* Neuroimage, 2, pp. 157165.

• Froger, J. & Pelissier, J. (2006). *Imagerie cerebrale fonctionnelle et reeducation.* Edition Masson, Problemes en medecine de reeducation.

• Gainotti, G., Miceli, G., & Caltagirone, C. (1977). *A neurolinguistic modelfor the study of aphasia.* European Neurology, 15, pp. 20-24.

• Gainotti, G. (2004). *A metaanalysis of impaired and spared naming for different categories of knowledge in patients with a visuo-verbal disconnection.* Neuropsychologia, 42, pp. 299-319.

• Gallese, V., Fadiga, L., Fogassi, L., & Rizzolatti, G. (1996). *Action recognition in the premotor cortex.* Brain, 119 (Pt 2), pp. 593-609.

• Gatignol, P., Marin Curtoud S. (2008). BIMM: Batterie Informatisee du Manque du Mot. *L'orthophoniste, 275, 18.*

• Habib, M., Giraud, K., Rey, V., & Robichon F. (2001). Neurobiologie du langage. In J.A. Rondal et X. Seron (Dir.) : *Troubles du langage. Bases theoriques, diagnostic et reeducation* (11-55). Liege: Mardaga.

* Hammelrath, C. (1999). *DVL 38: test de denomination de verbes lexicaux en images. L'ortho edition,* editor: Isbergues.

* Hauk, O., Johnsrude, I., & Pulvermuller, F. (2004). *Somatotopic representation of action words in human motor and premotor cortex.* Neuron 41(2), pp. 301-307.

* Hecaen, H. (1972). *Introduction a la neuropsychologie.* Paris: Larousse.

* Hillis, A.E. & Caramazza, A. (1991): *Mechanisms for accessing lexical representations for output: Evidence from a category-specific semantic deficit.* Brain and Language, 40, pp. 106- 144.

* Hillis, A., & Caramazza, A. (1995). *Representation of grammatical categories of words in the brain.* Journal of Cognitive Neuroscience, 7, pp. 396407.

* Hinojosa, J. A., Martin-loeches, M., Casado, P., Munoz, L., Fernandez- Frias, C., & Pozo, M. A. (2001). *Semantic processinf open- and close-class words: an event-related potentials study.* Cognitive Brain Research, 11, pp. 397-407.

* Hodgson ,C.,& Lambon Ralph, M.A. (2008). *Mimicking aphasic semantic errors in normal speech production: Evidence from a novel experimental paradigm.* Brain and Language, 104(1), pp. 89-101.

* Hotpof, W.H.N. (1980). *Slips of the pen. In U. Frith (Ed.), Cognitive processes in spelling.* New-York: Academic Press.

* Houk, J.C. (2005). *Agents of the mind.* Biol Cybern, 92(6), pp. 427-437.

* Kable, J.W., Lease-Spellmeyer, J.,& Chatterjee A. (2002). *Neural substratesof action event knowledge.* Journal of Cognitive Neurosciences, 14(5), pp. 795- 80

* Kable J.W., Kan, I.P., Wilson, A., Thompson-Schill, S.L.,& Chatterjee, A. (2005). *Conceptual representations of action in the lateral temporal cortex.* Journal of Cognitive Neurosciences, 17(12), pp. 1855-1870.

* Kacemi, S. (2009): *Magistere en orthophonie, sousla direction du professeur Zellal:* Universite Alger2.

* Kay, J., & Ellis, A.W. (1987). *A cognitive neuropsychological study of anomia: Implications for psychological models of word retrieval.* Brain, pp. 613-629.

* Kemmerer, D., & Tranel, D. (2000). *Verb retrieval inn brain-damaged subject: analysis of errors.* Brain and Language 73(3), pp. 393-420.

* Kemmerer, D., & Tranel, D. (2003). *A double dissociation between the meanings of action verbs and locative prepositions.* Neurocase, 9(5), pp. 421

* Kemmerer, D., Chandrasekaran, B., & Tranel D. (2007). A case of impaired verbalization but preserved gesticulation of motion events. Cognitive Neuropsychology 24(1), pp. 70-114.

* Kemmerer, D., Castillo, J.G., Talavage T., Patterson, S., & Wiley, C. (2008). *Neuroanatomical distribution of five semantic components of verbs: evidence from fMRI.* Brain and Language 107(1), pp. 16-43.

* Kertesz, A. (1993). *Clinical forms of Aphasia.* Acta Neurochirurgica Suppl, 56, pp. 52-58.

- Khon, S.E. & Goodglass, H. (1985). *Picture naming in aphasia*. Brain and Language 24, pp. 266-283.
- Kim, M., & Thompson, C.K. (2000). *Patterns of Comprehension and Production of Nouns and Verbs in Agrammatism: Implications for Lexical Organization*. Brain and Language 74(1), pp. 1-25.
- Kim, M., &Thompson, C.K. (2004). *Verb deficits in Alzheimer's disease and agrammatism: implications for lexical organization*. Brain and Language 88(1), pp. 1-20.
- Kiss, K. (2000). *Effect of verb complexity on agrammatic aphasic speakers' sentence production. In R. Bastiaanse & Y. Grodzinsky (Eds), Grammatical disorders in aphasia: a neurolinguistic perspective*. London: Whurr Publishers.
- Koechlin, E., Ody C., Kouneiher, F. (2003). *The architecture of cognitive control in the human prefrontal cortex. Science*, pp. 1181-1185.
- Koechlin, E., Jubault, T. (2006). *Broca's area and the hierarchical organization of human behavior*. Neuron, 50(6), pp. 963-974.
- Koenig, T., Lehmann, D. (1996). *Microstates in language-related brain potential maps show noun-verb differences*. Brain and Language, pp. 169.
- Kohn, S.E., Lorch, M.P., & Pearson, D.M. (1989). *Verb finding in aphasia*, Cortex , pp. 57- 69.
- Kourtzi, Z., & Kanwisher, N. (2000). *Activation in human MT/MST by static images with implied motion*. Journal of Cognitive Neurosciences, 12(1), pp. 48-55.
- Kremin, H. (1990). *La denomination et ses problemes. In: Linguistique et neuropsycholinguistique ; tendances actuelles. JL Nespoulous and M Leclerq*, Societe de neuropsychologie de Langue Francaise, Paris.
- Kremin, H. (1994). *Perturbations lexicales : les troubles de la denomination*. In Seron, X.,& Jeannerod, M., *Neuropsychologie humaine*, Bruxelles, Mardaga : pp.375-389.
- Kremin, H. (2002). *L'acces au lexique en denomination d'images: problemes actuels*.Psychologie francaise, 47(2), pp. 77-92. Lechevalier (eds), *Langage et aphasie*, Seminaire Jean-Louis Signoret, Brussels: De Boeck, 41-70.
- Le Dorze, G. (1985). *Aphasia and access to the mental lexicon*. These de Doctorat de 3° cycle. Universite de Montreal.
- Le Ny, J.F. (2005). *Comment l'esprit produit du sens*, Editions Odile Jacob, Paris.
- Lete, B., Sprenger-Charollres, L., & Cole, L. (2004). *MANULEX: A grade-level lexical database from French elementary-school readers*. Behavior Research Methods, Instruments & Computers, 36, pp. 156-166.
- Levelt, W.J.M. (1989). *Speaking: From Intention to Articulation,* Cambridge, MA, MIT Press.
- Levelt, W.J.M. Schriefers, H., Vorberg, D., Meyer, A.S., Pechmann, T.,& Havinga J. (1991). *The time course of lexical access in speech production: a study*

of picture naming, Psychology Review, 98, pp. 122-142.

• Levelt, W.J.M., Roelofs, A., & Meyer, A.S. (1999). *A theory of lexical access in speech production.* Behavioral and Brain Sciences, 22, pp. 1-75.

• Levelt, W.J.M. (1999). *Models of word production. Trends in Cognitive Sciences,* pp.223- 232.

• Liljestrom M., Tarkiainen, A., Parviainen, T., Kujala, J., Numminen, J., Hiltunen, J., Laine, M.,& Salmelin, R. (2008). *Perceiving and naming actions and objects. Neuroimage* 41(3), pp. 113- 114.

• Luria, A.R. (1966). *Higher Cortical Functions in Man.* New York: Basic Books.

• Luria, A.R. (1970). *Traumatic aphasia: Its syndrome, psychology and treatment.* The Hague: Mouton.

• Luzzatti, C., Raggi, R., Zonca, G., Pistarini, C., Contardi, A., & Pinna, G.D. (2002). *Verb-noun double dissociation in aphasic lexical impairments: Tne role of word frequency and imageability.* Brain and Language, 81, pp. 432444

• Luzzatti, C., Aggujaro, S., & Crepaldi, D. (2006): *Verb-noun double dissociation in aphasia: theoretical and neuroanatomical foundations.* Cortex 42(6), pp. 875-83.

• Machon, M. (2011), *Le lexique des verbes en denmination orale : etude exploratoire chez l'aphasique et étude en IRMF chez le sujet,* Universite Toulouse 2, Le Mirail (UT2 Le Mirail).

• Manchon, M., Magnin, E., Comte, A., Vuillier, F., Tatu, L., Duvignau, K., & Moulin, T. (2009). *Influence of the 'Static Action Scenes' vs 'Dynamic Action Scenes' Aid in Verb Naming: an fMRI Study.* Human Brain Mapping meeting in San Francisco, Proceedings of the H.B.M.

• Masterson, J. & Druks, J. (1998). *Description of a set of 164 nouns and 102 verbs matched for printed word frequency, familiarity and age-of- acquisition.* Journal of neurolinguistics, 11, pp. 331-354.

• Matzig, S., Druks, J., Masterson, J., & Vigliocco, G. (2009). *Noun and verb differences in picture naming: past studies and new evidence.* Cortex 45(6), pp.738-758.

• McCarthy, R. & Warrington, E. K. (1985). *Category specificity in an agrammatic patient: The relative impairment of verb retrieval and comprehension.* Neuropsychologia, 23, pp. 709-727.

• McCloskey, M. & Glucksberg, S. (1978). *Natural categories: Well- defined or fuzzy sets?* Memory and Cognition, 6, pp. 462-472.

• Nazir, T.A., Hauk, O., & Jeannerod, M. (2008). *The role of sensory-motor systems for language understanding. Foreword. Journal of Physiology, Paris,* pp1-3.

• Nespoulous, J.L., & Lecours, A.R. (1980). *Du trait au discours : les differents niveaux de structuration du langage et leur atteinte chez les aphasiques.* Grammatica *VII,* 1, pp. 1-36.

• Nespoulous, J.L. (1980). *De deux comportements verbaux de base : referentiel et modalisateur. De leur dissociation dans le discours aphasique.* Cahiers de Psychologie, pp. 195-210.

• Nespoulous, J.L. (1980). *Le manque du mot et ses manifestations. Study des difficultés d'encodage lexical chez l'aphasique.* Cahiers du Centre interdisciplinaire des Sciences du Langage, 2, pp. 97-115.

• Nespoulous, J.L. & Lecours, A.R. (1981). *Du trait au discours. In J.L. Nespoulous (Ed.).* Etudes Neurolinguistiques, 1-36, Service des Publications de l'Universite de Toulouse-Le Mirail, Toulouse, 1981.

• Nespoulous J.L., Dordain M., Perron C., Ska B., Bub D., Caplan D., Mehler J. & Lecours A.R. (1988). Agrammatism in sentence production withoutvcomprehension deficit: reduced availibility of syntactic structures and/orof grammatical morphemes? A case study. *Brain and Language*, 33, pp. 273- 295.

• Nespoulous, J.L. (1990). *De la difficulté d'interprétation des manifestations linguistiques de surface. In* Nespoulous, J.-L. &Leclercq, M. (eds), *Linguistique et neurolinguistique: tendances actuelles, 5-15*. Paris: Societe de neuropsychologie de langue franchise.

• Nespoulous, J.L. (1992). Le " manque du mot " et ses manifestations. Study of lexical encoding difficulties in aphasic patients. Lexique seminar, 21 and 22 January 1992, IRIT-UPS, Toulouse, pp. 173-186.

• Nespoulous J.L. (1994). *Linguistics, neurolinguistics and neuropsycholinguistics. Un parcours en quatre etapes.* In Seron X. & Jeannerod M., Ed. 1994. Neuropsychologie humaine. Liege : Mardaga.

• Nespoulous J.L. (1996). Palliative Strategies in Aphasia. *Reeducation Orthophonique,* 34, pp. 423-33.

• Nespoulous J.L. (1998). *En guise de postface : le traitement (specifique ?) des verbes par le cerveau/esprit humain des aphasiques agrammatiques : le retour du comparatisme?* In C. Fuchs & S. Robert (Eds.) Diversite des langues et representations cognitives, Paris.

• Nespoulous J.L. (1999). *De la linguistique ... a lapsycholinguistique et a la neuropsycholinguistique. Une illustration : le traitement (specifique?) des verbes par le cerveau/esprit humain.* In J. Francois & B. Victorri (Eds.) Semantique du lexique verbal, Universite de Caen & CNRS, UPRES-A 6047, 159-166.

• Nespoulous, J.-L. & Vribel, J. (2003). *Towards a revision of the notion of lexicalisation. Contribution a une vision dynamique du lexique mental : stock lexical, categories vs reseau lexico-semantique.* Revue intelligente.

• Nespoulous, J.L. & Virbel, J. (2004). *Apport de I'etude des handicaps langagiers a la connaissance du langage humain.* Revue Parole, 29-30, pp. 5- 42.

• Nespoulous, J-L., Rohr, A., Cardebat, D. & Rigalleau, F. (2008). *Symptomatology of oral expression and comprehension in acquired language disorders",* in B. Lechevalier, F. Eustache & F. Viader (Eds.) Traite de Neuropsychologie Clinique, Brussels, De Boeck Universite.

- New, B. & Pallier, C. (2006). *LEXIQUE 3, Bases de données lexicales du franqais contemporain sur Internet,* http:/www.lexique.org/.
- Newcombe, F., Oldfield,R.C., &Wingfield,A. (1965). *Object-namingby dysphasic patients.*Nature, 207, pp. 1217-1218.
- Newman-Norlund, R., Van Schie, H. T., Van Hoek, M.E.C., Cuijpers, R. H., & Bekkering H. (2009). *The role of inferior frontal and parietal areas in differentiating meaningful and meaningles object-directed actions.* Brain Research, pp. 63-74.
- Nickels, L., & Howard, D. (1995). *Aphasic naming: What matters?* Neuropsychologia, 33, pp. 281-303.
- Nickels, L. (1995). *Getting it right? Using aphasic naming errors toevaluate theoretical models of spoken word production.* Language and cognitive Processes, pp. 13-45.
- Pottier, B. (1964). *Vers une semantique moderne, Travaux de semantique et de litterature, 2, 107-137*; (1974). Linguistique generale, Paris, Klinksieck.
- Preissl, H., Pulvermuller, F., Lutzenberger, W., & Birbaumer, N. (1995). *Evoked potentials distinguish between nouns and verbs.* Neurosciences Letters, pp. 81-83.
- Pulvermuller, F. (1995). Agrammatism: Behavioral description and neurobigical explanation. *Journal of Cognitive Neuroscience* pp.165-181.
- Rizzolatti, G., Fadiga L., Gallese, V. & Fogassi, L. (1996). *Premotor cortexand the recognition of motor actions. Cognitive Brain Research*, 3, pp. 131-141.

Rizzolatti, G., Fadiga , L., Matelli M., Bettinardi, V., Paulesu, E., Perani, D. & Fazio, F. (1996): *Localization of grasp representations in humans by PET: 1. Observation versus execution.* Experimental Brain Research, 111, pp. 246-252.

Rizzolatti, G., Fogassi, L., & Gallese, V. (2002). *Motor and cognitive functions of the ventral premotor cortex.* Curr Opin Neurobiol, 12(2), pp. 149154.

Rizzolatti, G., & Craighero, L. (2004). *The mirror-neuron system.* Annual Review of Neuroscience, 27, pp. 169-192.

Rizzolatti, G., & Buccino, G. (2005). *The mirror-neuron system and its rolein imitation and language.* In Dehaene, S., Duhamel, G.R., Hauser, M. & Rizzolatti, G. (Eds), From Monkey Brain to Human Brain. MIT Press, *Cambridge,* pp. 213-233.

Rochford, G., & Williams, M. (1965). *Studies in the development and the breakdown of the use of names. Part IV. The effect of word frequency.* Journal of Neurology, Neurosurgery & Psychiatry, 28, pp. 407-413.

Roch-Lecours, A., & Lhermitte, F. (1979). *L'Aphasie.* Flammarion Medecine Sciences, Paris.

Rondal, J.A., & Seron, X. (1999). *Troubles du langage. Bases theoriques, Diagnostic et reeducation.* Liege: Mardaga.

Rondal, J.A. & Seron, X. (2003). *Troubles du langage. Bases theoriques, diagnostic et reeducation.* Collectif Broche, Mardaga Editions.

Rosch, E. (1975). *Classification of real-world objects: origins and representations in cognition.* In Ehrlich & Tulving, pp. 242-250.

Rosch, E., & Lloyd, B. (1978). *Cognition and Categorization.* Hillsdale, (N.-J.), (eds) Erlbaum L. London.

Roth, E.M., & Shoben, E.J. (1983). *The effect of context on the structure of categories.*Cognitive Psychology, 15, pp. 346-378.

Rosch, E., & Lloyd, B. (1978). *Cognition and Categorization.* Hillsdale, (N.-J.), (eds) Erlbaum L. London.

Roth, E.M., & Shoben, E.J. (1983). *The effect of context on the*
Cognitive Psychology, 15, pp. 346-378.

Sanfeliu, M.C., & Fernandez, A. (1996). *A set of 254 Snodgrass- Vandewart pictures standardized for Spanish: Norms for name agreement, image agreement, familiarity, and visual complexity.* Behavior Research Methods, Instruments, & Computers. pp. 537-555.

Schwartz, M.F., Saffran, E.M., & Marin, O.S.M. (1980). *The word order problem in agrammatism. I. Comprehension.* Brain and Language. pp.263280.

Schwitter, V., Boyer, B., Meot, A., Bonin, P., & Laganaro, M. (2004). *French normative data and naming times for action pictures.* Behavior Research Methods, Instruments, & Computers. pp. 564-576.

Segui, J., Frauenfelder, U., Mehler, J., & Morton, J. (1982). *The word frequency effect and lexical access.* Neuropsychologia, 20, pp. 615-628.

Shallice, T. (1987). *Impairments of semantic processing: Multiple dissociations. In M. Coltheart, R. Job & G. Sartori (Eds), The cognitive neuropsychology of language (p 111-127).* London: Lawrence Erlbaum Associates.

Tamba, I. (1994). *Une cle pour differencier deux types d'interprétation figuree, metaphorique et metonymique,* Langue Franchise, pp. 26-34.

Tesniere, L. (1959). *Elements de syntaxe structurale.* Paris: Klincksieck.

Tettamanti, M., Moro, A., Messa, C., Moresco, R.M., Rizzo, G., Carpinelli, A., Matarrese, M., Fazio F.,& Perani, D. (2005). *Basal ganglia and language: phonology modulates dopaminergic release.* Neuroreport, 16(4), pp. 397-401.223.

Thompson, C., Shapiro, L., Li, L., & Schendel, L. (1994). *Analysis of verbs and verb argument structure: a method for quantification of aphasic language production* In P. Lemme (Ed.), Clinical aphasiology, Vol. 23 (pp. 121e140).Austin, TX: Pro-Ed.

Thompson, C.K., Lange, K.L., Schneider, S.L., & Shapiro, L.P. (1997). *Agrammatic and non-brain-damaged subjects' verb and verb argument.*
structure production. Aphasiology, 11(4-5), pp. 473-490.

Thompson, C. K. (2003). *Unaccusative verb production in agrammatic aphasia: The argument structure complexity hypothesis.* Journal of Neurolinguistics, 16, pp. 151-167.

Thornton, I.M., & Hayes, A. E. (2004). *Anticipating action in complex scenes.* Visual Cognition, 11(2/3), pp. 341-370.

Tijus, C.A., & Zibetti, E. (2001). *The role of goal and object in the semantic determination of action verbs.* Journal des anthropologues- A.F.A., 85-86, pp. 157-182.

Tootell, R.B., Reppas, J.B., Kwong, K.K., Malach, R., Born, R.T., Brady, T.J., Rosen,B.R., &Belliveau, J.W. (1995). *Functional analysis of human MT and related visual cortical areas using magnetic resonance imaging.* Journal of Neurosciences, 15(4), pp. 215-230.

Tran, T.M. (2000). *A la recherche des mots perdus : etude des strategies denominatives des locuteurs aphasiques.* These pour le Doctorat en Sciences du Langage, sous la direction de Corbin, D. Universite de Lille III - Charles de Gaulle.

Tran, T.M. (2007). *Reeducation des troubles de la production lexicale. In Mazaux J.M., Pradat-Diehl & Brun V. (2007),* Aphasie et aphasiques, Issy- les-Moulineaux, Masson, 205- 215.

Uylings, H.B., Groenewegen, H.J.,& Kolb B. (2003). *Do rats have a prefrontal cortex?* Behav Brain Research, 146 (1-2), pp. 3-17.

Vendler, Z. (1967). *Verbs and Times.* In. Linguistics in Philosophy, NewYork, Cornell University Press, pp. 97-121.

Vinson, D.P., & Vigliocco, G. (2002). *Can independence be observed in a dependent system?* The case of tip-of-the-tongue states. Brain and Language, 68, pp. 118-126.

Von Hofmannsthal, H. (2005). *Words are not of this world.* Edition Rivages poche, coll. Petite Bibliotheque.

Warburton, E., Wise, R.J., Price, C.J., Weiller, C., Hadar, U., Ramsay, S., & Frackowiak, R.S. (1996). *Noun and verb retrieval by normal subjects.* Studies with PET. pp. 159-179.

Warrington, E.K. (1975). *The selective impairment of semantic memory*, Quartely Journal of Experimental Psychology, 27, pp. 635-657.

Warrington, E.K. (1981). *Neuropsychological studies on verbal semantic systems.* Philosophical transactions of the Royal Society of London, Series B,295, pp. 411-423.

Warrington, E.K. & McCarthy, R. (1983). *Category specific access dysphasia.* Brain, 106, pp. 859-878.

Warrington, E.K., & Shallice, T. (1984). *Category-specific semantic impairments,* Brain, 107, pp. 829-854.

Warrington, E.K., & Mc Carthy, R.A. (1987). *Categories of knowledge: further fractionations and an attempted integration.* Brain, 110, pp. 273296.

Warrington, E.K., & Mc Carthy, R.A. (1994). *Multiple meaning system in thebrain: A case for visual semantics*. Neuropsychologia, 32, pp. 465-473. Watson, J.D., Myers, R., Frackowiak, R.S., Hajnal, J.V., Woods, R.P., Mazziotta, J.C., Shipp, S.,& Zeki S. (1993). *Area V5 of the human brain: evidencefrom a combined study using positron emission tomography and magnetic resonance imaging.* Cerebral Cortex, 3(2), pp. 79-94.

Wernicke, C. (1874). *Der aphasiche Symptomenkomplex. Breslau: Cohn and Weigert. Republished as: The aphasia symptom complex: A psychological study on an anatomical basis. Wernicke's works on aphasia.* The Hague: Mouton.

White-Devine, T., Grossman, M., Robinson, K.M., Onishi, K., Biassou, N., & D'Esposito, M. (1996). *Verb confrontation naming and word-picture matching in Alzheimers disease.* Neuropsychology, 10, pp. 495-503.

Williams, S.E., & Canter, C.J. (1987). *Action-naming performance in four syndromes of aphasia.* Brain and Language, 32(1), pp. 124-136.

Wilson, M., Knoblich, G. (2005). *The case for motor involvement in perceiving conspecifics.* Psychological Bulletin, 131(3), pp. 460-473.

Wingfield A. (1967). Perceptual and response hierarchies in object identification. *Acta Psychologica*, 26, pp. 216-226.

Wingfield, A. (1968). *Effects of frequency on identification and naming objects.* American Journal of Psychology, 81, pp. 226-234.

Yamadori, A., & Albert, M.L. (1973). *Word category aphasia.* Cortex, 9, pp.83-89.

Yokoyama, S., Miyamoto, T., Riera, J., Kim, J., Akitsuki, Y., Iwata, K., Yoshimoto, K., Horie, K., Sato, S., & Kawashima, R. (2006). *Cortical mechanisms involved in the processing of verbs: An fMRI study.* Journal of Cognitive Neuroscience, 18(8), pp. 304-313.

Zeki, S., Watson, J.D., Lueck, C.J., Friston, K.J., Kennard, C., & Frackowiak, R.S. (1991). *A direct demonstration of functional specialization in human visualcortex.* Journal of Neurosciences, 11(3), pp. 641-649.

Zevin, J., & Seidenberg, M.S. (2004). *Age-of-acquisition effects in reading aloud: Test of cumulative frequency and frequency trajectory.* Memory andCognition, 32, pp. 31-38.

Zingeser, L.B., & Berndt, R.S.(1988).*Grammatical class and context effects in a case of pure anomia: Implication for models of language production.*Cognitive Neuropsychology, 5, pp. 473-516.

Zellal, N. (1986): *Contribution a la recherche en orthophonie : L'aphasie en milieu hospitalier Algerien etude psychologique et linguistique : These de doctorat sous la direction de Cohen, D.* Paris : Universite de la Sorbonne - Paris3.

Zellal, N., & Kacemi, S. (2017): *Le " MTA " Versions classique et informatisee : Test d'Evaluation et de Reeducation des cerebro-leses :* Salon National des produits de la recherche DGRSDT- Safex - Alger

Dictionaries

- Encyclopedie Medicale, Gaucher, Maurice, Quillet ,Aristit de Paris 1965.
- Nouveau Larousse Medical, rue de Montparnasse, Paris 1981.
- Dictionnaire Encyclopedique des Sciences du langage, Ducrot Oswald and Torodov Tezvetan, ed du Seuil, Paris, 1995.
- Dictionnaire de linguistique, Dubois. J et AL, ed Larousse-Brdas/VUEP, 2002.
- Dictionnaire de Petit Robert, Paris, 1993.

Sitography :

* www.vulgaris-medical.com
* www.aphasiequebec.org
* www.cen-neurologie.fr
* http://outilsrecherche.over-blog.com/pages/Notes_211_Speech_and_Cognition-3174356.html
* http://outilsrecherche.over-blog.com/pages/Notes_141_La_Phonetique-3083446.html
* http://lequotidienalgerie.org/2018/06/04/comment-lorthophonie-cree-t-elle-en-algerie-les-neurosciences-cognitives-de-la-neuropsycholinguistique-en-lien-avec-la-double-notion-economique/
* HTTP://LEQUOTIDIENALGERIE.ORG/2018/11/10/LETTRE-OUVERTE-A-MISTER-MINISTER-OF-INTERIOR-INTELLIGENCE-AND-SCIENTIFIC-RESEARCH/

Appendices

Appendix 1

A short aphasiological glossary (Lanteri, 1995)

	This is the disappearance or significant loss of grammaticality in language. It mainly affects the expressive side of language, but can also have an impact on grammatical and syntactic comprehension.
	Functional words, whose meaning is largely determined by the phrasal context, are tending to disappear: for example, verbal desinences, prepositions, conjunctions, etc., are no longer used.
Agrammatism	The composition of the sentence is reduced from the usual 6 to 7 words to one or two. It is characterised by the telegraphic style: both short and informative.
	Example: an "agrammatic" who was asked what he had done during the morning replied: "coffee: ... newspaper" (I drank my coffee and read the newspaper).
	The verb first reappears in the infinitive form.
	This is the loss of awareness of the disorder.
	This is not unique to aphasia.
Anosognosia	It varies in consistency and intensity, depending on the type of aphasia, circumstances and individual characteristics.
	Anosognosia culminates in Wernicke's aphasia.
	Total or partial loss of the verbal capacities of both sides of language: comprehension and expression, following an injury to the brain.
Aphasia	brain. In the vast majority of cases, this lesion is located in an extended area of the left hSmisphere cortex known as the "language area".

Difficulty understanding and expressing the voice effects produced in speech.

There's talk of a dual origin:

- articulatory: the movements of the phonatory organs,
- the limbic system.

The voice can be studied in terms of its physical characteristics: pitch, duration, intensity, and in terms of linguistic criteria: the intonation curve. Instrumental phonetic study can be used to characterise the various parameters.

Aprosodie

Aprosody is caused by a tesion of the right hemisphere and is therefore absent from aphasia.

Aprosody should be contrasted with dysprosody.

It's an expressive disorder.

In the spoken chain there is interaction, a combination of the "prosodic features" of the phonemes.

The pronunciation of a language is determined by the organisational rules that govern it.

Dysprosody or phonetic disintegration	In dysprosody, the combinatorics of linguistic sounds are impaired, phonemes are altered and syllabic structure is altered.
	Various manifestations of the disorder can be observed, which always

appear as difficulties in pronouncing the sounds of the language correctly: stammering, or exaggerated scansion, slowing down or rushing, pseudo-foreign accents, and so on.

These prosodic articulatory deviations are studied using acoustic instruments that allow comparison with normal articulation.

These terms receive their equivalents when we consider the 6tage physiological disorders: arthritic disorders, paretic-type disintegration and dystonic-type disintegration.

	or paragrammatism.
Dyssyntaxia	Incorrect or approximate use of sentence grammar, in terms of the choice of so-called functional words or sentence construction.

Example: "You see, I've been retired for 11 years now.

There are so many errors in jargon that the speaker cannot understand it. They are of two kinds:

• phon6mic: the sounds that make up words are poorly chosen, i.e. generally substituted, omitted or added.

• lexical semantics: words are replaced by others.

When productions cannot be recognised as words belonging to the language because of an accumulation of phon6mic and/or semantic errors, we find ourselves in the presence of neologisms.

Classically, there are three types of jargon, depending on the predominance of one type of error:

1. *paraphasic jargon* :

Jargon	words are used as if they had all possible meanings, i.e. none at all: the polysemy effect.

Example: "He took the master, yes, really, thief, like that...".

2. *asemantic or neological jargon* :

the words are "created", they don't exist in the language. "Indeed, the restonnes, they cramballent jusqu'ici . voila.".

3. *indifferent jargon* :

"a ti to ti . ti to ti

"yes, like 9a, one two ... so one, two ..." repSitive productions, very poor.

In practice, we see jargon where the forms are intertwined.

	Expressive overabundance opposed to controlled expression. The patient invited to speak seems to lose control of his expressive flow.
Logorrhee	which he does not channel, and which he has difficulty stopping. In a logorrheic expression, the information is poor and lacks conciseness.

The "lack of words" underpins this expressive behaviour.

Lack of the word This term is first and foremost an equivalent of the term aphasia. The lack of

word takes a different form depending on the type of aphasia.

It concerns the loss of the different grammatical categories, a lexical and grammatical deficit at the same time, and refers to the erroneous behaviours that are substituted for both comprehension and verbal expression. The term also has a more specific meaning when applied to a type of aphasia known as Pitres' amnesic aphasia or Anomie.

The lack of the word then means the loss of the ability to evoke nouns: proper nouns and the names of things, while the other words are normally emitted.

Verbal paraphasia or nominal paraphasia A word is replaced by another word:

- photo ? path

If the replacement word retains a relationship of meaning, we speak of semantic verbal paraphasia:

- fork ? spoon

If the replacement word retains a phonic form, we speak of morphological verbal paraphasia:

- cup ? face.

Stereotyping Verbal expression boils down to a single production that is always the same, whatever the linguistic circumstances: most often a refraction of one or two syllables: for example: "ma ma" or "ama" "to to".

The adverb "yes" is often used. It can be a complete sentence.

Speech disorders :

Speech abnormalities: the rate of oral expression (fluency, flow) can be altered

in the sense of a reduction (slow, pauses) or an acceleration (fast, difficult to interrupt, triggered by any external stimulus).

Suppression or silence.

Stereotypies: repetitive transmissions of the same linguistic segment; they constitute

They are sometimes the only broadcasts available and appear automatically during any verbal broadcast.

no

a word, or even a short phrase ("clac-clac", "tatata", "bonsoir les choses d'ici-bas").

Dysprosody: attenuation of melody (monotony), syllabification and sometimes pseudo-accent

(alsaeien,...).

Lack of words: difficulty or even impossibility of producing a word in an utterance situation (hesitations, pauses, "true", periphrasis: "c'est le nom d'un oiseau - P. Corneille", etc.).

enunciation is facilitated by the oral sketch and incomplete sentences.

Transformations in oral language :

Phonetic transformations: inadequate emission of phonemes anomaly in the realisation of the constituent features: Coquelicot = Cotlicot

Wednesday = Wednesday

Thursday = Teudi

Saturday = Tamedi

the changes are designed to simplify the articulation.

Phonemic paraphasias: addition, omission, displacement of phonemes :

Stool = Paturet

Fork = Fork

Match = Palumelle

Cigarette = Ciguerapette

Formal or semantic verbal paraphasia: word replacement
by another corresponding by the form or the conceptual relationship: Desk/
Executioner, Corpse/ Caviar, Table/ Bench, Foot/
Hand, Sock/ Sandal, Boulevard/ Pieton.

Repetition disorders:

Echolalia

Phonological dysphasia: the patient can repeat words but not logatoms (C.W.).

profound: repetition leads to the production of semantic verbal paraphasia,
concrete words are better repeated than abstract words, repetition of closed class
words and logatoms is almost impossible (B.C.).

semantics: the patient repeats without understanding (T.S.).

Mixed transcortical aphasia (= isolation of language areas)	++	-		++	+	-	-
Subcortical aphasia	++	-		-	++	-	+ or -

(+): Intense / (-): minimal / (+ or -): average

Main types of aphasia. Anatomo-clinical correlations generally observed:

Type of aphasia	Signs	Location	Etiology Usual	Associated signs
Global aphasia	Very good oral expression and comprehension Reduites	Extensive cortical (frontotemporopontal) or subcortical lesions)	Total sylvian infractus , tumour , trauma , haemorrhage .	Hemiplegia,
Broca's aphasia	Reduced oral expression , Agrammatism arthric disorder relatively preserved comprehension	Inferior frontal cortex , Grey nuclei and subcortical white matter of the frontal lobe	Superficial anterior sylvian infarction and/or deep Deep hematoma	Brachiofacial hemplegia Apraxia
Aphasia of Wernicke (type 1).	Abundant expression Comprehension disorders Paraphasia	Temporal lobe, sometimes thalamic lesions	Tumour Posterior sylvian infarction Herpetic encephalitis Lobar hematoma	Hemianopsia or quadranopsia Sensory disorders Few or no motor disorders

Conductive aphasia	Phonemic paraphasias Normal Comprehension Disturbed Repetition	Inferior parietal cortex External capsule	Posterior sylvian infarction (frequently of embolic origin)	Sensory disorders Quadranopsia
Pure verbal deafness (Wernicke type 2)	Comprehension and repetition disorders	Superior temporal gyrus (left or bilateral lesion)	Infarction Tumour Abces	No
Pure alexia (alexia without agraphia *)	Isolated reading disorder with retention and oral language impairment	Occipital lobe and splenium of the corpus callosum	Cerebral artery infarction Posterior tumour	Hemianopsy Visual agnosia
Anomic aphasia	Missing the word isole	Depth of temporal lobe Hippocampal region (low localisation value)	Tumour (or other expansive process) Alzheimer Infarction ACP Herpetic encephalitis	Apraxia Little or no sensitivomotor disorders Superior quadranopsia
Transcortical aphasia motor	Lack of incentives Verbal Repetition and comprehension Normal	Prefrontal region Additional motor area Grey cores	ACA infarction or ACA-ACM junction Hematoma Tumour	Frontal syndrome Dysarthria Crural hemiplegia
Transcortical sensory aphasia	Disturbed comprehension with retained repetition and "hollow" language. Missing word	Temporo-occipital junction Thalamus	Extended Alzheimer's PCA Posterior Junction Infarction	Demence Hemianopsy
Mixed transcortical aphasia	Echolalic language	Junction zones between the sylvian and anterior and posterior cerebral territories	Extended uni or bilateral junctional infarction	Attention disorders Hemiplegia uni or bilaterale crurale

*ACA: anterior cerebral artery;ACM: middle cerebral artery;ACP: posterior cerebral artery.

Symptoms	Lesions
Pure verbal deafness	Areas 41 and 42 (left or bilateral)
Pure Alexie	Left occipital lesion: - cortex + splenium - subcortical white matter
Lexico-semantic disorders - Comprehension disorders - purely verbal disorders - semantic disorders - dissociation according to content : - animated objects (predominantly identification processes) - inanimate objects (predominance of usage processes)	- Left temporal neocortex (areas 41, 42 and 22) - limited injury - extended lesion (22, 37, 40) - lower lesion (temporo-occipital) - superior lesion (temporoparietal) - temporal cortex - dorsolateral or parietal frontal cortex - perisylvian cortical areas and any extensive

- dissociation according to grammatical status - names - verbs - Anomie - spontaneous language and naming tests - spontaneous language only - by visual input	lesions - subcortical lesions - left occipital lesion
Verbal paraphasias	- Frontal, temporal and subcortical lesions
Perseverations	- Caudate core
Phonemic paraphasias	- Areas 40 and 22
Reduction in oral production "Non-fluent aphasias	• Posteroinferior frontal and subcortical lesions • Extensive frontal subcortical lesions • Putamen • Root and sub-root lesions
Syntax and discourse • Loss of verbal initiative, regressive mutism • Longer-lasting deficit • Speech disorders (incomplete, truncated, diffuse) • Syntax	• Supplementary motor area and/or anterior cingulate gyrus • Associated lesion of the corpus callosum and adjacent white matter • Prefrontal cortex • Subcortical structures • Broca area
Repetition	Insula and external capsule

Broca's aphasia

Broca's aphasia often begins with a phase of mutism or a very significant reduction in verbal production. In some cases, mutism is followed by a reduction in expression to a single stereotypy or a few automatic expressions.

More often than not, however, the progression is towards non-fluent verbal production, with the presence of articulatory disorders, dysprosody and a lack of words in conversational situations, accompanied by semantic and phonetic paraphasia. Gradually, but not necessarily, progress is made towards agrammatic production. On the other hand, auditory comprehension is relatively preserved, at least in conversational situations, because a more formal examination may reveal difficulties in understanding the syntactically expressed elements of the utterances. The repetition of words and phrases is altered.

The most common lesion pattern is a subacute or chronic infarction centred on the left frontal operculum but extending to the middle frontal cortex, inferior motor cortex, anterior and superior insula, anterior inferior parietal lobule and white matter deep to these structures (putamen, caudate nucleus) (Mohr, Pessin, Finkelstein, Funkenstein, Duncan, & Davis, 1978). In some cases, the lesion may be restricted to the subcortical white matter (Alexander & Hillis, 2008). A motor deficit in the right hemifield, of variable severity, is invariably associated with this aphasic syndrome.

We also often see apraxia of the upper limbs, oral-lingual-facial apraxia and, more rarely, sensory deficit. Patients are aware of their difficulties and experience considerable frustration in the face of these communication difficulties. They may display catastrophic reactions (crying and refusal to continue the examination). Major depression frequently occurs (Starkstein, Bryer, Berthier, Cohen, Price, & Robinson, 1991).

Wernicke's aphasia

This syndrome can be seen as the opposite of Broca's aphasia. Expression is fluent, even logorrheic, and well articulated, with numerous paraphasias of all types appearing in the context of grammatically rich utterances, which does not exclude the presence of dyssyntax. The frequency of paraphrases and dyssyntactic elements may be such that jargonaphasia is present. Auditory comprehension is very altered, as is the repetition of words and phrases, giving rise to numerous paraphasias and perseverations. Usually, this syndrome is caused by a central infarct in the left superior temporal gyrus extending into the middle temporal gyrus, superior supramarginal gyrus and inferior angular gyrus or by a hemorrhage in the posterior temporal lobe (Knepper, Biller, Tranel, Adams, & Marsh, 1989). The syndrome may not be associated with any neurological signs; in rare cases, there may be transient right hemiparesis of the face and upper limb and, more commonly, visual field deficit (superior quadranopia or right hemianopia). Awareness of the severity of the language deficit is highly variable. Patients are often unaware that their output is incomprehensible ("anosognosia") and therefore experience less frustration than those with Broca's aphasia. They may, however, become irritated by others' incomprehension of their utterances and develop paranoid tendencies or depression as awareness of the disorder improves.

Conductive aphasia

Expression is fluent, although generally less abundant than in Wernicke's aphasia, and grammatically well constructed. The dominant anomaly is a large number of phonemic paraphasias and a lack of words. Phonemic paraphasia is particularly common in phonologically complex words. Patients often make multiple attempts to correct their paraphasias ("approach behaviours"), although these attempts do not always bring them closer to the target (Valdois, Joanette, & Nespoulous, 1989). Auditory comprehension is relatively well preserved, particularly in conversational situations. Repetition of words, and even more so of sentences, is very poor. Patients may not be able to repeat the words presented to them at all, especially if they are functional words, or they may repeat them with numerous phonemic paraphrases and approach behaviours. However, comprehension of sentences that they are unable to repeat or read correctly is good, despite the presence of numerous paraphasias. The lesion at the origin of this syndrome is almost always an infarct in the supramarginal gyrus and the posterior and superior part of the insula, with variable extension into the inferior sensory and motor cortex, the superior parietal lobule and the deep parietal white matter (Palumbo, Alexander, & Naeser, 1992). The syndrome may not be associated with any neurological signs. However, right sensory loss, right hemiparesis or central facial paresis and right hemianopia may occur, but usually there is good recovery. The nosognosia of the disorders is obvious, but mood disorders are rare.

Transcortical motor aphasia

Expression is not fluent, and utterances are short, although usually grammatically well-structured. There are, however, some phonemic and verbal paraphasias, perseverations and phonetic distortions. Naming is less altered than spontaneous speech, although there are significant response latencies. Auditory comprehension appears normal in conversational situations, but is altered when tested formally. Repetition is intact with occasional echolalia. The usual lesion is caused by a left ventrolateral frontal infarct or intracerebral hemorrhage often involving the frontal operculum but centred on the more dorsal and anterior frontal cortex. A similar but less severe pattern is seen in large subcortical lesions centred on the periventricular white matter and the head of the caudate nucleus. Extensive medial frontal lesions can also cause transcortical motor aphasia, as can anterior thalamic lesions (Alexander & Hillis, 2008). Associated signs vary depending on the location of the lesion. In dorsolateral frontal lesions, there may be no associated signs apart from a mild contralateral grasping reflex and ataxic paratonia or paresis. Subcortical lesions usually produce hypophonia, dysarthria or even hypokinetic mutism, hemiparesis and postural instability. A medial lesion is often associated with a moderate grip reflex, paratonia and greater hemiparesis of the lower than the upper limb. In addition, patients with transcortical motor aphasia are often abrupt, lacking both motor and communicative spontaneity, particularly if they have an anterior thalamic lesion (Alexander & Hillis, 2008). Transcortical sensory aphasia Expression is fluent, with the presence of word gaps and semantic paraphasia; the content of utterances may be qualitatively reduced ("meaningless"). Auditory comprehension is very altered, and conversational comprehension seems to be better than comprehension of isolated words. Repetition of words and short sentences is preserved but may occasionally be echolalic. Patients usually present with initial anosognosia of their disorder. The usual lesion profile is a large infarct in the territory of the left posterior cerebral artery including the inferior temporal gyrus or a hemorrhage in the inferior temporal gyrus.

This syndrome has also been documented after lesion in various thalamic locations (Alexander & Hillis, 2008). According to Damasio (1988), the usual lesion site would be the posterior sector of the middle temporal gyrus and the angular gyrus, as well as the white matter located beneath these cortical structures. If the lesion is confined to the inferior temporal gyrus, the only associated deficit may be a right visual field deficit. In the case of infarction in the posterior cerebral artery territory, visual agnosia, alexia, amnesia (parahippocampal lesion), hemiparesis or abulia (thalamus) may be observed.

Global aphasia

As the name implies, global aphasics show an almost complete loss of the ability to understand and produce verbal messages. Global aphasia can thus be described as a combination of the expressive semiology of Broca's aphasia and the receptive semiology of Wernicke's aphasia. Verbal expression is non-existent or reduced to a few isolated perseverative words, insignificant syllables (stereotypy), emotional exclamations, or automatic short sentences ("I don't know"). Auditory comprehension is severely impaired and repetition is impossible. The typical lesion results from a large infarct of the perisylvian cortex and subcortical white matter. An extensive subcortical lesion can also cause global aphasia and a surprising number of global aphasics have little or no temporal lesion (Vignolo, Boccardi, & Caverni, 1986). Hemiplegia is usually, but not always, associated with global aphasia, as is often ideomotor or ideatory apraxia.

There may also be hemisensory loss, a visual field defect or postural extinction and instability (signs due to subcortical extension of the lesion).

In global aphasia without hemiplegia, deficits are less severe and recovery is better (Tranel, Biller, Damasio, Adams, & Cornell, 1987).

Mixed transcortical aphasia

This rare form of aphasia presents in a very similar way to global aphasia, with extremely reduced verbal expression - but stereotypies are less frequently observed than in global aphasia - and severely impaired auditory comprehension. In this case, however, echolalia dominates the pathological picture; consequently, repetition is relatively preserved. However, some highly echolalic patients are unable to repeat when prompted to do so in a repetition task. Mixed transcortical aphasia most often results from an extensive prefrontal lesion with deep extension. For this reason, it is usually the initial form of what will later manifest as severe transcortical motor aphasia. Anterior (polar) thalamic lesions may also cause mixed transcortical aphasia, which in this case rapidly progresses to anomic aphasia. Associated signs depend on the type of lesion. Extensive frontal lesions may cause no other signs, or a combination of paratonia, postural instability and moderate ataxic paresis. Abulia is common. Anterior thalamic lesions may result in significant executive deficit and amnesia (Alexander & Hillis, 2008).

Anomic aphasia

Expression is fluent, well-articulated and grammatically correct; there is little or no paraphasia, but there is a significant lack of words, manifested by pauses, periphrasis and non-specific filler words ("thing" for a noun, "do" for a verb).

When anomic aphasia corresponds to an initial picture, a lesion of the inferior temporal gyrus is most often the cause.

In the case of chronic anomic aphasia, corresponding to a residual state following recovery from more severe aphasia, no specific lesion site can be associated. The same applies to neurological signs, which vary according to the site of injury.

Appendix 4: Anatomy of the brain

The cerebral areas are different functional zones more or less delimited by the cerebral convolutions, which make up each of the four cerebral lobes:
- The frontal lobe (the most anatomically and functionally developed).
- The parietal lobe.

- The temporal lobe.
- The occipital lobe.

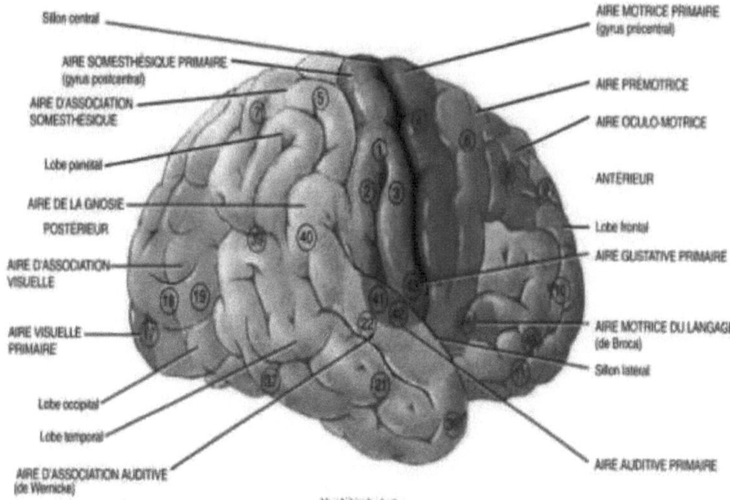

- The two **cerebral hemispheres are** made up of white matter and grey matter on the surface. The white matter, covered by the grey matter, is where the major ascending pathways pass through, i.e. the **nerve bundles** that carry information from the periphery to the cortex, in other words the sensory pathways that carry the messages picked up by the peripheral receptors that enable the information to be analysed. The other voices in the white matter are the descending pathways which originate in the cortex and reach the periphery. These are the motor pathways which transmit motor commands to the muscles from the **cerebral cortex, which is** made up of grey matter (cortex).

- The **internal capsule** is crossed by the pyramidal motor pathways, i.e. the nerve fibres coming from the pyramidal cells of the cortex, and the thalamic radiations, i.e. the nerve fibres coming from the thalamus to the cortex, in particular the parietal lobe. The cortex is divided into several lobes by more or less deep **scissures** and **sulci.**

- The lobes of the brain are in turn divided into cerebral convolutions. Each cerebral convolution corresponds to a different functional area.

o The **frontal lobe** is the largest lobe of the brain. It includes motor areas, in particular the **ascending frontal area** and motor areas, one of whose roles is motor programming. The other areas of the frontal lobe are responsible for behaviour, language (more specifically its expressive or motor component), planning, intellectual organisation and social conventions.

o The less voluminous **parietal lobe** is located behind the frontal lobe. This lobe is able to receive sensory impulses, particularly from the ascending parietal area. The ascending parietal area is situated immediately behind Rolando's sulcus, also known as the central sulcus. The parietal lobe is the site of sensitivity, language (as far as the comprehension component is concerned) and visual-spatial functions. Among other things, this lobe is responsible for gesture management (praxis) and recognition (of objects in particular, a deficiency of which is known as **agnosia**).

o The **temporal lobe** is located below **Sylvius' scissure,** also known as the lateral sulcus. We tend to forget this, but the temporal lobe extends into the lower, inner part of the encephalon. It contains the auditory areas, part of the language areas, and functional areas that play a role in the memory process. These include in particular the **hippocampal and entorhinal cortex.**

o The **occipital lobe**, the smallest, is located behind the **calcarine scissure**. It is essentially characterised by the presence of the visual areas.

·   **Primary areas** are :

o **Motor skills.**

o **Sensitive.**

o **Intellectual**. They receive information via underlying structures which send out **projections**. The information is then transmitted to adjacent areas, also known as **secondary** and **tertiary areas**. These areas have the capacity to integrate and analyse information from the primary areas.

·   The **associative areas** are located at the crossroads of the different cerebral lobes mentioned above. The associative areas are where the various inferences from the primary, secondary and tertiary areas are integrated. These associative areas also have the capacity to integrate very sophisticated information, from sensory and intellectual information.

Annex n°5 " Rendez- moi mes mots " (Give me back my words)

The "MTA" The work was launched in 1993, as part of the Algero-French Cooperation Programme Agreement (CMEP 91 MDU 177) co-signed by the University of Algiers and the J. Lordat Neurolinguistics Laboratory, directed by J. L. Nespoulous, the first co-author of the original battery.

This is a series of tests of oral and written expression and comprehension aimed at patients with aphasic syndromes.

Apart from the body part gnosias and oral-facial praxias, the practo-gnosic tests (constructive praxias, ideomotor praxias, colour gnosias, letter and word gnosias, auditory gnosias), which determine spatio-temporal structuring, the vector of communication, are absent in the original version.

Their inclusion in a small additional case (exhibited by the Toulouse team on 13 November 1993, during the GRAAL Day, Emile Roux Hospital, Limmeil-Brevannes) was motivated by the debate we opened on this subject, during the workshop led by Dr Michele Puel (neurologist at the CHU Purpan, Toulouse and member of the Franco-Canadian team which produced the battery published in 1992), as part of the SDORMP symposium (Toulouse, 6-9 June 1992).

This means that adapting the original assessment to the Algerian psycho-sociolinguistic context is not a translation of the original items into Arabic or Berber.

A theorisation of the act of communication and neuropsycholinguistic deficits guided this research, which led to the publication of the first Algerian-international clinical assessment of communication deficits in their linguistic and psychological parameters.

Even before its publication (which, as we knew, would require more than 10 years of scientific and technical work), in the mid-90s, its extension to the exploration of disorders in children (dysphasia, CMI, speech delays, surdites, dyslexia-dysorthographia), other neuropsychological disorders and cognitive deficits in neurodegenerative syndromes, proved to be effective.

Themes of numerous dissertations in the fourth year of the speech and language therapy degree; theses completed and in progress; paper presented at the international colloquium on "Child neuropsychology and psychoanalysis", Beni Abbes, 20-21-23 March 2003.

The theoretical book on the development of the "MTA", included in the case, through the method for adapting a foreign test to the Algerian reality that we propose, is now used as a basis for similar work on other clinical tools.

In particular, it emphasises **the direct relationship between the theory of disorders - the approach to test results - the therapeutic project**.

Through specialised training courses, we teach clinician-researchers, speech therapists and psychologists how to use the Patient Notebook, aphasiograms and qualitative grids.

In the third-year undergraduate module, the "MTA" is part of the Neuropsychology module programme.

Within the speech and language therapy LMD degree, the Methodology of speech and language therapy research techniques course in Semester 3 is reserved for the action programme offered by the 'MTA' within **cognitive neuroscience.**

"Give me back my words" computerised test software (MTA) adapted and calibrated by Professor Zellal Nacira, the aim of the software is to improve comprehension and recovery of oral language. It is a computerised programme for assessing language recovery in aphasics using a support: images, words, sentences, texts and video sequences. The programme is particularly suited to cerebro-lesional aphasia, using more than 200 words, 100 images and 40 video sequences. It measures the response time of aphasic subjects and calculates the percentage of different responses produced by aphasics (semantic, phonological and lexical paraphasias, semantic approximations, lack of words, etc.) and displays the results. detailed results in the form of an aphasiogram.

Ministere de 1'Enseignement Supĕrieur et de la Recherche Scientifique - University of Algiers 2

Cognitive Neuroscience-Orthophony-Phoniatry **Research Unit**

Ministerial Order no. 253 of 10 April 2013 - www.urnop-alger2.com

Director: Pr N. ZELLAL - zeUal.urnop@gmail.com - 0556996434

National Exhibition of Research Products DGRSDT

18-21 May 2017 - Safex - Algiers

Product name :

The "MTA" Classic and computerised versions:

Test d'Evaluation et de Reeducation des cerebro-leses

Nacira Zellal & Salah Kacemi

Cognitive Neuroscience - Speech Therapy - Phoniatry **Research Unit University of Algiers 2**

1. **By creating this Algerian-international test, we are demonstrating that the practice of speech therapy in university hospitals is scientifically justified.**

In fact, psychology, including speech and language therapy, as a result of the introduction of the linguistic criterion due to the emergence of acquisition theories in the 60s, is in fact the current or even future form of psychology, a profession which has been practised in Algeria since independence, using tests designed **for other countries, other languages and other cultures.**

The first and only Algerian-international neuropsycholinguistic clinical tool since independence, Nacira Zellal's "MTA", was published by the University of Algiers as part of CMEP 91MDU177 and by ANDRS, as part of Project 01/14/03/99/008, in 2002.

It has ёtë ёlaborё, in its adaptёe and ёtalonnёe version in a^rien context, as part of the CMEP 91MDU177 co-ёшдё Project by Nacira Zellal and Jean Luc Nespoulous, Director of the Jacques Lordat Laboratory at the University of Toulouse Le Mirail and at the same time first co-author of the 12-member Franco-Canadian team (linguists, neurologists, speech therapists, psychologists and psychomotor therapists), who developed and published the original battery under the name 'Le MT86' at Ortho-Edition (Icebergues, France) in 1992.

2. **Impact and contributions to the profession and to research by psychologists and speech therapists of the classic version by Nacira Zellal**

Objective

This battery of 33 praxis, gnosis, language and psychomotor tests provides an objective diagnosis of language and communication disorders, not only aphasic disorders, but also other disorders.

Usage

Professionally, it is used by speech therapists and practising psychologists in the care of **adults** suffering from neuropsychological deficits due to an acquired brain disorder (aphasia, neurodysfunction), in neurological, cardiology, neurosurgery and psychiatry departments.

In paediatrics, maxillofacial surgery and paediatricopsychiatry departments, its effectiveness in treating **child disorders**, including functional disorders (dysphasia) and neurodevelopmental disorders (autism), has also been proven, and it is also used in the treatment of auditory deficiencies in EJS and of children with implants in ENT.

In addition to CHUs, there are other organisations that employ psychologists and speech therapists: ëtablissements spëcialisës; UDSs; Structures scolaires et
extracurricular activities; Neighbourhood Centres; Sociëtës and national companies (e.g. Sonatrach, Ministëre de i'lnterieur : bilans et expertises).

At university level, since the years 90-2000, hundreds of mëmoires, magistëres, masters and doctorate courses spread across the country have been or are being developed using this clinical tool.

National and international conferences have included the results of its use in their programmes: see the URNOP website: www.urnop-alger2.com

3. Current developments in "MTA": the benefits of ICT and therapeutic contributions

In 2011, as part of the process of obtaining the magistëre d'orthophonie under the direction of Pr Nacira Zellal, the MTA was computerised, giving rise to the **'LogicielRendez- MoiMesMots'**. In fact, we are making ICT our ally, to bring us into the modern world of R&D in the Human and Social Sciences.

In 2017, we are offering this software not only for diagnostic purposes, but also for therapeutic purposes, since we have been able to experiment with it as a **means of reeducating** aphasics, by integrating "facilitation means" derived from reeducative theories such as :

1) Nacira Zellal's cognitive-behavioural approach (article published in 2011 in the French journal ANAE and posted on the URNOP website) and that :

2) the "MIT" Technique: The Melodic Intonation-Therapy by Philippe Van Eeckhout (2015-2016, CHU de la Salpetriere).

This result is the fruit of the doctoral thesis entitled :

"Proposition d'un iogiciei d^vaiuation et de Education des cërëbro-leses", carried out under the direction of Nacira Zellal, as part of the CMEP-TASSILI Project 13MDU902 - URNOP-Alger 2/LaboCHART Laboratoire de *Sciences Cognitives et d'Intelligence Artificielle-Paris* 8.

During our Junior stays at this CMEP, we benefited from courses run by Philippe Vaneekhout at La Salpetriere.

In conclusion, the MTA is both a **diagnostic** and **therapeutic** tool.

Case n°1 M.M.B

Exam results : Oral language

Test: InterviewDirigee

- quantitative reduction
- qualitative reduction
- agrammatism
- lack of word
- phonetic deviations
- phoneme deviations
- verbal deviations
- aspontaneitis

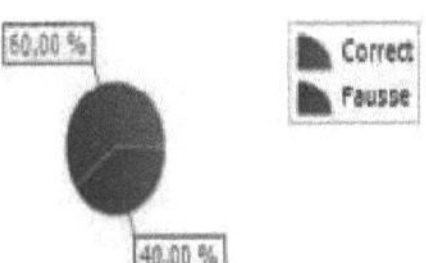

oral-facial apraxia

Test:Productiond'automatismes linguistiqueset recitation

- aspontaneitis
automatic-voluntary dissociation

Test: Paradigmatic lexical availability

- phoneme deviations

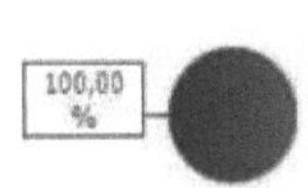

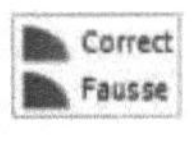

Test: Repetition of syllables, words, phrases and non-words

- phonetic errors
- errors proportional to item length
- grammatical errors
- errors in switching from one language to another

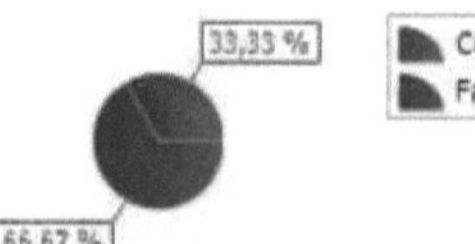

Test: Oral naming of words and actions

- lack of word
- confusion between actions that are close in meaning or configuration on the drawing
- difficulty channelling attention
- beginning to develop vocabulary
- purpose diagram
- gestural response

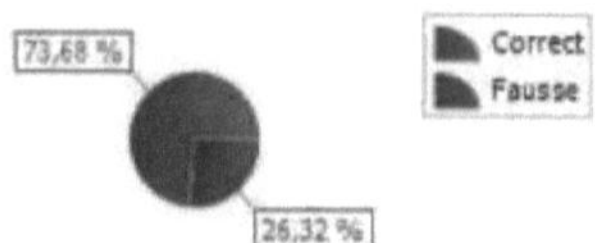

Test: Oral narrative discourse

- quantitative and/or qualitative reduction
- lack of word
- gestural responses
- jargonaphasia (paragrammatisms, semantic or mixed phonemic paraphasia)

Test: Oral comprehension of words and phrases

- confusion between words that are close to each other: semantic
- confusion between words that are close to each other: phonetically
- confusion between words that are morphologically close (house/building)
- confusion between similar actions

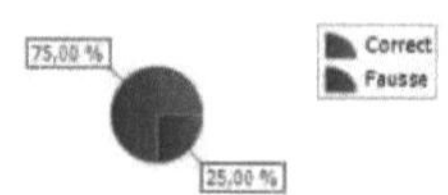

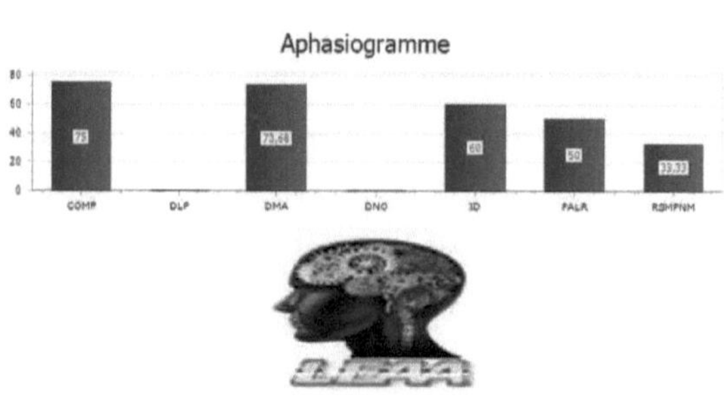

Appendix 6

Examination results : Oral language

Test: Interview Dirigee

- quantitative reduction
- qualitative reduction
- agrammatism
- lack of word
- phonetic deviations
- phoneme deviations
- aspontaneitis

Test: Production of linguistic automatisms and recitation

- aspontaneitis
automatic-voluntary dissociation

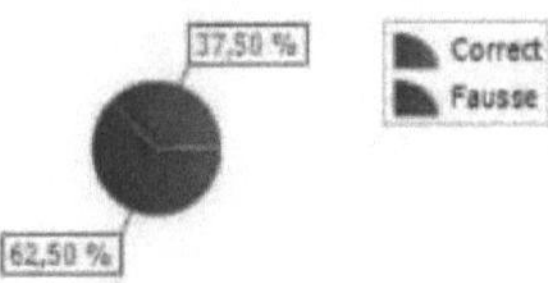

Test: Paradigmatic lexical availability

- qualitative reduction
- phonetic deviations
- phoneme deviations

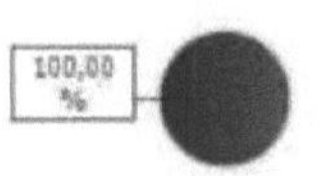

Test: Repetition of syllables, words, phrases and non-words

- phonetic errors
- p onemic errorsuargonap asia
- errors proportional to item length
- grammatical errors
- errors in switching from one language to another

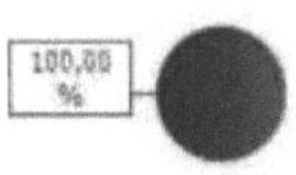

Test: Oral naming of words and actions

- lack of word

- difficulty channelling attention
- beginning to develop vocabulary
- purpose diagram
- response through use
- gestural response
- possible facilitation methods

Test: Oral narrative discourse

- lack of word

Test: Oral comprehension of words and phrases

- confusion between words that are close to each other: semantic
- confusion between words that are close to each other: phonetically
- confusion between words that are morphologically close (house/building)
- confusion between similar actions

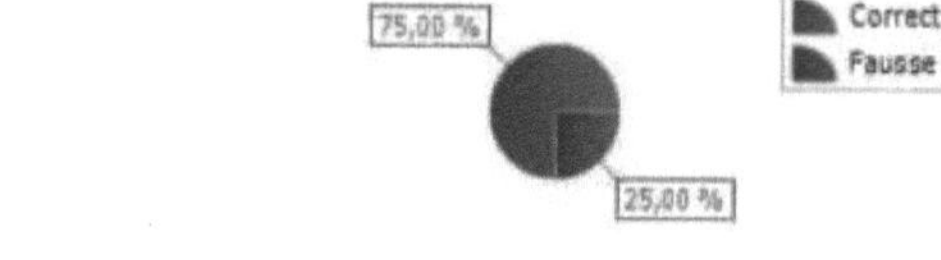

Aphasiogram

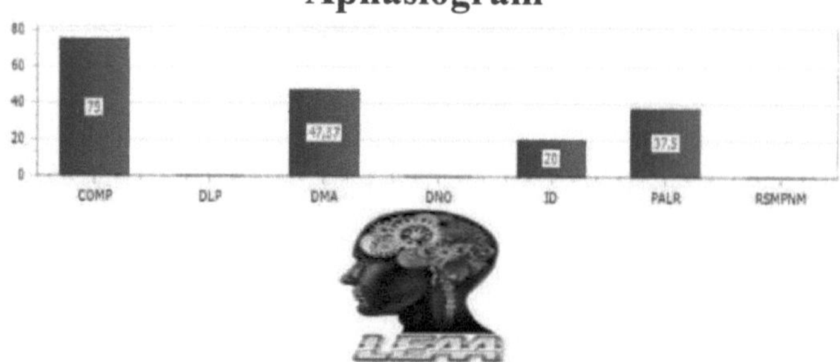

Annex 6 **Monday 4 June 2016**

Case n°3 M.T.S

Exam results : Oral language

Test: Interview Dirigee

- quantitative reduction
- lack of word

- aspontaneity

gestural response, cold disorder

Test: Production <u>of</u> linguistic automatisms and recitation

- aspontaneitis
- automatic-voluntary dissociation

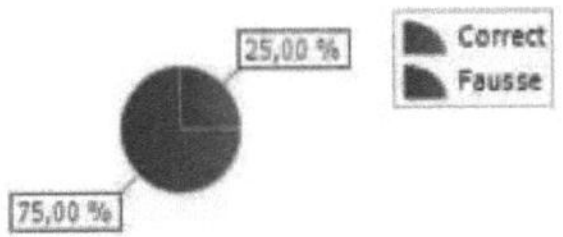

Test:Lexical availabilityparadigmatic

-    qualitative reduction
-    temporal difficulties (production reader)
-    phonetic deviations
-    phoneme deviations

Test: Repetition of syllables, words, phrases and non-words

-    phonetic errors
-    p onemic errorsuargonap asia
-    errors proportional to item length
-    grammatical errors
-    errors in switching from one language to another

Test: Oral naming of words and actions

lack of word
-    confusion between actions that are close in meaning or configuration on the drawing
-    difficult^ to channel l'attention
-    phonemic approach
-    response through use
-    gestural response
-    confusion with different paradigms; studying paradigmatic distance

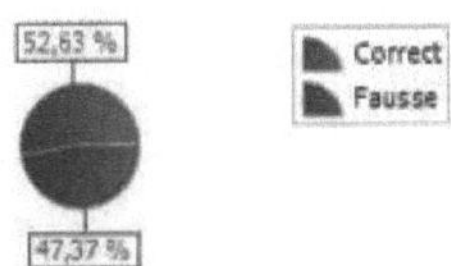

Test: Oral narrative discourse

-    loss of redundancy

- quantitative and/or qualitative reduction
- lack of word
- gestural responses

Test: Listening comprehension of words and sentences

- confusion between similar actions

Aphasiogramme

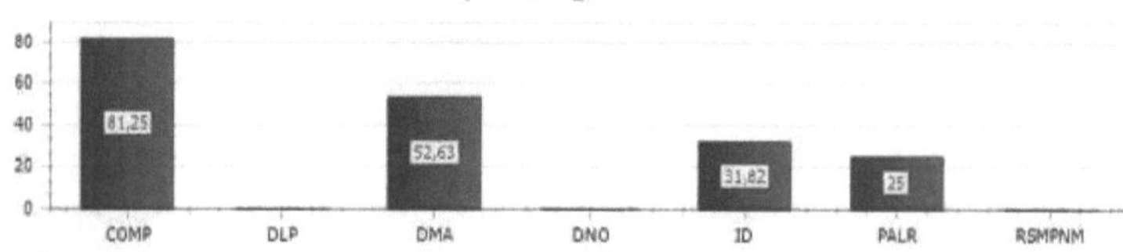

Appendix 6: Examination results: Oral Language

Cas n°4

M.J.K

14 July 2016

Test: InterviewDirigee

- quantitative reduction

- qualitative reduction

- agrammatism

- lack of word

- phonetic deviations

- phoneme deviations

- aspontaneitis

Test:Production of linguistic automatisms and recitation

- aspontaneity
- automatic-voluntary dissociation

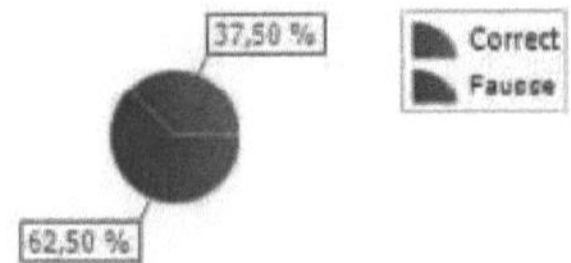

Test: Paradigmatic lexical availability

- quality reduction
- phonetic deviations
- phonemic deviations

Test: Repetition of syllables, words, phrases and non-words

- phonetic errors
- p onemic errorsuargonap asia
- errors proportional to item length
- grammatical errors
- errors in switching from one language to another

Test: Oral naming of words and actions

- lack of word
- difficulty channelling attention
- beginning to develop vocabulary
- purpose diagram - response through use
- gestural response - possible modes of facilitation

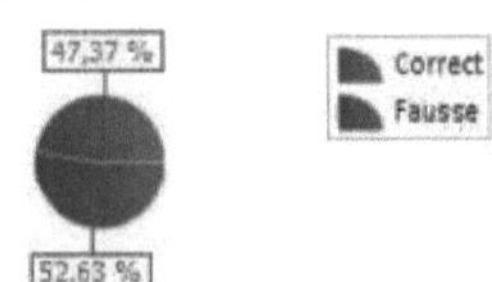

Test: Oral narrative discourse

- lack of word

Test: Listening comprehension of words and sentences

- confusion between words that are semantically close
- confusion between words that are close to each other: phonemically
- confusion between similar words in morphological terms (house/building)
- confusion between similar actions

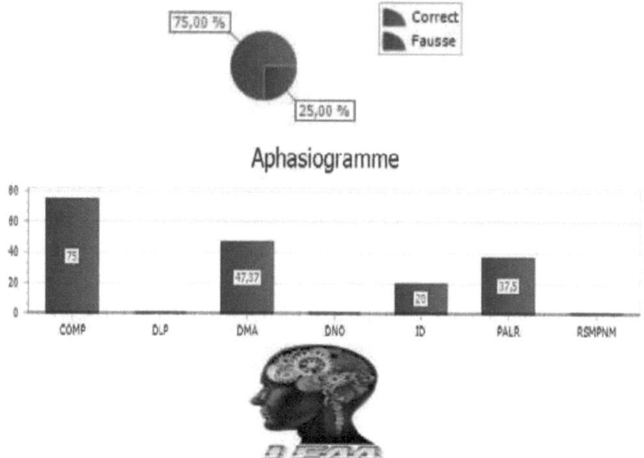

Annex 6 Examination results: Oral language

Monday 4 July 2016

Case 5
M.R.F

Test: Interview Dingee

-   quantitative reduction
-   qualitative reduction
-   agrammatism
-   lack of word
-   phonetic deviations
-   phoneme deviations
-   verbal deviations
-   aspontaneitis

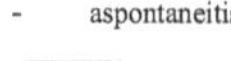

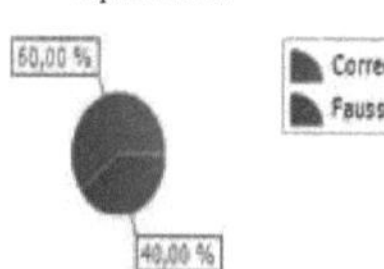

oral-facial apraxia

Test: Production of linguistic automatisms and recitation

-   aspontaneitis
-   automatic-voluntary dissociation

50,00 %
50,00 %

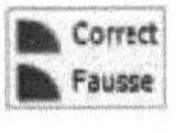

Correct
Fausse

- qualitative reduction
- phonetic deviations
- phoneme deviations

Test: Repetition of syllables, words, phrases and non-words

- phonetic errors
- errors proportional to item length
- grammatical errors
- errors in switching from one language to another

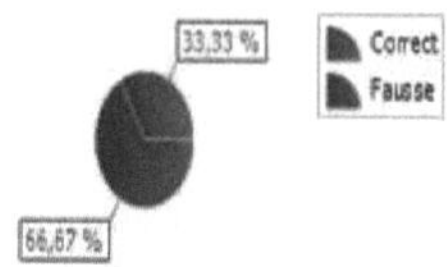

Test of oral naming of words and actions

- lack of word
- confusion between actions that are close in meaning or configuration on the drawing
- difficulty channelling attention
- beginning to develop vocabulary
- purpose diagram
- gestural response

Test: Oral narrative discourse

- quantitative and/or qualitative reduction
- lack of word
- gestural responses
- jargonaphasia (paragrammatisms, semantic or mixed phonemic paraphasia)

Test: Oral comprehension of words and phrases

- confusion between words that are close to each other: semantic
- confusion between words that are close to each other: phonetically
- confusion between words that are morphologically close (house/building)
- confusion between similar actions

Aphasiogramme

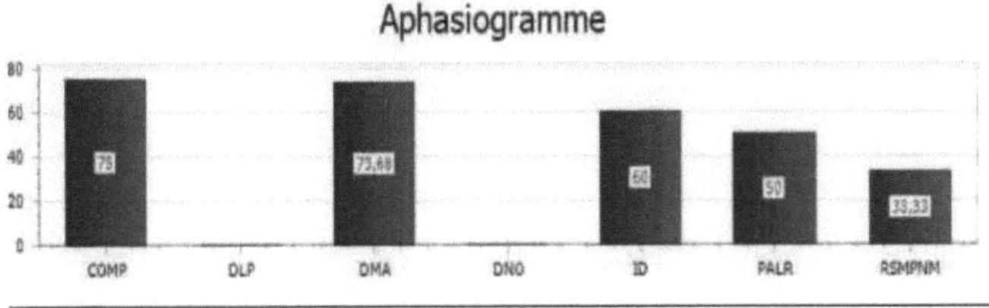

Printed by Books on Demand GmbH, Norderstedt / Germany